Intervention
in the Caribbean

D0742698

Intervention in the Caribbean

The Dominican Crisis of 1965

General Bruce Palmer, Jr.

THE UNIVERSITY PRESS OF KENTUCKY

WITHDRAWN
UTSA LIBRARIES

Copyright © 1989 by The University Press of Kentucky
Scholarly publisher for the Commonwealth,
serving Bellarmine College, Berea College, Centre
College of Kentucky, Eastern Kentucky University,
The Filson Club, Georgetown College, Kentucky
Historical Society, Kentucky State University,
Morehead State University, Murray State University,
Northern Kentucky University, Transylvania University,
University of Kentucky, University of Louisville,
and Western Kentucky University.
Editorial and Sales Offices: Lexington, Kentucky 40506-0336

Library of Congress Cataloging-in-Publication Data

Palmer, Bruce, 1913-
    Intervention in the Caribbean :   the Dominican crisis of 1965   /
  Bruce Palmer, Jr.
      p.   cm.
    Includes bibliographical references.
    ISBN 0-8131-1691-0
    1. United States—Relations—Dominican Republic.
  2. Dominican Republic—Relations—United States. 3. Dominican
  Republic—History—Revolution, 1965. 4. Organization of American States. I. Title.
  E183.8.D6P35   1989
  303.48'27307293—dc20   89-16761

This book is printed on acid-free paper meeting
the requirements of the American National Standard
for Performance of Paper for Printed Library Materials. ∞

Library
University of Texas
at San Antonio

To the American diplomats, soldiers, sailors, marines, and airmen who have faithfully served in Central America and the Caribbean

Contents

[Illustrations follow page 100]

Maps

Figures

Preface

Many motivations underlie the writing of this book. One is to tell the story of the U.S. military involvement in the Dominican affair—especially that of the U.S. Army, which virtually all writers ignore; the usual reference is to "25,000 marines" when in fact the army's 82d Airborne Division, under the superlative leadership of Maj. Gen. Robert H. York, played a dominant military role. Another motivation is to describe the closely interacting political-military relationships that developed during the crisis, including those between the United States and the Organization of American States (OAS), the heroes of which were the redoubtable American diplomat Ellsworth Bunker, who masterminded the OAS negotiations, and the tenacious William Tapley Bennett, United States ambassador to the Dominican Republic, who skillfully guided the complex activities supporting U.S. objectives in the country. Still another purpose is to tell the story of the Inter-American Peace Force (IAPF), the first—and perhaps the last—in OAS history to be put in the field with an operational mission.

Throughout history, the most successful statesmen and diplomats have recognized that the key to the art of negotiations lies in the fundamental interrelationship of diplomacy and force. The two must work hand in glove, seeking to achieve national objectives with a minimum of force—ideally, not even having to threaten the use of force but simply to make its availability clear to the other side. This relationship is not an either/or proposition. Diplomacy and force are not black-and-white alternatives but must be closely intermeshed for the best prospects for success; neither can accomplish national aims alone. No one knew these fundamental truths better than Ambassador Bunker, a consummate negotiator. The Dominican Republic experience of 1965-66 was not only a unique example of the skillful employment of diplomacy and force in tandem but also an achievement rare in the annals of statesmanship: a polarized civil war situation was resolved peacefully through a political solution.

In the course of my research and study for this book, I found myself more and more looking at the Caribbean Basin as an entity; that is, the Caribbean Sea, the Gulf of Mexico, and the land region that encompasses Mexico, Central America, the northern littoral of Columbia and Venezuela, and all the islands in the Caribbean. The importance of this region to the United States has been recognized by U.S. leaders since our beginnings as a nation. In my judgment (although to develop this thesis fully is beyond the scope of this narrative), no geographic area of the world outside our borders is now or will be more important to the United States—strategically, politically, economically, and sociologically—than the Caribbean Basin.

For all these reasons, I hope this book will prove to be useful to Americans, both civilian and military, in positions of national leadership. Further I am hopeful that it will contribute to the thoughtful development of sound doctrine, thoroughly grounded in experience, with respect to the conduct of lesser military operations or so-called "small wars," the kind of conflict situation in which the United States in the future is most likely to become involved. The question of how to prepare for and conduct "small wars" and special operations has generated much study and discussion within our government, both in the executive branch and in the Congress. It has resulted in, among other things, an agreed-upon term for this sort of action: in the best tradition of bureaucratic jargon it is called "low intensity conflict." The Dominican Republic experience involved the use of force in both combat and noncombat situations and thus usefully illustrates what future limited-intensity conflict may well entail.

It seems clear that limited conflict will see increasingly violent pressures and more sophisticated weapons and techniques used against the Western democracies. These will require not only close international cooperation to counter but also closely knit national organizations to handle. Moreover, international terrorism and drug trafficking have added a global dimension to so-called low intensity conflict; the flow of drugs across U.S. borders constitutes a deadly assault on the nation's very foundations. It goes without saying that only close civilian-military relationships within the governmental structure can cope successfully with such complex threats. Ideally, in any given operation, one individual should be charged with planning and carrying out approved actions and programs, especially in the field. Again, the Dominican Republic sets a good example: Ambassador Bunker was clearly in charge. With respect to the United States role, even President Lyndon B. Johnson deferred to his judgment and decisions, while his prestige and international stature allowed him to assume the lead in OAS efforts.

In this endeavor, I am particularly indebted to the late Ambassador Ellsworth Bunker and Ambassadors William Tapley Bennett, Carol Laise Bunker, and William Leonhart; Ambassador Richard T. McCormack, U.S. Permanent Representative to the OAS, and his assistant Russell Wapenski; the late Generals Harold K. Johnson, Robert H. York, and Robert R. Linvill, U.S. Army; General Roy K. Flint, Dean of the Academic Board, U.S. Military Academy; retired U.S. Army Generals Donald D. Blackburn, Chester V. Clifton, Eugene P. Forrester, and William E. Klein; retired U.S. Army Colonels Robert Abraham, Dwight L. Adams, Harold E. Dill, Jack Gardner, James R. Hughes (my West Point roommate and classmate, whose first love has been the Caribbean), Eldredge R. Long, and William R. Swarm; General Lincoln Jones III and Colonels Thomas H. Brett, John J. Costa, and Rod Paschall, all active duty U.S. Army; and Professors Roger J. Spiller and Lawrence A. Yates. Particularly supportive have been retired U.S. Army General John T. Carley, author and journalist; and professor, author, and retired U.S. Army General Douglas Kinnard.

Finally, I must acknowledge the ever constant and good-humored support of my patient wife, Kay Sibert, whose judgment I have come to rely upon; and the faithful support of our daughter, Robin, her husband, Albert L. Sessler, Jr., our son, Bruce III, his wife, Deborah, my older brother and mentor, Harding, his wife, Sarah, and my youngest sister, Sylvia Johnsen.

Prologue

When the United States intervened in the Dominican Republic in late April 1965, bitter controversy broke out in the United States and all over Latin America. Indeed, the action found few supporters in the West and was categorially denounced throughout the Communist world. It was not popular—but then, no American intervention in Latin America has ever claimed general approbation. Virtually all the civilian authors who have written about the crisis have condemned the U.S. action with little, if any, sympathy for official American views. Relatively few commentators have acknowledged the fact that the Dominican Republic in a political sense has been a success story for the more than twenty years since, while others say that the intervention worked, but for the wrong reasons.

Although numerous military men have written excellent brief papers with a relatively narrow view of the Dominican affair, this book is the first comprehensive examination of the subject by a senior military officer. My perspective is that of a military professional—as an army deputy chief of staff in the Pentagon when the crisis began, then as commander of U.S. forces in the Dominican Republic early in the operation, and subsequently as deputy commander of the Inter-American Peace Force. Thus I could judge events initially from the point of view of officials at the seat of government and later from that of the participants on the scene.

In April 1965, when the Dominican crisis erupted, the Joint Chiefs of Staff (JCS) were preoccupied with the deepening U.S. commitment in Vietnam. Indeed, the last months of 1964 and the early months of 1965 had been largely taken up with soul-searching discussions about the true nature of the war, the feasible military options open to the United States, and the ultimate depth of U.S. involvement. By April 1965 the United States was beyond the advisory stage, having committed American air power against North Vietnam and deployed the first U.S. ground combat troops, army and marine, in South Vietnam. Everyone involved in war planning and operations knew that the time was near for a fateful decion (it came in July) that would engage the United States in major ground warfare in Vietnam.

The JCS chairman at the time was Gen. Earle G. Wheeler, who had moved up from army chief of staff in July 1964 when Gen. Maxwell D. Taylor, the incumbent chairman, went to Saigon as the U.S. ambassador; Gen. Harold K. Johnson had succeeded Wheeler as army chief. Gen. Curtis E. LeMay was air force chief; Adm. David L. McDonald was the chief of naval operations; and Gen. Wallace M. Greene was marine commandant. These were all men who had come through the crucible of World War II and were familiar with the complexities of global cold war.

To help them in their duties, the JCS have a subordinate group known as the operations deputies (OPSDEPS), who accomplish a good deal of minor business for their chiefs with minimum rhetoric and wasted motion. This group consists of the director of the Joint Staff and the service operations deputies, a total of five three-star officers. I was the army's deputy chief of staff for operations (DCSOPS) at the time of the Dominican crisis and thus principal assistant to General Johnson. The director at the time was Lt. Gen. David S. Burchinal, U.S. Air Force, an articulate and intelligent man who was adept at achieving consensus among us when he wanted to. Occasionally we would lock horns over some issue but managed to be civil about it. When things got dull, Burchinal liked to liven them up by making a crack, for example, about the limited usefulness of aircraft carriers, which would invariably draw a hot retort from Vice Adm. Andrew Jackson, the navy's feisty operations deputy. Jackson, who had served a total of fifteen years in the joint military arena in Washington and was familiar with every interservice issue known, would sputter when he got excited over something of this sort. So the rest of us— smooth, canny Lt. Gen. John Carpenter, U.S. Air Force; Lt. Gen. David Buse, a big, gruff no-nonsense marine; and I—would sit back and enjoy the verbal fireworks between the two, which would usually end in a draw.

Like our chiefs, in late April 1965 we were not overly concerned about the Dominican situation and had only sketchy information about the crisis. There were reasons for this state of mind in addition to our preoccupation with Vietnam. One was that numerous false alarms about possible U.S. military intervention in the Dominican Republic had been raised ever since Rafael Trujillo's assassination in 1961. But another reason, and a significant one, was that President Lyndon Johnson did not see fit to include any military personnel—not even the JCS chairman—in the high-level deliberations that went on in the White House during the first days of the crisis, beginning on 24 April. Only late on 29 April was General Wheeler included for the first time.

Until then, we in the Pentagon were aware of only the bare facts: that a revolution had broken out on Saturday, 24 April, in Santo Domingo, the capital; and that the crisis had worsened on Sunday, prompting the president that day to order preparations for evacuating U.S. citizens. By 2:00 A.M. on Monday, 26 April, the USS *Boxer* with an amphibious fleet was a short distance off the southern coast of the Dominican Republic. At the president's direction, U.S. marines had gone ashore, carried out the initial evacuation on Tuesday, 27 April, and continued the operation the next day. We also knew that the JCS, as a precaution, had alerted part of the 82d Airborne Division.[1] However, we did not realize that the president had been discussing further options with Secretary of State Dean Rusk, Secretary of Defense Robert S. McNamara, National Security Council (NSC) adviser McGeorge Bundy, and personal advisers Clark Clifford and Judge Abe Fortas.

On the morning of Friday, 30 April 1965, I attended a long meeting of the operations deputies in the JCS conference room, commonly called the "Tank" because it was windowless and severely functional. Although most of our business centered on matters relating to southeast Asia, we were mostly in the dark on details and were expecting to be enlightened about Santo Domingo just as soon as Wheeler returned from the White House, where he had been all morning.

When I went to my office at about 11:30, Maxine Clark, my typically efficient, smart, and attractive civilian secretary,[2] told me to head back at once because Wheeler wanted to see me. My walking route to the JCS complex took me past the offices of the army chief of staff, the secretary of the army, and the secretary of defense, all on the third floor, then down the escalator leading to the River Entrance of the Pentagon and the special entrance to the restricted JCS area used by the chiefs. En route, I stuck my head into General Johnson's office, anticipating that I would be accompanying my chief to the chairman's office, only to learn that he was in the dentist's chair at the Pentagon dispensary. Normally, I could make the walk from my office to the Tank in three minutes at a fast walk. That morning, sensing that something special was up, I made it in two minutes flat, arriving breathless and mentally saluting the portrait of kindly-looking, horsefaced Gen. Omar Bradley, first chairman of the Joint Chiefs, that hung outside Wheeler's office. A navy yeoman and an air force lieutenant colonel in the outer office waved me into a large room on the E Ring, rating a couple of good-sized windows to the outside world. Wheeler, a big dark-haired man, was sitting at his desk diagonally facing the door; standing on either side of him were his special assistant Lt. Gen. Andrew Jackson Goodpaster, U.S. Army, and Joint Staff Director Burchinal. All three men had a grim look about them, thin-lipped and serious. I had expected a much larger meeting with all the service chiefs present, but there was no one else in the room. I had no inkling as to what was about to happen.

Wheeler wasted no words getting to the point: President Johnson had just decided to intervene in the Dominican Republic with the force necessary to prevent a Communist takeover. Not only did he fear that the leftist side would win the

ongoing civil war and sooner or later be subverted and over-
powered by the Communist elements of the revolution; he
believed that a sudden, direct takeover was a distinct possibility and that the swift introduction of powerful U.S. forces on
the ground was the only sure way to nip a Communist coup in
the bud. The president was also determined to bring an end to
the fighting in Santo Domingo and avoid a festering sore in the
Western Hemisphere, particularly at this critical juncture
when the United States was about to become deeply committed
in Vietnam.

This was the president's personal decision; all civilian advisers, including Rusk and McNamara, and Wheeler (the only
military adviser), had recommended against immediate intervention. Looking back, I believe that Wheeler was simply noting the advisers' reservations about military intervention *at
that time*. According to other accounts, all present agreed that
the United States had to prevent a Communist takeover; the
question was how to accomplish that aim. The advisers wanted
enough time to secure OAS support and gather credible, hard
evidence of the imminent danger of a Communist coup.[3] But
the president had directed Rusk "to make it look good" in the
OAS, meaning to get OAS acceptance and participation.

The president, Wheeler said, had personally selected me (I
took this with more than a grain of salt) to take command of
all U.S. forces in the Dominican Republic as soon as I could
get there. My stated mission was to protect American lives and
property; my unstated mission was to prevent another Cuba
and, at the same time, to avoid another situation like that in
Vietnam. The U.S. forces needed to assure the success of that
mission would be made available. I never received any such
unequivocal directive in writing. The closest thing was a "back
channel" message (a special private channel restricted to a very
few senior users) from Wheeler on 1 May 1965, after I had
arrived in the Dominican Republic. It is paraphrased as follows:

EYES ONLY from Wheeler for Palmer.

As you know, mission of US forces deployed to Dominican Republic area is to protect the lives of Americans and other foreign na-

tionals. In so doing, those forces have evacuated a large number of noncombatants and have secured certain areas contiguous to and in the city of Santo Domingo and at San Isidro airfield. If the current strife continues with communist-dominated forces obviously gaining the ascendancy so as to threaten a communist takeover of the Island, the mission of US Forces is expected to be broadened to one designed to prevent such an outcome.

This message is extremely sensitive. It is intended for your personal information only.

Wheeler went on to say that the forces immediately available, if needed, included the 4th Marine Expeditionary Brigade (MEB) with three marine battalions plus the marine battalion already on the scene, and the 82d Airborne Division with nine parachute infantry battalions, two of which had just arrived in the Dominican Republic; the 101st Airborne Division with nine parachute infantry battalions had also been alerted for possible commitment. The U.S. Air Force and Marine Corps would provide air cover and other tactical air support from bases in Puerto Rico, and the U.S. Navy would maintain general air surveillance of the northern coastal areas of the island of Hispaniola, looking for any attempts to infiltrate forces from other countries by sea.

I was to proceed to Santo Domingo as quickly as possible, going through Fort Bragg, North Carolina, on the way to pick up a staff and communications element to take with me. (I was already slated for assignment to Bragg in June, to take command of the XVIII Airborne Corps headquartered there; the corps included the two airborne divisions, the 82d at Bragg and the 101st at Fort Campbell, Kentucky.) Wheeler said that he had not yet had a chance to tell "Johnnie" (Army Chief of Staff Johnson). He again urged me to make all possible speed in getting to Santo Domingo where a very uncertain and confused situation existed. His only bit of advice was to seek out the U.S. ambassador and "stick to him like a burr." It was good advice that was to pay off.

Finally, although the present chain of command ran from the joint task force commander—Vice Adm. K.S. Masterson, who had just arrived off Santo Domingo—to Adm. Thomas H.

Moorer, Commander in Chief Atlantic Command (CIN-
CLANT) at Norfolk, Virginia, and thence to Washington.
Wheeler told me that it was his intention to have the U.S.
commander in Santo Domingo eventually report directly to
Washington, thus taking CINCLANT out of the chain of command; meanwhile, I was to keep the chairman informed directly, reporting to Admiral Moorer at the same time, until the
situation cleared, because communications with the crisis area
had been slow, erratic, and unreliable, and up-to-date information hard to come by. When I asked about adequate support
for long-line strategic communications, Burchinal replied that
we could have anything available in the United States. Specifically, however, all he could promise was the temporary loan
of an air force "talking bird," a specially equipped C-130 aircraft
belonging to the Air National Guard.

Wheeler then shook my hand and wished me luck, and I
departed. It was exactly noon on the clock over a world map
covering the wall near the entrance door; other clocks showed
the local time in Saigon, Seoul, Pearl Harbor, and Frankfurt,
where major U.S. military headquarters were located overseas.
(The time in Santo Domingo, as in San Juan, Puerto Rico, to
the east, is one hour ahead of Washington time.) As I closed
the door behind me, I mentally noted that Goodpaster had not
uttered a word during the meeting. Later I learned that he had
been slated to command the XVIII Airborne Corps but that his
hopes had been dashed because he was too valuable to President
Johnson as liaison with former President Eisenhower, especially at this critical time when Johnson needed Eisenhower's
support for proposed U.S. actions in Vietnam. And so Goodpaster was denied the troop and command experience he
wanted and needed and had to continue in high-level Washington staff jobs, while lucky Palmer was assigned to the corps.
I didn't blame him—I would have felt the same way.[4]

My deputy, Maj. Gen. Arthur S. Collins, Jr., was waiting for
me when I returned to my office. "Art, you are now the army
DCSOPS," I said, handing him my voluminous notebook covering JCS and other meetings over a two-year period. A combat-
experienced leader and skilled staff officer, Collins did not bat

an eye but simply told me in his best South Boston brogue to forget Washington and get on my horse. So I waved goodbye to all, asking my ever reliable executive officer, Col. Ben Carroll, to tidy up after my hasty exit, and headed for home: Quarters No. 2, Fort Meyer, Virginia. It is right next to the chief of staff's quarters, No. 1, but I never got a chance to touch base with the chief before I left.

Nor was I able to say goodbye to my wife and son; Kay had gone to the hairdresser, and Bruce III was at St. Stephens School in Alexandria, Virginia. The only person I found at home was my senior enlisted aide, Sgt. Perry Castle, a hardworking, faithful noncommissioned officer who later served with me in Vietnam. He helped me throw some combat boots, fatigues, socks, and underwear in a duffel bag, and I was off. I left a note for Kay to say that I should be back in two or three weeks—a poor estimate, because I never did make it back to Quarters No. 2. Kay and our son moved to Bragg on schedule in June 1965; I finally reported there in early 1966.

By two o'clock that afternoon a young lieutenant colonel from army intelligence and I were airborne out of Davison Army Airfield at Fort Belvoir, Virginia. En route, the intelligence officer informed me about such things as the major ports, landing beaches, and transportation system in the Dominican Republic. He also briefed me on some of the leading Dominican personalities, this information serving to confuse rather than enlighten me. The truth was that no one had a handle on what was going on in Santo Domingo. At about four o'clock we touched down at Simmons Army Airfield at Fort Bragg, North Carolina. A few minutes later we arrived at the headquarters of the XVIII Airborne Corps, where our reception was lukewarm at best. The incumbent corps commander, Lt. Gen. John Bowen, would have been the logical man to command U.S. forces in the Dominican Republic but had not been selected, apparently because he was slated to retire shortly. Moreover, he had not been informed of my mission at Bragg until we landed at Simmons. Understandably, he took a dim view of this interloper from the Pentagon with instructions to raid his command for anything I wanted.

Nevertheless, the corps chief of staff, Brig. Gen. Robert R. Linvill, had already organized a small but complete staff for the expedition, headed by Col. Frank Linnel, the corps deputy chief of staff, as well as a provisional communications unit using people and equipment from the corps's 50th Signal Battalion. This group, to double in brass as both joint staff and senior army staff in the Dominican Republic, made an outstanding team, earning the admiration of the American ambassador and U.S. mission personnel in Santo Domingo and working smoothly with the other major military commands in the area. (Later, Linvill took over as the chief of staff at the insistence of Gen. Harold K. Johnson, who wanted the corps's first team in the action. Likewise, Stanley Resor, secretary of the army, made certain that U.S. forces committed to the Dominican Republic were fully supported even though they were competing for available resources with the growing number being committed to Vietnam.) Other key staff members were Cols. Herbert Bowlby, G-3, Plans and Operations; John Foulk, G-2, Intelligence; Jean Holstein (later Mike Murley), G-4, Logistics; James Royalty, G-1, Personnel, and G-5, Civil Affairs; Robert Terry, Signal Officer; Roy Bass, Provost Marshal; Robert Abraham, Liaison Officer to the U.S. Air Force, and Harold ("Doc") Hayward, G-3 Plans Officer. The corps sergeant-major, Kenneth Merritt, headed the enlisted contingent of the staff, which was made up of combat veterans, all experienced paratroopers. General Bowen was kind enough to lend me also his junior aide, Lt. Bernard Rethore, a tall, gangly, bespectacled youngster just out of school with a degree in economics. He was intelligent, courageous, and loyal, and from the beginning we hit it off well together.

Before we left Bragg, my new staff briefed me. They had good information on the air movement of forces between Pope Air Force Base, North Carolina (adjoining Fort Bragg) and San Isidro air base in the Dominican Republic, as well as on the 82d Airborne Division elements and other units that had arrived there, but their knowledge of the political and military situation was even less complete than mine, which was skimpy at best. So in a sense we were all starting out at the same zero base. By

5:00 P.M. we had finished our business at Bragg and moved to our assigned chalk mark (aircraft spotted at a specific place ready for loading) at Pope field.

Before takeoff, I visited the joint airlift coordination and control center at Pope, the nerve center of the gigantic air movement already under way. Here Brig. Gen. Robert C. Taber, an assistant division commander of the 82d, controlled the loading of army troops, equipment, and supplies as called forward from the Dominican Republic by the division commander, Maj. Gen. Robert H. York. The sequence of takeoff, however, was a joint function, coordinated between Taber, the army representative, and Brig. Gen. Ernest M. Hardin, U.S. Air Force, the commander of the troop carrier division conducting the airlift. One wing of the division was based at Pope, the other at Sewart Air Force Base, Tennessee. Both Taber and Hardin were at Pope during the movement. Hardin controlled the U.S. end and was responsible for feeding in the air force elements that were being airlifted to the Dominican Republic. This impressive operation was working well. Taber, a slender, incisive, and tough-minded soldier, was very much on top of the situation. (Later I was fortunate to have him as my chief of staff in Vietnam.) Equally hard-nosed and efficient, Hardin was a big raw-boned, cigar-chomping Kentuckian whose troops, air force or army, would go to hell for him. Military professionals and leaders don't come much better than "Moose" Hardin.[5]

Refueling difficulties and a cranky outboard turboprop engine delayed our takeoff until 7:30 P.M., well after dark. The flight from Pope to San Isidro is about 1,100 nautical miles and takes four and a half hours in a C-130, at that time the workhorse of the Tactical Air Command's airlift fleet. The C-130 is both a strategic and a tactical aircraft, with a range of 2,000-3,000 miles carrying a full load of paratroopers (sixty-six men ready for parachute assault) or other cargo, plus a unique tactical ability to perform either parachute assault operations or landings on short, rough, unimproved airfields. Given the ambiguous situation in the Dominican Republic—we were uncertain whether a landing could be made at San Isidro airfield or whether a parachute assault would be necessary—an aircraft that could carry out either kind of operation was the ideal choice. Moreover, the C-130 could make the turnaround at San Isidro and return to Pope without refueling.

The weather, both local and en route, was good and our flight uneventful, so I was able to catnap in the bunk on the flight deck behind the crew and above the troop compartment. I also enjoyed talking to the pilot and his crew, as well as admiring this highly professional team in action. As we neared San Isidro, the weather turned sour, and we made our final approach over water in a blinding tropical rainstorm. At the last minute the airfield lights failed, and I had a grandstand seat for a demonstration of the superb flying skill needed to put the big heavily loaded aircraft safely down on a wet, dark strip in a severe squall. It was just past midnight in the first minutes of 1 May 1965 when we rolled to a stop near the airfield control tower. As we stepped off the ramp just behind the port engines onto the concrete, U.S. Army jeeps were getting into position to light the field with their headlights. The field was clearly in the hands of U.S. paratroopers in battle dress, steel "pots," M-16 rifles, and all.

CHAPTER 1

Origins of the Revolution

The origins of the 1965 Dominican revolution go back to the early 1900s, when the United States time and again intervened in the Caribbean to protect its national interests—strategic, political, and economic. After the ejection of Spain from the region as a result of the Spanish-American War, the United States was ever alert to any attempted foreign penetration that would jeopardize the political or territorial integrity of the area or the substantial U.S. economic investments there. Of major strategic importance, the Panama Canal was built during these first years of the twentieth century. In the Dominican Republic, as in many other Caribbean countries, sugar, fruit, and mineral production were especially profitable enterprises. During these early years of the century, the United States exercised political and financial control over Dominican affairs and in 1916 even established a military government under the U.S. Navy and Marine Corps, an occupation that lasted eight years.

In the late 1930s, after repeated interventions in the region, from Mexico to Nicaragua, in Panama, and in Haiti and the Dominican Republic, the United States began to have second thoughts about the wisdom of its Caribbean policy. The world-wide economic depression that began in the early 1930s contributed to a concurrent U.S. decision to adopt an explicit policy of nonintervention in Latin American affairs. President Franklin D. Roosevelt in 1933 adopted a Good Neighbor Policy toward Latin America, leading to the withdrawal in 1934 of U.S. marines from Haiti, the last of our "occupation" forces in the area.

Then World War II brought home to the United States the vital importance of Latin America. Fifty percent of the raw materials needed to supply U.S. defense industries came from the area, while allied bases in the Caribbean and South Atlantic proved essential in overcoming the German submarine threat to allied forces and materials transiting the area. After the war, however, the United States forgot its Latin American allies. Their economies devastated during the war, they now became orphans of the cold war. Although an inter-American system, the Organization of the American States (OAS), was created, the United States was unwilling to lend the economic aid that Latin American nations desperately needed to bring about meaningful social and economic reforms, and regarded the OAS as primarily a security system to block the expansion of communism in the Western Hemisphere.

During the Eisenhower years, the United States woke up too late to "save" Cuba from defecting to the Soviet orbit in 1959-1960, and the "Cuban problem" was passed on to John F. Kennedy and succeeding U.S. presidents. Meanwhile in the mid-1950s, the United States began its twenty-five-year involvement in southeast Asia. This was the overall situation when the Dominican crisis arose in 1965.

The Dominican Republic, with an area roughly the size of Vermont and New Hampshire combined and with a mid-1960s population of about five million people (about seven million in the 1980s), occupies the eastern half of the island of Hispaniola lying midway between Cuba to the west and Puerto Rico to the east along the northern rim of the Caribbean Sea. Jungle-covered mountains separate the Dominican Republic from its historically unfriendly neighbor Haiti, which occupies the western part of the island; and the Cordillera Central, a high mountain spine running generally northwest to southeast, splits the Dominican Republic about in half. (It also boasts the highest peak in the Caribbean region—Pico Duarte, 10,417 feet. Indeed, most of the western part of the republic is mountainous. The eastern areas enjoy the most desirable land for agriculture. Another rugged mountain range, the northern

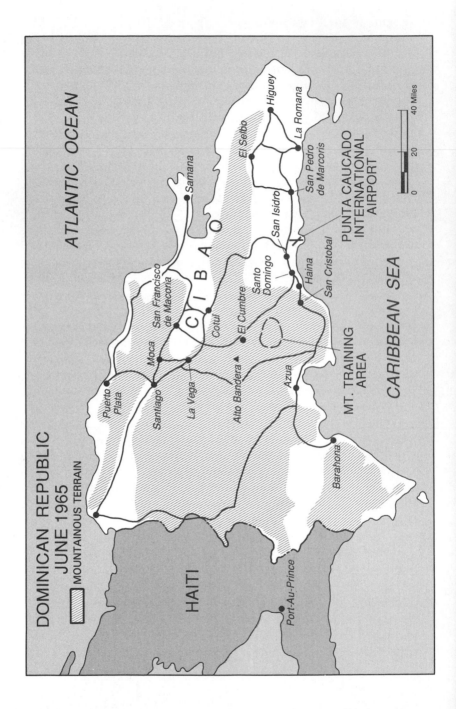

cordillera, runs along the northern coast. Between this range and the Cordillera Central lies a lush, rich region—the nation's breadbasket—which the Spanish named the Cibao. Some of the earliest New World cities were founded in the Cibao: Moca, La Vega, San Francisco de Macoris, and Santiago de los Caballeros (Santiago for short), the country's second largest city. Santo Domingo, the capital and largest city, with a population in 1965 of half a million (today about 1.4 million), lies on the south central coast. As in many Caribbean nations, the capital is the heart and brain of the republic: "As goes Santo Domingo, so goes the Dominican Republic."

Three-fourths of the Dominican people are *mestizos* (of mixed blood), and as in Cuba there are significant Spanish (15 percent) and black (10 percent) minorities. Typical of the Caribbean region, there is a nexus between race and socioeconomic class, as expressed in an old folk saying: "A rich Negro is a mulatto, but a rich mulatto is a white man." There are no Jim Crow laws against racial or ethnic groups, but subtle and inexorable economic law bars disproportionate numbers of blacks and persons of mixed black and European blood from staying in the better hotels, attending the best theaters, eating in the famous restaurants, or living in the more prosperous residential areas. Likewise, senior positions in civilian professions and higher military rank tend to be denied to people of mixed race. In the educational system, both public and parochial, blacks and *mestizos* are usually found only in the lowest grades and rarely progress upward, especially into the college level. Thus, social and racial inequities, although not founded in law, are widespread and severe, with white and predominantly white people controlling the social and power structure.[1]

Also typical of the Caribbean are overpopulation and the high rate of unemployment. Most jobs are only seasonal; many Dominican males with much time on their hands enjoy such pursuits as gambling, cockfighting, and baseball, the national sport. At the lower levels the Dominican society is a matriarchy: the mothers raise and feed large families, eking out a bare existence, while the men brag about how many children they have sired. To make life more interesting, however, Dominicans have a tradition of violence in settling the disputes that erupt all too frequently. It is said that a Dominican boy becomes a man when he starts wearing a pistol in his belt.

In 1930, six years after the U.S. Marines had departed, Rafael Trujillo, now in command of the Dominican National Guard, seized power during a revolution brought on at least in part by the American stock market crash of 1929. Trujillo had gotten his start during the occupation when the United States created the national guard, a national constabulary initially officered by Americans. He was an early graduate of the Dominican Military Academy, also founded by the U.S. occupiers and intended to develop professional, apolitical officers for the national guard. According to U.S. Marine Corps documents, however, Trujillo's record there was a tarnished one.[2]

During the 1930s and 1940s, including the wartime period, Trujillo's rule appeared to be benign, and the country made some progress. Old industries were revived, new ones were created, and the number of jobs increased; trade likewise increased, especially with the United States. The quality of public education improved as well, although literacy remained below the 40 percent mark during Trujillo's time. Modern highways were built, a sophisticated telecommunications system was installed, magnificent public buildings were erected, and the arts were encouraged and supported by the government. In this climate the relatively small middle class grew larger, as did the number of affluent families.

On balance, Trujillo's popularity as a benefactor rose among the people, and the perception of him abroad was generally favorable; he was considered at worst a benevolent despot. Handsome, physically impressive, bright, and dynamic, Trujillo paid for advertisements in newspapers and on billboards in the United States to enhance his image with the U.S. public and officialdom. But in the 1950s sinister stories about oppression, atrocities, and corruption began to leak out, and the world came to realize his regime's true nature. By 1961 the Catholic Church was denouncing him as a bloodthirsty tyrant.[3]

Altogether, Trujillo's reign was truly incredible. Even his

notable success in developing the infrastructure of the nation was achieved at the expense of the people and their social and economic development, because he milked the country like a cow. In 1961 his family, with a new worth of $800 million, owned one-third of the cultivated land and controlled two-thirds of the sugar industry, the nation's largest asset. He became a cruel, barbaric despot who killed off any opposition, or anyone he didn't like, and destroyed anyone courageous enough to demonstrate leadership ability. Upper-class families in Santo Domingo learned to conceal any visible sign of affluence, and they kept their maturing daughters out of sight because Trujillo liked to abduct beautiful young girls who caught his fancy. He left a legacy of violence, hate, distrust, and intrigue that will take generations to overcome.

When the OAS Human Rights Commission issued a damning report on conditions in the Dominican Republic in June 1960, Trujillo's standing in Latin America hit a new low. Not surprisingly, having already established that the Dominican dictator was backing a plot to assassinate President Betancourt of Venezuela, the OAS imposed political and economic sanctions against the Trujillo regime in August 1960. President Eisenhower promptly suspended all diplomatic and economic relations with Santo Domingo.[4]

Trujillo's bloody thirty-one-year rule came to an abrupt end in May 1961 when he was killed by gunfire while riding in a car to one of his ranches outside Santo Domingo. The country immediately plunged into an even more unstable phase of its turbulent history. Following a bitter power struggle during 1961-62—involving Trujillo's heirs, returning political exiles, and military leaders—free elections with official OAS observers on the ground were held in December 1962. Juan Bosch, leader of the liberal, leftist Dominican Revolutionary Party (PRD), emerged with a large majority as the victor. In the meantime the United States, seeking to stabilize the situation, inaugurated both economic and military assistance programs under a new ambassador, John Bartlow Martin, while the OAS lifted its sanctions. Bosch, however, by such actions as legalizing the previously outlawed Communist parties, alienated the right wing, especially the military, many of whose members were corrupt. The outcome was a bloodless coup in September 1963 engineered by Col. Elias Wessin y Wessin, commander of the elite Armed Forces Training Center (CEFA), which sent Bosch into exile in Puerto Rico. After an outraged President John F. Kennedy stopped all U.S. aid and withdrew his ambassador, the newly promoted General Wessin bowed to American pressure and in September 1964 turned the government over to a three-man civilian junta headed by Donald Reid Cabral, a well-known, American-educated businessman in Santo Domingo. Meanwhile Lyndon B. Johnson had become the U.S. president following Kennedy's assassination in November 1963.

With the military holding power behind the scenes, the new triumvirate found itself trapped between the political extremes of the far right and far left, the fundamental Dominican problem being the absence of any substantial group of moderates at the center of the political spectrum. The renewed outlawing of all Communist and extreme leftist parties triggered guerrilla and terrorist activities against the government, which felt compelled to respond with an intensive counterguerrilla campaign. At this juncture, unfortunately, an economic setback to the sugar industry helped increase civil unrest amid numerous rumors of planned coups, particularly on the part of Juan Bosch and his PRD followers in Puerto Rico. Meanwhile, the United States had recognized the new civilian government and late in 1964 had sent as the new ambassador William Tapley Bennett, an experienced and well-thought-of career diplomat who had served in Bolivia and Panama.

The Reid government, in spite of its problems, made strong efforts to reform the military and reduce corruption within its ranks. These actions caused friction between older and very conservative senior military leaders who resisted any change and younger, restless junior officers who favored fundamental change. As a result, both older and younger factions were involved in planning separate coups against Reid, to take place before the promised free elections scheduled for September 1965.[5]

On the eve of the 1965 Dominican crisis, the United States was facing a changing global situation. Although serious problems remained in Berlin and western Europe, hostilities in southeast Asia had taken center stage. The Caribbean, however, was no less strategically important to the United States than before, and the Dominican question confronted President Johnson with the need to take swift, decisive action in this area if U.S. forces were to undertake a major commitment in Vietnam halfway around the world. But Johnson also faced a large domestic political problem. Having seen Eisenhower criticized for "losing" Cuba and Kennedy humiliated by the Bay of Pigs failure, Johnson was determined that no similar disaster would befall him: there would be no "second Cuba" while he was president.[6]

On 23 April 1965, Ambassador Bennett returned to the United States to visit his ailing mother. He had been personally assured by Reid, who was fully aware of the multiple coups being planned, that no overt attempt would occur for several months. But unknown to Bennett or Reid, the stage was already set for civil war in the Dominican Republic.[7] The very next day, a Bosch-inspired PRD coup attempt was prematurely triggered, apparently several days earlier than planned, when army troops in two separate barracks on the western outskirts of Santo Domingo revolted. The chief of staff of the Dominican armed forces and other military leaders, who had gotten wind of the plot and had gone to one of the camps hoping to head it off, were taken prisoner. Army officers and men in rebellion totaled about 1,500. The elite navy "frogman" element also defected, but the rest of the navy and virtually all of the air force remained loyal to the Reid government. Gen. Wessin's CEFA national police in downtown Santo Domingo declined to oppose the rebels but remained steadfast in the rest of the country.

Taking advantage of the situation, the PRD, whose ranks included some Soviet-oriented Marxists, almost immediately began to mobilize. Its leaders seized control of the official Radio Santo Domingo (which had numerous relay sites and could transmit simultaneously throughout the country) and began to broadcast appeals for the people to demonstrate in the streets for the return of Juan Bosch, the deposed *presidente*. A Castorite group, the "1J4" party (named for an aborted Cuban invasion of the Dominican Republic on 14 June 1959), immediately joined the PRD. Using the estimated 10,000-12,000 weapons taken from the two army camps, the PRD and 1J4 soon had large numbers of armed civilians in the streets. When roving armed bands began shooting on sight any member of the national police on duty in downtown Santo Domingo, the policemen discarded their uniforms and melted away. Another active but relatively small Communist-oriented party, the Movimiento Popular Dominicano (MPD), which was Maoist in outlook, seized commercial gasoline stations, where numerous Molotov cocktails were assembled and distributed to the crowds. Armed bands burned the offices of conservative parties and the premises occupied by the anti-Communist newspaper *Prensa Libre,* and erected barricades on the main streets. By the morning of Sunday, 25 April, the law and order previously maintained by the national police had disappeared in downtown Santo Domingo.[8]

Meanwhile, on Saturday night the rebel military under Colonel Francisco Deno Caamano, Dominican Army, who had been an adviser to Donald Reid but had joined the rebellion, had moved into downtown Santo Domingo. There they established defensive positions on the Duarte Bridge over the Ozama River, marking the eastern boundary of the city, as well as in various large parks from which they could command the major avenues in the vicinity. These forces had not only individual weapons but also mortars and machine guns. The arms stocks available to the rebels were enlarged a short time later when they overran and captured the Ozama Fortress in the southeastern part of the city, the main government arsenal.[9]

Before the revolt, the Dominican Army, numbering about 10,000 men, comprised seven infantry brigades stationed about the country. It was neither trained nor equipped for mobile tactical operations but was oriented, like the rest of the armed forces, to defend against an external conventional attack—for example, from Haiti. The Dominican Navy, with about 3,500 personnel, owned one obsolete destroyer, a few patrol boats, and some service aircraft; the Dominican Air Force, some 4,000 strong, possessed about 120 aircraft, mostly obsolescent. The loyal armored force was from CEFA, in effect separate from the army and stationed with the air force at San Isidro airfield, the principal air force base. About 2,500 in number, CEFA acted autonomously and was seemingly responsible only to its commander, General Wessin y Wessin. The Dominican National Police numbered some 8,500 countrywide at this time, with about half of the so-called *cascos blancos* and their headquarters located in the capital. This police force had its own chief but was considered to be part of the Dominican military under the minister of armed forces.

In the ambassador's absence, the deputy chief of the U.S. mission, William Connett, was in charge of the U.S. embassy. The defense attaché, a navy commander, and the army and air force attachés were also present and actively engaged in a liaison role with their Dominican counterparts, but the chief and most members of the U.S. Military Assistance and Advisory Group (MAAG) were in the Panama Canal Zone attending a MAAG chiefs conference conducted by the U.S. unified commander for Latin America (known as the Commander-in-Chief U.S. Southern Command, or CINCSOUTH), with headquarters at Quarry Heights in the Canal Zone. At that time CINC-SOUTH was responsible for all military aid programs in Central and South America, as well as in the Caribbean. Since a different unified commander, CINCLANT, with headquarters at Norfolk, Virginia, was responsible for the strategic overwatch of and operational contingency planning in the Caribbean (as well as for the North Atlantic and South Atlantic), U.S. military responsibility with respect to the Dominican Republic was split between two widely separated headquarters. Moreover, CINCSOUTH has traditionally been an army billet and CINCLANT, a navy one.[10]

At any rate, the revolt began when both the U.S. ambassador and the MAAG chief, Colonel Joseph Quilty, were out of the country. Quilty, a burly, outspoken marine, was naturally unhappy about the circumstances because he felt that the presence of American MAAG personnel with modern mobile communications might have cleared up some of the early confusion within the Dominican military and kept matters from getting out of hand. Because the rebellion spread so swiftly, however, it is very doubtful that the MAAG could have prevented the breakdown of Dominican security forces in the capital.

On 25 April a prominent PRD leader, José Rafael Molina Urena, at the urging of Juan Bosch in Puerto Rico, declared himself the provisional president of the republic and leader of the revolution, pending Bosch's return. The rebels took the name "Constitutionalists" in reference to the 1963 constitution instituted by Bosch when he was president (a constitution that conservatives considered Communistic because, for example, it circumscribed the right to own private property). In response, the opposing Dominican military leaders adopted the name "Loyalists" and belatedly decided to support the government, or what little was left of it. But it was too late: rebel forces under Colonel Caamano had that morning stormed the Presidential Palace and taken Donald Reid prisoner. Caamano later that day allowed Reid to escape to a sanctuary in Santo Domingo.[11]

At this time, the Dominican chiefs included General Wessin y Wessin, who had been appointed chief of the armed forces by Reid just before the government was overturned; Adm. Francisco Rivera Caminero, chief of the Dominican Navy; Gen. Jésus de Los Santos Céspedes, commander of the Dominican Air Force; Gen. Jacinto Martinez Arana, commander of the Dominican Army; and Col. Hermano Despradel Brachs, chief of the Dominican National Police. When the loyalist government was left without a political leader, General Wessin technically became the de facto head of state. The Dominican chiefs, however, could mount only ineffectual actions. On the afternoon of 25 April, the air force strafed the rebel-held Presidential Palace with four World War II–vintage P-51 Mustangs, losing one to ground machine-gun fire, while the navy, operating from the Ozama River, lobbed four shells over the palace from a gunboat, which then quickly left the area. Neither attack did any real damage. Indeed, Chargé d'Affaires Connett telephoned Secretary of State Rusk on 25 April to report that constitutionalist military forces were in control of downtown Santo Domingo (the governmental, business, financial, telecommunications, and news center of the country), while the loyalist military seemed to be "divided, ineffectual, and undecided."[12]

By the next day it seemed clear to the U.S. embassy that armed civilians under the control of the PRD and 1J4 now outnumbered the original rebel regular soldiers under Caamano. Connett, moreover, was convinced that the rebel movement was being dominated by the more radical leftist political party leaders (many of whom were known Communists), who had gained ascendancy over the relatively moderate rebel military leaders. Radio Santo Domingo, now firmly in rebel hands, renewed its calls for increasingly violent actions against any opposition.[13]

As the situation deteriorated, the U.S. Joint Chiefs of Staff, without direct presidential authority, ordered precautionary measures to protect U.S. citizens in the country. As a result, by early Monday, 26 April, the Caribbean Ready Amphibious Squadron, with one marine battalion landing team afloat, was in position near Santo Domingo prepared to evacuate American citizens when so directed. And very early on Tuesday a brigade of the 82d Airborne Division at Fort Bragg and appropriate airlift and other elements of the Tactical Air Command (TAC) headquartered at Langley Air Force Base, Virginia, were alerted for possible movement to the crisis area.[14]

On 27 April, General Wessin's CEFA troops based at San Isidro (about twenty miles east of Santo Domingo) advanced on the capital from the east, while another loyalist force from the Mella Camp in San Cristobal (about fifteen miles west of Santo Domingo) entered the western suburbs. The CEFA force crossed the Duarte Bridge against rebel opposition and established a firm bridgehead on the western bank of the Ozama River, while the other loyalist force recaptured the Presidential

Palace. That same day, the Dominican navy again fired a few futile rounds at the palace, but the air force did not fly any operational sorties.

On the same day the rebels, unopposed, consolidated their hold on downtown Santo Domingo, taking the Ozama Fortress and seizing a store of government arms, estimated at five to ten thousand in number, including some automatic weapons. In the western residential environs, despite the presence of loyalist troops, rebel paramilitary groups entered the grounds of the Hotel Embajador and harassed U.S. citizens gathering there in anticipation of being evacuated. Outside the hotel, rebels lined Americans up and fired shots over their heads, while others fired at the building's upper-story windows. These actions were conspicuous indicators that discipline and control were lacking on the rebel side.[15]

Returning to Santo Domingo early that afternoon, Ambassador Bennett was almost immediately visited at the embassy by Constitutionalist President Molina Urena, accompanied by Colonel Caamano. Urena asked that the United States intercede to stop loyalist attacks against rebel forces that also endangered innocent civilians and to mediate a negotiated settlement. The request tacitly admitted that Urena and his PRD military leaders had little control, much less influence, over the disparate rebel forces. Bennett refused, reminding Urena that he had started the rebellion in the first place and noting the ascendant Communist role in the uprising, but did agree to help arrange a cease-fire and eventual settlement.[16] Molina Urena and the civilian PRD leaders, apparently taking Bennett's response as a suggestion to throw in the towel and fearing for their lives, took refuge in the Colombian Embassy, where they were granted political asylum. Caamano thereupon assumed the titular leadership of the self-proclaimed Constitutionalist Government, although it seemed clear that he was only a figurehead as far as the more radical leftist groups were concerned.[17]

In later months Bennett was severely criticized for his actions, even by some of his own colleagues in the State Department. The thrust of their argument was that this was the last opportunity open to the United States to stop the fighting and avoid the necessity for an American military intervention, and that Bennett should not have rejected out of hand Molina Urena's request for help. But such hindsight judgments do not square with the factual knowledge available to Bennett at the time. Bennett told me later how deeply and personally he felt affronted by the PRD's coup attempt in his absence, and that at the time of Urena's plea for help he was not about to let the PRD wiggle out of its self-inflicted predicament. Doing so would have been buying a pig in a poke, because he had no assurance that a constitutionalist government could maintain a moderate stance, while wooing the leftist groups, without inviting a Communist takeover—and Bennett was under direct, urgent, and personal presidential instructions to take no chances on that score.[18]

On the same day, 27 April, the evacuation of U.S. and other foreign nationals began. President Johnson's decision to begin the evacuation, influenced by the rebel attempts to intimidate American citizens at the Hotel Embajador, was relayed to General Wheeler shortly after noon on 27 April through Assistant Secretary of State for Inter-American Affairs Jack Vaughn—not an unusual occurrence inasmuch as State is normally in charge of such contingencies, and the situation was as much political as military. The people assembled at the hotel were convoyed in motor vehicles under national police guard along the coastal highway to Haina, the main Dominican naval base about ten miles west of the capital. From Haina, the evacuees were taken by U.S. boats and helicopters to U.S. ships off shore and then by sea to safety in Puerto Rico. Since the overland evacuation route passed through an area still held by loyalist forces, an armed U.S. escort was not provided at that time. These initial operations were completed by late afternoon.[19]

At San Isidro air base, also on 27 April, loyalist generals chose a new three-man military junta: an army colonel, a navy captain, and an airman, Col. Pedro Bartholomé Benoit, who acted as the head. The Dominican chiefs apparently believed that a new and less senior junta might achieve a better effort from the rank and file of the loyalist forces, who no doubt were in a confused state of mind at this point. The Dominican Air Force did launch a small attack against rebel positions in the city, but it caused little damage. This was the only loyalist operation conducted that day. The next day, 28 April, saw the balance swing against the loyalists at about the same time that moderate PRD influence within the constitutionalist leadership all but disappeared.

When rebel snipers began shooting at the U.S. embassy on 28 April, Ambassador Bennett asked the U.S. naval commander offshore in charge of evacuation operations, Capt. James A. Dare, to reinforce the marine guard protecting the embassy compound, which included the ambassador's residence. At about the same time, having been warned by National Police Chief Despradel that he could no longer guarantee the safety of American citizens in Santo Domingo, and having also received an informal request for U.S. military help from Colonel Benoit at San Isidro, Bennett recommended to Secretary Rusk that the president approve the deployment of U.S. Marines not only to reinforce the embassy guard but also to protect Americans in the city. Johnson approved such an action, and that evening about two companies of the marine battalion afloat went ashore at Haina. From there they moved overland to the Embajador, securing the hotel grounds and the adjacent polo field as a base for further evacuation direct by helicopter to the USS *Boxer*. The first American casualty occurred during the march from Haina, a short distance from the hotel, when a marine was killed by sniper fire. Concurrently, a marine platoon moved by helicopter directly from the *Boxer* to secure the embassy compound (some distance to the east of the Embajador) in the international section of Santo Domingo where most of the foreign embassies were located.[20]

Back home that night, in a national TV address to the nation, President Johnson announced the marine presence in Santo Domingo, explaining that it was necessary to protect Americans and other foreign nationals caught in the civil war, as well as to protect the U.S. embassy, which had been hit with hostile small-arms fire. Ambassador Bennett, realizing that the situation might well worsen and that the president might need more than verbal requests from Dominican authorities to justify a U.S. decision to intervene in force, let it be known that the U.S. government would give serious consideration to a formal request for military support. He was rewarded for his foresight around midnight when Colonel Benoit provided an official written request for direct U.S. military support on the grounds that Dominican security forces could no longer handle the situation.[21] (Some time later President Johnson would cite this request as the legal basis for American military intervention.)

One of Bennett's most difficult problems during this period was to convey to Washington a sense of immediacy, of the "clear and present danger" inherent in the situation. Record communications to Washington were secure and reliable; the communications center in the embassy was shared with CIA Chief of Station David Philips. (Although the State Department had its own separate, confidential code, CIA personnel who operated the center did have access to embassy traffic passing though it.) But written dispatches transmitted electronically can neither keep pace with a fast-moving situation nor express adequately the critical effect of a swift succession of traumatic events, and telephone service within Santo Domingo had been completely disrupted when the city's telecommunications center fell into the hands of the rebels. Bennett's only means of communication with the loyalist junta at San Isidro air base, for example, was by liaison officer flying in a rickety old French Alouette helicopter. Normal voice communications with the outside world likewise had been interrupted. As a result, keeping Washington fully informed about an unclear, dynamic situation was almost impossible. Nevertheless, Bennett did succeed in getting the message of immediate urgency across to the president, who grasped the nettle of the problem.

At the outset of the crisis, the president had dispatched to Santo Domingo a former U.S. ambassador to the Dominican Republic, John Bartlow Martin, as his special emissary. Martin, with impressive credentials as a liberal, was very knowledgeable about Dominican affairs but had been unable to find a way to bring the two Dominican political extremes to the conference table; nevertheless, he played an influential role because he satisfied himself that the rebellion had in fact taken on a definite leftist/Communist coloration and so informed Johnson. Martin's conclusions no doubt had a major effect on the president's thinking and probably helped Johnson reach his own judgment that stabilizing the political and military situation without risking the loss of the Dominican Republic to Communism would require intervention with American forces.[22]

Domestic and international reactions up to this time, 28 April, had generally been sympathetic. Polls indicated the U.S. public opinion supported the evacuation operations, and for the most part Latin America had also favored U.S. actions— although Argentina, for example, expressed shock and indignation. Within the OAS, however, the United States got off on the wrong foot, even though its representative to the OAS, Ambassador Ellsworth Bunker, was one of the most experienced and successful American diplomats of the time. It was on 27 April, as the initial evacuation from Santo Domingo was about to begin, that Bunker approached the Inter-American Peace Commission, a standing subordinate organ of the OAS Council, and asked for the first OAS discussion of the Dominican crisis. The commission, however, prudently decided to pass the matter to the OAS Council, scheduled to meet the following morning. Accordingly, on the morning of 28 April, Bunker informed the council that the evacuation operations carried out by U.S. Navy and Marine Corps contingents in the area on the preceding day had been necessary to save lives and that these actions were solely for that purpose. The reactions of the council members were cool but not adverse. That evening, as the situation in Santo Domingo worsened, Bunker called for another council meeting the next day, 29 April, at which he explained that American marines had landed in Santo Domingo the day before to protect the continuing evacuation and to secure the U.S. embassy from hostile attack. He also obtained the council's agreement to raise the subject before the OAS foreign ministers, who function collectively as the highest organ of the OAS and the only one empowered to take military action against a member state. The foreign ministers' meeting, however, could not be convened until Friday, 30 April.[23]

On Thursday, before the foreign ministers could meet, OAS Secretary General José A. Mora, a distinguished Costa Rican diplomat, received word from Monsignor Emanuel Clarizo, papal nuncio and dean of the diplomatic corps in Santo Domingo, that the situation was very serious, that he was attempting to arrange a cease-fire, and that he thought the OAS should lose no time in offering its good offices to resolve the dispute. This prompted the OAS Council's first resolution on the Dominican civil strife, calling for a cease-fire and the establishment of an International Security Zone (ISZ) in the western part of the capital in its diplomatic quarter. The vote, coming during the early hours of 30 April 1965, was 16 to 0 with four abstentions (Chile, Uruguay, Mexico, and Venezuela). Immediately after the 2:00 A.M. vote, the council adjourned, unaware that President Johnson had already committed the 82d Airborne Division, whose leading elements were at that moment landing at San Isidro. Moreover, U.S. marines had already deployed into the area of Santo Domingo that was to be designated the International Security Zone—several hours before the ISZ resolution was passed by the Council.[24] The timing of these troop deployments, which could not disguise the fact that the United States had acted unilaterally, would prove awkward at best for the U.S. government, particularly in its Latin American relations.

CHAPTER 2

Initial U.S. Operations
29 April–3 May 1965

Shortly after the president made the crucial decision at about 7:30 P.M., 29 April, to intervene with force to prevent a hostile takeover in the Dominican Republic, the leading elements of the 82d Airborne Division took off from Pope Air Force Base, North Carolina. (The 3d Brigade with two parachute infantry battalions constituted the initial "package" of the 82d Airborne's deployment plan called "Power Pack.") At about the same time the remainder of the U.S. Marine force afloat off Santo Domingo came ashore to secure the area of the city that a few hours later was designated an International Security Zone by the OAS Council. Neither the OAS Council, meeting in Washington on the night of 29-30 April, nor the OAS foreign ministers, scheduled to meet on 30 April, had any knowledge of these unilateral U.S. decisions and troop movements until after the fact.[1]

The U.S. diplomatic problem caused by the ensuing contretemps within the OAS, which had repercussions among the other Western allies, was truly a horrendous one. President Johnson's advisers, keenly aware of the potential for trouble, had pleaded with him to delay the paratrooper movement for at least a few hours, but to no avail. Johnson expected a loud public outcry both domestic and foreign, especially from Latin America, but he was confident of his own ability, supported by his administration, to allay any lasting resentment. Following his political instincts, the president went ahead full steam.

Arriving in the Dominican Republic as the designated U.S. commander on 1 May, I was not completely aware of the international complications involved and concentrated on the operational aspects of the intervention. But it wasn't long before I became attuned to the critical political dimensions, both at home and abroad, of our Dominican actions.

The U.S. operations put into motion on the night of 29 April were part of a family of CINCLANT contingency plans for the Caribbean. Known as CINCLANT OPLAN 310/2, and developed during the final days of the Trujillo dictatorship in the Dominican Republic, it was simply a movement plan involving a marine amphibious brigade and an army airborne brigade. After Juan Bosch's ouster in 1963, the plan had been revised at President Kennedy's suggestion to include several other options—a show of naval force, a naval blockade, and army troop movements to Puerto Rico—before the ultimate step of committing U.S. troops on Dominican soil.[2] The revision provided more flexibility with respect to the initial stage of any U.S. military intervention but added nothing in the way of specific planning beyond the first troop movements into the country.

Taking advantage of these additional options, the State Department had been able to persuade the president to approve flying the lead elements of the 82d Airborne Division first to Ramey Air Force Base, a Strategic Air Command (SAC) base in the northwest corner of Puerto Rico, where they would stage for the next move: a parachute assault against San Isidro, the main air base of the Dominican Air Force, a few miles east of Santo Domingo. Although State intended the move to Ramey as a show of force, hoping thereby to avoid actually engaging the paratroopers in the Dominican Republic, it seems quite clear that the president had no such reservation.

In any event, the 3d Brigade of the 82d took off in the dark from Pope Air Force Base for Ramey in a parachute assault configuration: that is, the troopers had their parachutes and assault gear with them. Loaded on separate aircraft were their heavier weapons and equipment, as well as their vehicles, all secured on heavy platforms that were each rigged with three large cargo chutes ready for "heavy drops." Most of the aircraft

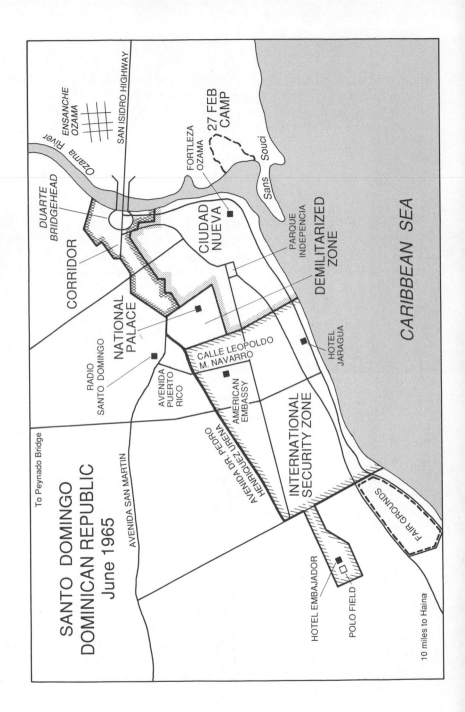

SANTO DOMINGO
DOMINICAN REPUBLIC
June 1965

To Peynado Bridge

AVENIDA SAN MARTIN

HOTEL EMBAJADOR

POLO FIELD

10 miles to Haina

FAIR GROUNDS

INTERNATIONAL
SECURITY ZONE

AVENIDA DR. PEDRO
HENRIQUEZ UREÑA

AVENIDA PUERTO
RICO

AMERICAN
EMBASSY

CALLE LEOPOLDO
M. NAVARRO

RADIO
SANTO DOMINGO

NATIONAL
PALACE

CORRIDOR

DUARTE
BRIDGEHEAD

Ozama River

ENSANCHE
OZAMA

SAN ISIDRO HIGHWAY

FORTLEZA
OZAMA

27 FEB
CAMP

Sans Souci

CIUDAD
NUEVA

PARQUE
INDEPENCIA

DEMILITARIZED
ZONE

HOTEL
JARAGUA

CARIBBEAN SEA

involved, whether loaded with men or with heavy gear, were C-130 troop carriers with four turboprop engines, designed especially for assault operations by either parachute or air landing. Taking off from Pope at five-minute intervals, with a flight time to Ramey of about five hours, the 150 or more C-130s assigned to the operation created an air stream of about sixty aircraft in the air at one time between the departure and arrival airfields.

As the lead aircraft were winging across Atlantic waters, intense discussions were under way in Washington as to the wisdom of staging the paratroopers through Ramey in light of the parlous situation in Santo Domingo. Mindful of the president's concern about being faced with a *fait accompli* before the airborne troops could arrive, McNamara and his deputy, Cyrus Vance, favored redirecting the airstream of troop carriers directly to San Isidro, prepared for either parachute assault or air landing, depending on whether the field at San Isidro was in friendly hands or not. Both CINCLANT and CINCSTRIKE (Commander-in-Chief Strike Command) were opposed to such a diversion, because they thought San Isidro was too small to accommodate the landing of the large number of C-130s involved and because it lacked the ground equipment needed to handle the heavy-drop loads efficiently. Late in the hour, the overall joint commander, Vice Adm. Masterson, who had arrived on the scene on 29 April, sent word that San Isidro, although not ready for night operations, was still in friendly hands. Consequently, Vance ordered the last-minute switch to San Isidro at a time when the lead aircraft was about halfway to Ramey. The final decision to land at San Isidro was reportedly made by Vance with Gen. Wheeler's reluctant concurrence.

There then unfolded a dramatic episode of joint army–air force operations of an unprecedented nature. When the final word came, Maj. Gen. Robert H. York, commanding the 82d Airborne Division, and Col. William Welch, commanding the troop carrier wing at Pope Air Force Base, were aboard the lead aircraft together, while Brig. Gen. Robert Deleshaw (assigned to the TAC's 9th Air Force) was flying near the formation in an EC-135 airborne command post from which he could direct the flight of the huge air armada. Turning this airstream around in flight and redirecting it to a different destination at night while flying over strange territory, mostly water, involved no mean navigational, communications, and control feats. Meanwhile, a navy pilot from the USS *Boxer* managed to contact the loyalist junta at San Isidro, put the control tower into operation, and get the landing lights turned on, although they worked only spasmodically. The first trooper carriers landed safely at about 2:15 A.M., 30 April.[3]

During the next few hours some forty troop-carrying C-130s landed, unloaded, and took off immediately for the return flight to Pope field. Heavy-load aircraft were a different matter, however. Sheer manpower and ingenuity managed to get the cargo off without the aid of ground-handling equipment, but ramp space on the airfield was soon saturated, even though arriving aircraft taxied in circles, "trunk to tail" like a herd of elephants, awaiting their turn to unload. Consequently, many of the following aircraft were directed to Ramey Air Force Base after all. Because Ramey, a SAC base, also lacked TAC ground-handling equipment, heavy-drop loads had to be manhandled off the aircraft there, too, and then loaded back on for an air-landing operation.

My arrival at San Isidro field in the early hours of 1 May occurred not long after the initial brigade of the 82d had closed at the air base. As I stepped down from the C-130, I spotted an old friend, Brig. Gen. Edward P. Smith, waiting there in the drenching rain under a poncho. A small, muscular man and a master parachutist, Smith was one stout fellow whom I was very happy to see at this moment. We walked away together, not trying to talk above the shrill whine of the inboard turboprop engines—which the pilot had not cut, since the aircraft had to taxi to a parking apron and prepare for immediate return flight. (Smith and Taber were the two assistant division commanders of the 82d: Taber ran the outloading operation at Pope airfield; Smith was York's second in command in the Dominican Republic.)

As we walked toward the division's command post, set up

temporarily in Hangar 2 of the air base, Smith told me that our arrival was pretty much a surprise—the 82d had only just received a message that we were en route—and that York was asleep and so did not know yet we had landed. Although I was reluctant to awaken the 82d's commander, an experienced, tough leader who no doubt needed some sleep, I felt that the sooner we got together the better. And so, a few minutes later, York and Smith and I were gathered around the division situation map in a corner of the hangar, where Lt. Col. Eugene P. Forrester, the division G-3 (plans and operations officer), briefed us.[4] All around us were sleeping men, some on cots but most on blankets or bedrolls laid on the concrete floor. The wind and rain made a din on the hangar roof, and the acoustics were awful. Nevertheless, Forrester did an outstanding job of laying out the current situation as the division staff saw it.

First, to the east of the capital, one U.S. airborne battalion (1st Battalion, 505th Infantry) had secured San Isidro airfield; another (1st Battalion, 508th Infantry), the first to arrive in the country, had secured the Duarte Bridge over the Ozama River about eighteen miles west of the air base. Inasmuch as the river marked the eastern boundary of Santo Domingo, the U.S. bridgehead controlled the main eastern exit from the city. The headquarters of the 3d Brigade of the 82d was located within the bridgehead, which also encompassed the main power plant serving most of the city—a factor of major importance, it turned out, in the unfolding struggle for control of the city. Rebel forces had resisted the U.S. seizure of the Duarte Bridge, and both sides had suffered some casualties. Between San Isidro and the Duarte Bridge, however, no rebel activity was reported, and the connecting highway appeared to be under loyalist control.

On the western side of Santo Domingo, Forrester continued, the 3d Battalion, 6th U.S. Marines, had secured the ISZ, and the area farther west along the coastal highway to Haina, the principal naval base of the Dominican Navy, seemed to be in loyalist hands. Between the marines and the paratroopers, however, most of the heart of the capital city, the downtown area, was entirely in the hands of the rebel constitutionalists, who were proclaiming the absent Juan Bosch, still in Puerto Rico, as their leader. Downtown Santo Domingo, bounded by the Ozama River on the east and the Caribbean Sea to the south, was clearly the city's vital nerve center because, we discovered, it contained most of the important government office buildings, including the Presidential Palace; the nation's telecommunications, including major radio and TV stations as well as the telephone center and mainland and overseas cable terminals; the business and financial center; the newspaper presses and other media offices; and the customs offices and main port facilities.

Significantly, U.S. paratroopers advancing west from San Isidro had not been fired upon until they reached the Duarte Bridge, where they encountered long-range small-arms fire from the tops of buildings on the western (or city) side of the Ozama. It was presumed to be rebel fire because the junta's loyalist forces reacted to the paratroopers only with friendly waves. The loyalist military had been told to identify themselves by putting their caps on backward or sideways; they presented a comical appearance, but for recognition purposes it worked.

Within the U.S. bridgehead around the Duarte Bridge, there had been a small CEFA force under a Dominican army colonel. Earlier, it had been hoped that these government troops would move west and fill the gap in the city between the U.S. paratroopers and marines, but for reasons not completely known this never happened. Perhaps the Dominican commander felt that the rebels were too strong for his force to handle, or perhaps he had received orders to return to the CEFA base at San Isidro and leave the problem to the intervening American troops. Later, I learned from Lt. Col. Eldredge R. Long, the U.S. battalion commander in the bridgehead during the night of 30 April–1 May, that he had asked the Dominican commander at the bridge site to take his men off the front-line positions, where their presence resulted in frequent fire fights. Long hoped that this might quiet things down in the area and was glad when the Dominican commander did as requested.[5] That night the CEFA forces withdrew through the 82d's bridgehead and returned to San Isidro.

York also told me about the papal nuncio's efforts to maintain a cease-fire. From the point of view of the United States, cease-fire at that time made no sense either politically or militarily. It froze the situation in an inconclusive, ambiguous way, leaving U.S. forces widely separated and with no means to exert military pressure except by offensive action. It left the ISZ with no secure overland route to the principal airfields in the area—San Isidro air base and the civilian international airport at Punta Caucedo, the latter not then operational—both lying to the east of the capital. It left most governmental, economic, financial, communications, and media facilities in the hands of the self-proclaimed "Constitutionalist Government." In areas outside the ISZ, it left the rebel forces free to organize and fortify Santo Domingo, as well as to export arms, ammunition, mob violence, and guerilla warfare into the countryside. Finally, it left the loyal Dominican forces and the rebels free to get at each other's throats. Certainly, the humanitarian aspects of the cease-fire could not be denied (even though it was also evident that the papal nuncio had more than a passing political interest in the outcome of the rebellion); nevertheless, I could see no way to accomplish our assigned mission if the status quo were maintained.

I told York, therefore, that I did not recognize the cease-fire and that it was imperative to link up the U.S. marine and paratrooper forces as soon as possible, making every effort to avoid casualties, civilian or military. However, since we needed both U.S. and OAS approval for any such operation, we first had to demonstrate its feasibility using the U.S. forces at hand. Accordingly, I instructed York to conduct a reconnaissance in force, beginning at first light that day, 1 May, in order to confirm the presence, strength, and location of the main rebel forces in the city and to find a linkup route that would avoid our having to fight any more than necessary.

Later that day we got the results: a strong combat patrol, composed of elements from the 17th Reconnaissance Troop and the the 1st Battalion, 508th (all from the 82d Airborne) shortly after noon made contact with the marines in the northeast part of the ISZ perimeter. En route they encountered several hastily prepared roadblocks and scattered sniper fire but no effective resistance—although two paratroopers were killed and five wounded when a small element of the patrol became separated and blundered into the heart of rebel-held territory. After contacting the marines, the rest of the patrol returned safely to the Duarte bridgehead. This reconnaissance confirmed the presence of strong rebel forces in the city and uncovered a route, appearing to be only lightly defended, that eventually would become the U.S.-held corridor (about 2.5 kilometers long) through Santo Domingo between the ISZ and the Duarte bridgehead. Some valuable information about new road construction downtown, as well as details about parks, the configuration of major buildings, and the like, was also gathered by the patrol.

Early on 1 May, a beautiful sunny day, my aide and I took off in an army "huey," a UH-1B helicopter, for the U.S. embassy in the western part of Santo Domingo. (In addition to the UH-1B hueys that belonged to HQ XVIII Airborne Corps and the 82d Airborne Division, we had a separate assault helicopter company, also flying mostly hueys, which had been training at Fort Bragg for deployment to Vietnam before being sent to the Dominican Republic. These helicopters were invaluable—we simply could not have accomplished what we did in the Dominican Republic without them.) Col. Frank Linnel, my chief of staff, and the rest of the XVIII Airborne Corps staff stayed behind to establish a temporary command post (CP) near the 82d's CP. At about the same time, the U.S. Air Force elements ashore also established a command post at San Isidro near the headquarters of the 82d. My plan was to assume command of all U.S. land forces ashore as soon as the corps headquarters could communicate with Vice Adm. Masterson, commander of Joint Task Force (JTF) 122 afloat off Santo Domingo, and with the commander of the marines ashore.

Our chopper route took us along the highway from San Isidro

to the Duarte Bridge, thence south along the east bank of the Ozama River to the coast, west along the water-front, and finally north to the embassy; we thus avoided overflying territory known to be held by the constitutionalists. From a few hundred feet of altitude we got a good look at the area. Not far from San Isidro air base, passing over the drop zone where the originally planned parachute assault would have taken place, we were shocked to see the area pockmarked with large outcroppings of coral, not to mention several huge sinkholes full of water in the coral. They looked beautiful from the air but would have been dangerous obstacles for an assault parachute force. Since they had not shown up in the aerial photos furnished to us, it seemed obvious that the U.S. military attachés and MAAG personnel on duty in the Dominican Republic had not made an adequate personal reconnaissance of the ground. It was pretty country, however; we could see ripe fields of sugarcane inland to the north, and the coral-fringed water along the coast reminded me of the beautiful water and beaches of the Florida Gulf Coast. The highway between San Isidro and the capital was deserted except for military traffic, mostly American. From the air Santo Domingo looked deceptively peaceful for the moment, while out in the Caribbean Sea there was quite an impressive array of U.S. naval amphibious power.

We decided to land in a small patch of open ground in front of a large white palatial-looking building just west of the American embassy. It turned out to be a former residence of Trujillo's, which the Dominican Department of Agriculture had taken over for offices but had abandoned when the rebellion started. Leaving the crew with the helicopter, Rethore and I headed for the high wire fence between the grounds of the empty government building and the embassy. He had an M-16 rifle slung over his shoulder, while I was wearing a .38 Colt pistol in a shoulder holster on the outside of my uniform. As we clambered over the fence a burst of automatic fire, apparently coming from the old Trujillo "palace," erupted behind us, and we ended up in a heap on the ground, almost on top of the marine lieutenant commanding the platoon that guarded the embassy.

He explained that they had been receiving sporadic hostile fire from that direction and our sudden chopper appearance had probably set off a little action.

We left the marines, wishing them luck, and double-timed about 150 yards through a small grove to the embassy. A marine corporal on guard inside the front door passed us through into a scene of much activity and tension, an atmosphere much like that of a building under seige. We found ourselves in a large anteroom full of people, mostly male civilians plus a few women and several American military men. The embassy had become the center of U.S. and other foreign activity in Santo Domingo, and practically all American officials assigned to Dominican duty were using it as their base of operations, having been forced to abandon their own offices at other locations in the city.

We headed for the ambassador's office in the west wing of the building, where the deputy mission chief's smaller office adjoined it, access being through a small reception room serving them both. The reception area, with its couch, chairs, and a small table cluttered with books and magazines, was unoccupied. But the door to the deputy's office was ajar, disclosing a man sitting on the floor next to the desk, his legs stretched out, leaning back on both arms. He wore no coat, and his shirt was open at the collar, his tie loosened. Three other men squatted around him.

My first startled impression was that the man was a prisoner being interrogated. He turned out to be William Connett, the deputy U.S. mission chief, who had been chargé d'affaires when the rebellion broke out and acted in Ambassador Bennett's absence until his return on 27 April. Later, Connett was to be instrumental in establishing a close working relationship between the embassy staff and my military staff next door. A handsome, youngish-looking man, he shook hands without getting up, explaining that he preferred the floor to his desk because the building had been under hostile fire. The two windows in the room, one on the front and the other on the west side of the embassy building, were closed and shuttered on the outside. He waved me toward the door leading to the ambassador's office, a spacious, tastefully furnished room and, like Connett's, blacked out with shuttered windows and drawn curtains.

Ambassador Tap Bennett got up from his desk and greeted me with a warm smile. A tall, slim, reddish-blond man, he spoke in a cultured accent with only a trace of the southern flavor that befitted a descendant of a proud old Georgia family. He was expecting me, and I briefly explained my mission, assuring him that our forces would support him and U.S. policy to the best of our ability. As we discussed the situation, it was obvious that he had little solid information on what was going on downtown in the rebel sector. It was also clear that his only reliable communication with Vice Adm. Masterson was by helicopter messenger. Bennett agreed completely with our plans and was delighted that we would place our CP in the building next door. It was the beginning of a close, warm relationship, and I soon found it a pleasure to work with this courageous man of intelligence and good will.

Before I left Bennett, he pulled aside the drapes to reveal the shattered window almost directly behind his desk and recounted how he had been conversing on the phone with President Johnson when rebel fire hit the embassy. He had finished the conversation on the floor, and the president claimed that at his end he could hear the shots over the phone. As Bennett spoke, I glanced up at the large autographed photograph of the president that adorned the wall behind the desk. In a slyly serious pose, Johnson seemed to be listening to our conversation. I told the ambassador that I had to fly back to my temporary CP at San Isidro but that I would return the next day and thereafter remain in Santo Domingo.

My aide and I next visited the marines in the ISZ, where we met Lt. Col. P.F. Pederson, commander of the 3d Battalion, 6th Marines, whose command post was in an open area on the grounds of the University of Santo Domingo, which had been a hotbed of discontent just prior to the outbreak of hostilities. In most Latin American countries the universities are essentially autonomous, and even the police have limited authority over them. The presence of our troops no doubt deeply offended this tradition in Santo Domingo, but it could not be helped, because the campus offered one of the few open places inside the ISZ where troops could be bivouacked. When the head-quarters of the 4th MEB arrived a short time later, the brigade took over a hotel for its HQ, and we tried to minimize troop presence in the university area.

Pederson showed me his dispositions on a city map; his battalion was spread pretty thin over the ISZ, which covered about seven square kilometers in a mostly residential and governmental area of the city. He also related that the marines had initially pushed out to the north of the designated ISZ, planning to place their checkpoints at the main intersections along the next major street to the north, Avenida Puerto Rico, but they ran into such intense fire at its intersection to the northeast with Avenida San Martin that they pulled back to the present line along Avenida Dr. Pedro Henriquez Urena. We learned later that the troublesome northeastern intersection, which the marines had dubbed the "hot corner," was only a block and a half from the main operating site of Radio Santo Domingo, which the rebels understandably wanted to hold at all costs.

Unfortunately, the ISZ, which included most of the foreign embassies and the best residential part of the capital, had some serious flaws as initially drawn. The U.S. embassy found itself right on the front line (on Calle Leopoldo M. Navarro) marking the zone's eastern edge, and à la Berlin the ISZ was an island with no secure overland access route to any other area in friendly hands. Lacking an airfield within its boundaries, it could not be reached except by helicopter or over the beach from the sea.

The "hot corner" episode pointed up a major weakness in CINCLANT's contingency plans existing at the time: basically, they went no further than the introduction of U.S. forces into an area for missions involving simply the evacuation of American citizens and the protection of U.S. property. Lacking was an appreciation of the key places—government buildings, foreign embassies, telecommunication centers, TV and radio sites, news media offices, major utilities, and the like—that would have a significant bearing on broader missions involving stability or peacekeeping operations. Our initial military maps lacked such vital information, but fortunately, we found the local and Texaco road and city maps to be excellent for our needs. We soon received some sharp, clear, low-altitude aerial photographs of Santo Domingo made by the 9th Air Force and, later, some high-quality U.S. Army tactical maps. But in the early critical days it was the American oil corporation maps that saved the day.

Rethore and I returned to San Isidro to learn that our corps headquarters had established good communications with Masterson's JTF 122 headquarters aboard the *Boxer,* as well as with the marine headquarters ashore. And so, with Masterson's concurrence, at about 3:30 P.M. on 1 May I assumed command of all U.S. land forces in the country but reporting to JTF 122. We soon learned that there had been frequent communications outages, especially at night, between Masterson's HQ and CINCLANT at Norfolk. Navy communicators were inclined to blame the problem on adverse atmospheric conditions rather than on equipment or operator deficiencies.

The small field detachment from the army's Special Security Office (SSO) at Fort Bragg, which had accompanied me to the Dominican Republic with its own communications and cryptological capabilities, had already established excellent contact with Bragg from our initial corps CP at San Isidro and with the Department of the Army in Washington. (Each service has such a special, highly secure communications capability to handle sensitive and highly classified material on a top-level personal basis. Only a handful of senior officials are authorized to use this so-called "back channel" system. Messages are marked "eyes only" for specified addressees, as distinguished from open channel messages, which get much broader distribution.) That afternoon I was able to send my first personal message to General Wheeler, giving him the situation as we knew it as well as our intentions in the Dominican Republic.

In those early hectic days I sent daily back channels directly to the JCS chairman, sending each one also to CINCLANT for information, in keeping with Wheeler's original instructions. It was not long, however, before I received an irate message from Admiral Moorer, CINCLANT, telling me in no uncertain terms to start reporting directly to him or he would ask promptly for my relief. At about the same time I received a message from Wheeler, informing me that it would not be possible to have U.S. forces in the Dominican Republic report directly to Washington, that our chain of command would have to be through CINCLANT; nevertheless, we were to "info" the JCS chairman direct on all messages: that is, include the chairman as an information addressee on messages sent to CINCLANT. This settled the issue, and I soon established a close and warm relation with Moorer, which was to prove helpful several years later when as vice chief of staff, U.S. Army, I had quite a bit of business with him in his capacity first as chief of naval operations (CNO) and then as the chairman of the Joint Chiefs.

In the military support of U.S. forces in the Dominican Republic, CINCLANT had a major role to play; however, since the political guidance and political-military decisions we needed could come only from Washington, he was in effect a relay station, although of course his views were always taken into consideration. He was invariably supportive—I cannot recall a single instance when Moorer and his staff did not back us up completely—but it might have been more logical and efficient to have the commander in the Dominican Republic report directly to the JCS chairman or secretary of defense.

On the night of May 1-2, the last night I spent in San Isidro, President Johnson called me twice by phone, at 10:00 P.M. and at 4:00 A.M., using the C-130 "talking bird" flown in by the Air National Guard. It was a strange feeling to stand in front of the console on the dimly lit cargo deck of an aircraft crammed full of electronic gear and converse with the president of the United States. He was primarily interested in whether the fighting had stopped and repeatedly asked about casualties, particularly among our own troops. I told him about the 82d's reconnaissance probe and U.S. casualties (up to that time, six killed and sixteen wounded in action), assuring him that in all our operations the minimizing of loss of life and of property damage was an integral part of our planning. The president seemed to be satisfied.

Early on the morning of 2 May, my aide and I again took off by huey for the U.S. embassy. Previously, I had told Frank Linnel and the corps staff that my presence near the American embassy was imperative, that the embassy would be my forward CP for the present, and that the staff's priority task was to join me in Santo Domingo as quickly as possible. The staff accomplished the transfer, making shore-to-shore movements by navy lighters and using army hueys to lift sling loads, and by 3 May our headquarters had been established at the old Trujillo mansion next to the embassy, where we stayed for the duration. The corps signal people also installed a direct field phone line between Ambassador Bennett's desk and mine—a reasonably secure means of discussing something privately and in a hurry.

Meanwhile, on the morning of 2 May Bennett and I visited Masterson and his deputy commander of JTF 122, Maj. Gen. Thomas Tompkins, USMC, to discuss the situation and settle on future operations. We flew in an army huey to the *Boxer* without incident, landing on the ship's small helicopter pad (the first such landing for our young army pilot), where Masterson, an outgoing man with a salty manner, greeted us enthusiastically. It was a brief, pleasant interlude, and we enjoyed the fine navy chow—invariably outstanding at sea—as a welcome respite from army K-rations, which most of the Americans at the embassy had been eating. (In fact, these "emergency" rations were so popular at the embassy that a few days later, when we could no longer keep up with the demand and had to stop supplying them, the protesting howls could be heard all over Santo Domingo.) In our conference aboard the *Boxer*, we agreed that an overland linkup between our marines and paratroopers was imperative and would be our immediate goal.

Accordingly, Bennett and I returned to the embassy, accompanied by Tompkins, where we were joined by York and his G-3, Lt. Colonel Forrester; Brig. Gen. John Bouker, USMC, the recently arrived commander of the 4th MEB and senior marine ashore; and Colonel Quilty, the MAAG chief. Our purpose was to plan the linkup operation that would establish a U.S.-held corridor through the city between the ISZ and the Duarte Bridge. The light in the ambassador's office was not very good because the embassy was still blacked out (I made a mental note to change this condition at the first opportunity), and the dark paneling of the room did not help. We all sat down on a huge oriental rug covering most of the floor and gathered around my Esso street map of Santo Domingo, while York showed us the route taken by the 82d's reconnaissance patrol. We decided that the axis of the operation to open the corridor would generally follow that route, along which we anticipated meeting the least rebel resistance. At the western end we avoided the "hot corner" mentioned earlier, still unaware that in doing so we were bypassing Radio Santo Domingo—an almost fatal mistake. We also agreed to make the move in darkness, hoping to maximize surprise and minimize civilian noncombatant casualties and property damage.

By this time on 2 May we had two marine and four airborne infantry battalions available in the Dominican Republic, the president having approved the deployment of the rest of the 82d Airborne from Bragg and the 4th MEB (with three marine battalions) from Camp Le Jeune, North Carolina.[6] Because Bouker, the marine commander, felt that securing the ISZ was all that his marine force could handle at the time, we gave the corridor mission entirely to the 82d Airborne Division. York decided to use three paratrooper battalions for the task, leaving one to secure the San Isidro air base. I told him to be ready to move that night, and we then went our separate ways.

In consonance with President Johnson's desire to bring the U.S. intervention under some kind of OAS umbrella, my next chore was to get our proposed operation blessed by the newly appointed OAS commission, which had arrived in Santo Domingo that morning, as the first step in securing approval. Bennett and I found the commission, composed of five ambassadors (one each from Argentina, Brazil, Colombia, Guatemala, and Panama) and headed by Ambassador Ricardo Colombo of Argentina, at the Embajador Hotel. Here we were joined by the versatile and effective OAS Secretary General José Mora.[7] They were all sensible men and readily understood the necessity for the corridor, particularly in view of the immediate need to establish a secure evacuation route overland between the ISZ and the airfields east of Santo Domingo. Although they were understandably leery about setting off any renewed fighting, they nevertheless quickly assented.

Getting final Washington approval proved to be much more difficult. Returning to the U.S. embassy, I got on the phone with the Pentagon. By this time, the embassy had established with the White House a single open, insecure voice circuit, active twenty-four hours a day, which American officials in Santo Domingo shared on an informal basis. Unfortunately, this line went through the rebel-held telecommunications center in downtown Santo Domingo, where the constitutionalists could readily listen to our phone conversations. Nevertheless, talking to General Burchinal over this open line, I learned that the Joint Staff had no problem with our plan—which by this time had been transmitted by secure electronic means—but that General Wheeler was reluctant to approve it. Later, I discovered that part of Wheeler's doubt concerned a message sent on 1 May from Vice Admiral Masterson, estimating that a force of one to two divisions—much larger than we had on hand at the time—would be required to handle the situation in Santo Domingo. Wheeler was also concerned about the unpredictable hazards of a night operation. Eventually, however, he was persuaded by his Special Assistant, Andy Goodpaster, to accept our plan, and late on 2 May the president personally approved it, with the admonition that the advance was not to begin before midnight.

And so we turned the 82d loose exactly at midnight, and one hour and fourteen minutes later the division had established the initial four-block-wide corridor and had linked up with the marines. York's three paratrooper battalions had used a leapfrog maneuver in advancing from the Duarte Bridge: the leading battalion went about one-third of the way and held, allowing the following battalions to pass through its lines, and this scheme of movement was repeated until linkup was ac-

complished. The operation's superb execution under York's
personal command surprised the constitutionalists, who, as we
had hoped, were totally unprepared and offered virtually no
resistance.

At daylight on 3 May, U.S. military traffic started to use the
corridor without incident, and by that afternoon our troopers
were providing food, water, and medical attention to a starving,
thirsty, and tense population that showed friendliness and
gratitude right from the start. It was evident that the presence
of many black American soldiers (about 30 per cent in the
average battalion of the 82d Airborne Division), as well as some
who spoke Spanish, helped establish friendly relations between
our troops and the people of Santo Domingo. This good spirit
generally prevailed during the entire period of the U.S. presence, despite the sustained efforts of the rebel opposition to
arouse the people against us.

In order to take advantage of the open telephone line to the
White House, I had remained near the embassy until the corridor operation was completed. When I left at about 2:00 A.M.,
3 May, not wanting to return to San Isidro, I decided to spend
the night with the marines guarding the perimeter around the
embassy grounds. Rethore and I found ourselves in a small
outbuilding on the southeast corner of the grounds, right on
the marine front line. Since the structure also housed a marine
machine gun, we spent a noisy, sleepless, but educational few
hours; rebels from houses across the street kept sniping at the
marines, who would promptly return the compliment with
long and heavy bursts of fire, burning up far more ammunition
than was expended on the rebel side. It seemed a futile and
hardly productive exercise—both sides were well protected
from such small-arms fire—and we were playing into the hands
of the *constitutionalistas*, whose intent was to keep things
boiling and to harass the embassy. A quiet, stabilized situation
in Santo Domingo was the last thing the rebels wanted. It forcibly struck me that not only did we need to secure the U.S.
embassy from direct hostile fire as soon as possible but also,
if we were to achieve an effective cease-fire, we had to improve
our own discipline and discourage firing on the part of our

troops unless there was sufficient and good provocation. I decided to do something about both points as soon as I could.

On 3 May, apparently after learning where I had spent the rest of the previous night (I didn't tell him), Ambassador Bennett was kind enough to put me up in a guest bedroom in his official residence, a graceful and elegant structure located about 200 meters behind the embassy. (Its sister building, an exact duplicate, is the official residence of the U.S. ambassador in Port-au-Prince, Haiti.) The residence had turned into a sort of emergency dormitory for U.S. officials and employees when private homes had become too dangerous. (Most families of American officials and female U.S. employees had been evacuated, although a courageous and stalwart handful insisted on staying, at considerable risk.) The marine platoon guarding the grounds was bivouacked in the area between the two main buildings and near a large swimming pool, which the marines put to good use when Santo Domingo finally quieted down.

Several weeks later I established official quarters with Brig. Gen. Robert R. Linvill, the combat-seasoned paratrooper who took over as my chief of staff, in a small house just south of and across the street from our headquarters building. The house was owned by an absent American family who were happy to rent it to the U.S. government until the unpleasantness was over.

On 4 May HQ U.S. Land Forces (JTF 120) was "chopped" to CINCLANT; this meant that I now reported directly to Adm. Moorer at Norfolk, Virginia. Still later, on 7 May when the U.S. Air Force could control air activities in the area, JTF 122 was disestablished and all U.S. forces ashore came under the control of our corps HQ, which was now called U.S. FORCES DOM REP. The amphibious forces of the 2d Fleet, under Vice Adm. Jack McCain, remained separate from our command on land but continued to support us in the Dominican Republic.

CHAPTER 3

Stabilizing the Situation
3–15 May 1965

Realizing that getting the American embassy off the front line of the ISZ would go a long way toward calming the situation in Santo Domingo, on 3 May Bennett and I sought the approval of the OAS commission to move the eastern boundary of the ISZ well to the east at the first opportunity. OAS agreement was readily given because several other embassies in the area, notably, those of Ecuador and El Salvador, had also been harassed by rebel fire and had urgently requested protection. Marines of the 4th MEB swiftly accomplished this objective, making several advances under cover of darkness that moved the perimeter four blocks east by 4 May. (On 12 May one last extension of the ISZ straightened out the eastern boundary.) Some twenty-five embassies now lay within the ISZ, Japan's being the only major exception. During the same period the 82d Airborne widened the corridor by one block each on the northern and southern sides in order to protect the traffic flowing through it from direct fire.

From 3 to 5 May the U.S. paratroopers gained valuable experience in city street, backyard, and rooftop operations that demonstrated the suitability of the organizations, weapons, and equipment of the airborne rifle company and battalion for this kind of urban warfare. Skilled military police were also critically needed, however, and early in the deployment were given equal priority with combat units in the air movement from Fort Bragg. Crowd control was a special challenge, particularly considering the restrictions Washington placed on our use of such riot control agents as tear gas and smoke.

Once the corridor configuration was set, we precisely delineated our troop dispositions on local maps, supported by up-to-date aerial photographs of the actual front-line locations of our forces on roofs, balconies, street intersections, and so on, and of their barricades of concertina wire, sandbagged checkpoints, and the like, which allowed them to control access to the corridor from any direction. This positive and detailed evidence of exact troop positions later proved invaluable when the constitutionalists repeatedly accused us of cease-fire violations.

By now it was abundantly clear that the corridor operation was the key military move in the entire Dominican venture. Although it left Colonel Caamano, the rebel commander, with some good hole cards, it had trapped 80 percent of his forces and his best men downtown in the southern part of the city in an area bounded on the west by the eastern edge of the ISZ, on the north by the corridor, on the east by the Ozama River, and on the south by the sea. Never fully recovering from this maneuver, the rebels could no longer reinforce their smaller groups in the northern part of Santo Domingo, nor could they readily move arms or revolutionaries into the interior of the country. Finally, the corridor operation allowed the United States to act more impartially in achieving a political settlement because U.S. troops were in a position to prevent either side from defeating the other.

During the next ten days we consolidated our military positions and unequivocally supported the loyalists. On 5 May Ambassador Mora and the OAS commission were able to get the junta and the rebel side to sign "The Act of Santo Domingo," a formal cease-fire arrangement by which both belligerents agreed to respect the ISZ and the corridor.[1] By this time Colonel Caamano had been proclaimed the *presidente* of the Constitutionalist Government; shortly thereafter the loyalist junta, with the support of Ambassadors Bennett and Martin, succeeded in forming a "Government of National Reconstruction" (GNR) headed by Antonio Imbert, one of the heroes of the Trujillo assassination and a self-proclaimed general.[2] Imbert was willing to make the effort, a courageous act in itself in the Dominican Republic, and he had the support of the extreme rightists, other conservatives, and what few moderates existed in the country. One of Imbert's first actions was to appoint Adm. Francisco Rivera Caminero, formerly head of the Dominican Navy, as minister of the armed forces.

Having secured the U.S. embassy from further harassment, we could now turn to the troublesome problem of how to bring "peace and tranquility" to Santo Domingo. Extending the ISZ to cover most of the foreign embassies was helpful because it removed tempting targets from the range of direct harassing fire from the revolutionaries. Another logical step was to put into effect more restricted rules of engagement for our troops along the corridor and on the ISZ perimeter. As the troop positions became more permanent and better protected with sandbag emplacements and overhead cover, stricter rules of engagement became more feasible. However, disciplined troops who understood the nature of their mission and what the United States was trying to accomplish remained an indispensable ingredient of any peacekeeping success.

In essence, we developed our own ground rules for the use of force by our troops: in the beginning, no firing first, and returning fire only in self-defense. Later, these guidelines were expanded to allow fire and maneuver if troop positions were in danger of being overrun; and still later, we added the rule that troops would normally return to their original positions after such fire and maneuver. We also restricted the employment of weapons to small arms: that is, rifles and pistols, machine guns, the LAW (a small, light antitank weapon fired from the shoulder), and the 40mm grenade launcher normally fired from the shoulder. The one exception, the 105mm recoilless rifle mounted on a jeep (quarter-ton truck), was restricted to firing only at specific point targets—such as through a window in a concrete building—where small-arms fire would be ineffective.

Because we were operating in a populous urban area, all weaponry more suitable to open terrain—mortars and artillery, tanks, naval gunfire, and close air support—were prohibited. Before this rule went into effect, a direct-support artillery battalion ashore did fire eight rounds of illuminating fire in the air over the Duarte bridgehead on the night of 30 April–1 May, but the artillery battalion commander ordered the illumination stopped for fear that the burning remains of the shells would touch off fires in the crowded slums near the bridge. This was the only artillery battalion to bring its tubes (105mm) ashore, and these were the only rounds fired operationally (later, the battalion engaged in service practice at a Dominican Army range). Thus, artillery troops on Dominican soil were used basically as infantry or military police troops.

The oddest weapons employment occurred on the first day of the 82d Airborne Division's presence in the Dominican Republic when the troops used a 105mm recoilless rifle against a freighter berthed at the Santo Domingo docks, putting a large hole in its hull and grounding it at the pier. Rebels had seized the ship and had made the mistake of firing from its bridge at U.S. paratroopers on the east bank of the Ozama River. Fire from the 105 routed the rebels and thwarted their attempt to take the vessel to sea. It was the 82d's first and probably last "naval" encounter.

We also established rules for the control of the ISZ and the corridor, as well as for access to these areas and the rebel sector. No armed individuals, whether loyalist (GNR) or rebel (constitutionalist), were allowed to enter the ISZ from any direction or leave it (there were some loyalist troops within the zone at the time of the cease-fire), or to traverse the corridor in either direction east or west, or to cross it north or south. Our own peacekeeping forces were likewise excluded from the rebel zone. We placed no such restrictions on areas outside the ISZ or corridor.

At established checkpoints on the eastern edge of the ISZ and along the corridor, unarmed individuals were allowed to pass back and forth from the rebel zone. Checkpoints were also established on primary roads leading into the ISZ and at the east end of the Duarte Bridge, the only access route into the city from the east across the Ozama River. All pedestrian and vehicular traffic moving into or out of the ISZ, the corridor, or the rebel zone was funneled through these checkpoints, which handled a daily average of about 22,000 vehicles and 35,000 persons and effectively stopped the flow of arms and ammunition and other contraband such as explosives. Concertina and barbed wire soon formed an unbroken land obstacle, manned by our troops, around the rebel sector, the sea on the southern side effectively restricting movement in that direction. When it was later discovered that the rebels were getting through the corridor by using the underground maze of sewers that honeycombed the city, U.S. engineers countered this move by opening the manholes, placing lights in the sewers, and maintaining twenty-four-hour surveillance of those sewers leading into and out of the rebel zone.

Dominican National Police presented a special problem because they had become demoralized and disorganized in Santo Domingo. As they slowly regained effectiveness, we allowed armed policemen to traverse the corridor and to move in and out of the ISZ, on the grounds that they were needed to maintain law and order. They were not, of course, allowed in the rebel sector—indeed, the rebels would have given them short shrift—nor were they allowed to make any political arrests in the ISZ.

Frustrated militarily by the cordon placed around their zone, the constitutionalists launched a psychological offensive against the United States, the OAS, and the GNR. Radio Santo Domingo, with its numerous outlets, studios, transmitter and relay sites throughout the country, was their primary weapon. Well known to the Dominican people for many years as the voice of the government, Radio Santo Domingo was expertly exploited by the rebels, who made every effort to incite the rest of the nation to revolt.

We responded with jamming operations, using Army Security Agency (ASA) units ashore, air force units in the air, and navy ships afloat, while a reinforced company from the army's 7th Special Forces Group under the skillful leadership of Col. Edward Mayer attacked major relay sites outside the capital. Our initial efforts were not effective, however, and rebel broadcasts continued to make their influence felt countrywide. Recognizing that this might be our Achilles heel, we attempted physical disruption on the ground of the telecommunications linking the main studio in Santo Domingo with its numerous transmitter sites, again employing our own special forces working with loyalist Dominican special forces. Colonel Mayer led the combined group on this hazardous night mission, accompanied by the 82d's General York. The attempt failed to hurt the radio operation but did cripple the commercial telephone system upon which the rebels relied for their principal tactical communications in the city. Outside Santo Domingo, U.S. and Dominican special forces conducted several highly successful operations: one on 5 May at a major telecommunications center at Alto Bandero (in the mountains to the northwest of the capital), where they seized and removed vital equipment, making the center nonoperational; and another on 6 May at a major TV station at El Cumbre, near La Vega, an important city in the Dominican interior.[3]

On 13 May Imbert's government threw caution to the wind and ordered the Dominican Air Force to attack Radio Santo Domingo and its main transmitter sites near the Peynado Bridge north of the city. U.S. troops near the radio studio, initially believing that *they* were under attack, opened up with small arms and shot down one of the Dominican aircraft, a P-51 Mustang of World War II vintage. Dominican special forces then on 14 May attacked and destroyed the alternate studio and transmitter site north of the Duarte Bridge. These actions, taken together, did succeed in weakening Radio Santo Domingo to the extent that it could no longer broadcast outside the capital, and thus we weathered that particular crisis. In the process, we discovered the enormous difficulty of conducting effective jamming operations against a powerful commercial broadcasting complex, particularly with military jammers designed for use against military frequencies. It had not been normal U.S. policy to conduct such operations, and it occurred to me that there was a sound practical rationale behind that policy, quite apart from other considerations.

While this struggle was going on, we sent special teams out

into the countryside, deploying them by U.S. Army helicopters (hueys) painted solid green without any identifying insignia. Aboard were army special forces and medical and intelligence personnel, all in civilian clothes, with at least one Dominican national to assist them in finding their way and in speaking to the people. The idea was to take the pulse of the country outside Santo Domingo and to see what was going on; a secondary mission was to carry some basic medical care and food to areas where they might be needed.

These teams rapidly covered the major cities and regions of the republic and soon brought back a broad estimate of the situation. Generally, they found the country tense and wary, watching what was going on in the capital and verifying the saying that "as Santo Domingo goes, so goes the Dominican Republic." They also found that Dominican security forces had things under control. This was reassuring, at least in part, because it told us that the rebellion could probably be confined to the capital if matters were handled with discretion and common sense, and that relatively few foreign troops would be needed. We therefore immediately started planning to reduce the U.S. forces involved.

This intelligence operation, which we had dubbed the "Green Hornet Caper," gave us another kind of insight: the Dominicans encountered, who invariably concluded correctly that most members of the Green Hornet teams were Americans, reflected a great reservoir of good will and friendship toward the American people. As we were to note later, there was an almost childlike faith in the belief that the United States could accomplish anything and make things right again. In fact, we used to joke that had General York run for the Dominican presidency, he could easily have been elected. After the Green Hornet operation was completed, we returned some U.S. special forces teams to operate along the northern coast of the republic, ostensibly as weather observers but with the real purpose of keeping watch for possible unfriendly infiltration attempts from outside the island of Hispaniola.

Over the next few weeks, while the loyalists consolidated the GNR position, a major U.S. policy shift emerged: instead of developing and supporting a strong loyalist government, the United States adopted a policy of strict neutrality between the two warring sides. One immediate fallout from this change was an order to neutralize the Dominican Air Force and Navy, which we received just after the Dominican air attack on Radio Santo Domingo on 13 May. At San Isidro, where practically all the Dominican Air Force was based, the U.S. Air Force headquarters used friendly verbal persuasion on Dominican air leaders, while the 82d Airborne Division physically blocked the runways with vehicles and other heavy equipment. No more Dominican aircraft took off. We asked the U.S. amphibious fleet offshore to handle the naval problem, and thereafter U.S. ships overwatched the Dominican naval base at Haina with the objective of intercepting any sortie out of the harbor. These efforts were successful except for one instance in July, when a Dominican frigate got by the naval screen and dashed up the mouth of the Ozama River in a show of force. We were unloading bunker fuel for the city's power plant from a large tanker at a pier on the east bank of the river into a tank farm near the mouth of the river, and so we held our breath, fearing that a fire fight might break out between the rebels on the west bank and the frigate maneuvering in the river near the tanker. Fortunately, nothing happened, and the frigate returned peacefully to Haina.

On 15 May the most senior group of U.S. officials from Washington to visit the scene arrived to take over the negotiating task in a unilateral attempt to resolve the situation. Headed by the president's national security adviser McGeorge Bundy, the team included Deputy Secretary of Defense Cyrus Vance, Thomas Mann, and Jack Vaughn, the latter two with wide experience in Latin American foreign affairs. Intending to stay for only forty-eight hours, the group soon discovered that there was no ready political solution. One proposed quick solution they did explore revolved around a coalition government to be formed under wealthy Dominican farmer/rancher Antonio Guzman, who was a follower of PRD leader Juan Bosch. Bosch insisted, however, on the immediate departure from the country of the Dominican military chiefs and the appointment of Caamano's choices to the key positions of minister of the armed forces and army chief of staff, thus risking the integrity of loyalist forces and control of the country. Naturally, Imbert and his provisional government, the GNR, not to mention the Dominican military chiefs, were dead set against any such proposal.[4]

At about 2:00 A.M. on 17 May, President Johnson polled us by telephone as to our individual assessment of the Guzman solution. We were assembled in the small room in the U.S. embassy that held the one terminal on our only reliable but still insecure phone connection with Washington. One by one, the president called us to the phone and spoke to each man personally and exclusively, members of the Washington team first and then Ambassador Bennett; I brought up the rear. When my turn finally came, Johnson asked whether I could "guarantee" a free and democratic Dominican Republic that would not slide under Communist domination. I replied that Guzman was an unknown quantity to me personally, that I was seriously concerned about Bosch's proposals for control of the military, and that in good conscience I could give no such guarantee. I also said that it would take a long time to find and carry out a proposal agreeable to both sides. Johnson said, wisely, that he would sleep on it, and the next day we learned that the Guzman gambit had been abandoned.

Mann stayed for two days and Vaughn for three; McGeorge Bundy stuck it out until 26 May, and the last member of the Washington team, Cy Vance, did not depart until 29 May. This was the last serious attempt to find a unilateral solution; thereafter, the United States was content to let the OAS take over the negotiations. In late May the OAS agreed to send a three-man Ad Hoc Committee to Santo Domingo: Ilmar Penna Marinho of Brazil, Ramon de Clairmont Duenas of El Salvador, and Ellsworth Bunker of the United States. No chairman was designated, but Bunker in reality was first among equals, his stature as a veteran American diplomat and his skill, experience, and vigor ensuring him the leading role in the ensuing negotiations.[5]

Personally, I enjoyed the May visit of the senior Washington group and profited from their presence. We were all house guests in Ambassador Bennett's spacious residence and held many long, fruitful discussions. I particularly liked talking with Bundy and Vance. Youthful-looking, ruddy-faced Bundy was articulate and attractive; tall, gangly Vance, with a strong mountaineer twang and a twinkle in his eye, was likewise impressive. In view of Vance's position in the U.S. defense establishment, I escorted him on several tours of marine and army troop locations. On his first visit to the corridor we ascended to the roof of a combined Catholic church and parochial school and then climbed the bell tower to get a better look at the constitutionalist sector. We stayed only briefly because we came under sniper fire from the direction of the rebel zone. One bullet embedded itself in the brick bell tower right alongside the head of my aide, who was the last man down, and we lost no time getting off the roof.

As we went downstairs inside the church, I said to myself, "That was a dumb thing to do—suppose you had gotten the deputy secretary of defense killed?" But I did not change my ways: because I have always felt that there is no better way for the top people to get a feel for a problem than to visit the front in whatever form it takes, I likewise escorted Ambassadors Bunker and Bennett, Admiral Moorer, and other distinguished visitors through the corridor. Manning the area was a brigade of the 82d Airborne Division, initially commanded by Col. George Viney and later by Col. Robert C. Kendrick, a colorful veteran paratrooper with much combat experience. "Butch" Kendrick had a flair for the dramatic and established a degree of rapport with his rebel counterpart, who often appeared as if on cue, when there was a distinguished visitor, in the large park located in the middle of the rebel sector. The "opposing commanders" would exchange informal salutes, and the visitors invariably went away with a vivid impression of the Dominican revolution, many being surprised by the common sense and good understanding of their mission demonstrated by the young American soldiers.

On 18 May the original five-member OAS commission, having accomplished its basic task of assessing the situation in the

Dominican Republic and having reported to the OAS Council its strong support of U.S. actions, permanently departed the country. Secretary General Mora stayed on to carry out the OAS role in Santo Domingo until the Ad Hoc Committee arrived on 4 June to assume overall responsibility for OAS efforts to resolve the political-military problem.

The directed new policy of U.S. neutrality soon brought us some severe military headaches. Although we could physically prevent fighting between the loyalist forces outside the rebel sector and the rebels inside their own zone in Santo Domingo, it was quite a different matter in other parts of the city and the rest of the country. Caamano's weakest forces were located in the northern (also the industrial) part of Santo Domingo, north of the corridor, where they held Radio Santo Domingo; it was easy for Imbert to concentrate his best ground forces against them without violating the corridor or the ISZ. He proceeded to do so, moving CEFA troops from San Isidro and Dominican Army troops from garrisons to the northwest of the capital and launching a coordinated and systematic sweep eastward through the northern part of the city on 15 May. Imbert's drive was successful, capturing the much prized and fought-over Radio Santo Domingo on the first day and reaching the banks of the Ozama River after clearing the area. The operation bolstered the prestige of the GNR and helped restore some measure of confidence to the Dominican Army, which had been demoralized by the rebellion.

While this was going on, we came under heavy pressure from Washington to intervene and stop the fighting. In my opinion, establishing what would have amounted to another corridor would have been a serious mistake, both militarily and politically. It would have forced U.S. troops to confront both loyalist and rebel forces and would have involved an attempt to drive a wedge between two hostile groups in close contact. We would have been the ham in the sandwich, possibly with both sides shooting at us. As it was, the fighting between the Dominican factions during the sweep did result in our receiving some fire within our lines along the northern edge of the corridor. Those who felt that we were allowing Imbert to annihilate the northern rebels in Santo Domingo did not seem to realize that all a rebel had to do in order to leave the area safely was to cross the corridor unarmed through an established checkpoint, and he would be home free in the rebel sanctuary protected by U.S. forces.

Before Imbert's drive, as a matter of fact, we had been under pressure from other quarters to clear the rest of the city using American troops and, in accordance with guidance from the JCS, had made such plans in case we were ordered to do so. But we were overtaken by events: Imbert simply made his move before a U.S. decision could be reached one way or the other.

Press stories of alleged U.S. partiality toward Imbert's forces in violation of the declared policy of neutrality were numerous at this time. President Johnson was quoted as saying at one press conference that he would "bust General Palmer right down to a buck private" if he were guilty of such violations. Asked about this in Santo Domingo, I told the press that I was not about to disobey the instructions of the commander-in-chief, but this did not satisfy the newsmen. I then explained that the president could reduce me to my permanent grade of major general but that only a court-martial could strip me of my commission and dismiss me from the service. As for becoming a private soldier, I was beyond draft age, and voluntary enlistment would not be a credible act under the circumstances. Finally, I said that Johnson was speaking figuratively, for effect, not literally.

After Imbert completed his sweep through northern Santo Domingo, Johnson personally reiterated the U.S. policy of neutrality, ordering Vance and me to sign a statement "in blood" to the effect that U.S. forces had not given any unauthorized aid to Imbert's troops. The statement had to include a list of all materials furnished by our forces directly to loyalist troops, both military and police. It was not much of a list: several thousand rounds of 50-caliber machine-gun ammunition, about 100 armored vests, a few small tactical (walkie-talkie) radios, and about 5,000 K-rations—all of which had been provided early in the crisis before the shift in U.S. policy. That was the last we heard of the matter.

During his last few days in the Dominican Republic in late May, Vance concentrated on persuading the Dominican chiefs to leave their country voluntarily, at least temporarily, as a step toward lowering tensions and enhancing the possibility of a political settlement. Although his all-out efforts were to no avail at the time, they did lay the groundwork for later negotiations with the chiefs that ultimately led to their stepping down from their positions. Vance suspected that one major factor working against his efforts was the presence of the U.S. naval, air, and army attachés, who were on close terms with their Dominican counterpart service chiefs and were in their corner. The U.S. attaché was also the defense attaché, in good standing with Dominican minister of the armed forces, Rivera Caminero. Normally, U.S. defense attaches not only receive guidance from the Pentagon but also respond to the needs of the local U.S. ambassador and participate as members of the U.S. country team, which operates under the supervision of the ambassador. In this instance the attachés had been invaluable to Ambassador Bennett, who used them skillfully in seeking the cooperation and support of the Dominican chiefs. But Vance felt that the serving attachés had become emotionally involved and did not fully accept the drastically changed circumstances brought about by the revolution, and so he arranged for their immediate replacement without prejudice to the individuals concerned. Bennett was not particularly happy about the matter, but I agreed with Vance's actions; they made my job easier.

While these efforts by Vance were under way, Bennett undertook to persuade General Wessin y Wessin to accept voluntary exile. Wessin, as commander of the elite CEFA forces, was for all practical purposes independent of the other Dominican chiefs. I accompanied Bennett when he visited Wessin and appealed to his patriotism, calling on him to leave the Dominican Republic for the good of his country. The conversation was in Spanish, and I got only the drift of its substance.

A small, sallow, harmless-looking man with a furtive expression, Wessin would not look either one of us in the eye but did finally agree in writing to make the sacrifice. Not surprisingly, however, he reneged the very next day.

On 14 May, just before Imbert's drive began, a new and significant influence had arrived on the scene: a team of United Nations observers, which had been requested by the constitutionalists. Headed by José Mayobre of Venezuela,[6] the team included Maj. Gen. Indura Rikhye of India and a Canadian Army lieutenant colonel. Mayobre immediately called for a cease-fire but was unable to arrange one until after GNR troops had reached the Ozama River. In sending the team, the UN gave the unfortunate impression that one of its goals was to degrade the OAS as an effective international regional system and to embarrass both the United States and the OAS. Alleged cease-fire violations by U.S. forces, for example, were quickly reported by the team to UN headquarters in New York without any investigation and were promptly exploited publicly. Since we meticulously investigated every such allegation and had to report the results through Washington, we could not compete with the UN tactics: by the time we could establish and make known the facts, the damage had already been done. About confirmed rebel cease-fire violations—and there were many— the UN team remained mute. Moreover, General Rikhye lived in the rebel zone, seeing Caamano and other constitutionalist leaders daily but rarely visiting the GNR side.

The United Nations also dispatched a human rights team to investigate alleged atrocities and the like; again, however, the UN representatives were interested mainly in allegations against the GNR and ignored reports of violations committed by leftist groups. To put it mildly, we were annoyed with the frustrating methods employed by the seemingly biased UN group. This was when we learned that the State Department had certain favorite words to convey special meanings, just as the military uses "Pentagonese" and other professionals have their own private way of expressing things. To describe Rikhye, State used the word "mischievous," which meant that he was out for no good, while the Canadian colonel was "unhelpful," which meant that he was not above thwarting U.S. and OAS aims.

During this early period of stabilization, the role of the press came forcibly to my direct attention. Representatives of many different national and international press agencies had preceded U.S. forces into Santo Domingo by several days, but the American media got my closest attention and brought home the drastic change that had occurred since World War II in the nature of the relationship between the U.S. military and the press. In the Dominican Republic, Defense Department public information matters were handled by the Joint Information Bureau (JIB), established in Santo Domingo in late April and manned by personnel from all the services. The bureau provided guidance to the public information officers (PIOs) of the major subordinate headquarters involved in the operation, such as the XVIII Airborne Corps, the 82d Airborne Division, and so on, with respect to such as matters as assistance to media representatives and release authority for specific items of press interest. The JIB offices were located in the Embajador Hotel, which, in addition to being the assembly point for noncombatants wanting to be evacuated, had become the hangout of virtually every foreign correspondent in Santo Domingo. Col. George A. Creel, U.S. Army, a veteran military PIO, was put in charge of the JIB. Aware of the poor relationship then existing in Saigon between the senior military headquarters and the media, he was determined to get off on the right foot with the press in the Dominican Republic.[7]

Creel succeeded under difficult circumstances in satisfying the press's need for electronic means of communication with the outside world—almost nonexistent in the beginning—as well as transportation within the country. He also established excellent rapport with the U.S. embassy and the U.S. Information Service (USIS) in Santo Domingo. But a good climate of military-press relations was not in the cards.

Before the outbreak of hostilities on 24 April, major press entities had had only "stringers" in Santo Domingo—local, usually inexperienced people who tried to keep their eyes and ears open for possible news stories. But shortly after the revolution broke, the city was swarming with some 250 correspondents of many nationalities, who varied in experience from seasoned journalists to "freshman war correspondents." In the uncertain, hectic early days of the rebellion, many highly exaggerated and inaccurate reports were filed: for example, inflated civilian casualty figures. Not surprisingly, such reporting hurt relations between the U.S. military and the press from the outset. Indeed, one correspondent's emotional, biased, book-length story, full of inaccuracies, was rushed into print and later won a Pulitzer Prize for journalism.[8] Regrettably, the damage done to the truth was never rectified.

In all fairness, however, it should be pointed out that many correspondents who tried to be fair and impartial had no control over the slant given the stories by their editors. Moreover, when an issue as controversial as U.S. intervention in the Dominican Republic was being hotly debated in Washington, and when the major networks—not to mention senior members of the Congress—were taking sharp exception to executive-branch actions, correspondents in the field were bound to be influenced if not intimidated by their home offices.

Like Creel, I too wanted to establish good relations between our forces and the press. In particular, I hoped that we could avoid what had happened in Vietnam in the early 1960s, when the press simply did not believe military releases with respect to progress in the war. (Relations in Vietnam began to deteriorate in the early advisory period and worsened in 1965 with the commitment of U.S. ground troops. The feeling of mutual distrust between American forces and the press that took root then still exists today.) But in the spring of 1965, several incidents occurred in Santo Domingo that damaged our good intentions.

The first of these occurred on 10 May when 2d Lt. Charles T. Hutchinson III, a platoon leader in the 82d Airborne, was killed by rebel fire in the corridor of the city controlled by our forces. Hutchinson, a U.S. Military Academy graduate, class of 1964, had been a football star at West Point and was much liked by his fellow paratroopers. A young American correspondent covering the story reportedly antagonized the other soldiers in Hutchinson's platoon with unfriendly questions and statements that showed little sympathy for the death of a youthful American doing his duty, reflecting instead the reporter's bitter hostility toward the U.S. intervention. Word of this incident, however accurately or inaccurately repeated, spread rapidly through the 82d, causing great indignation.

Then in late May a CBS videotape was aired in the United States, supporting the allegations that our forces in Santo Domingo were collaborating with loyalist Dominicans and violating the policy shift that defined the U.S. role as one of strict neutrality between the two Dominican factions. The tape was made at a U.S. checkpoint on the western boundary of the ISZ. Something in the film struck us as being wrong; we couldn't put a finger on it at first, but we undertook a formal IG (Inspector General) investigation of the matter. We finally found the discrepancy when we ran the film in slow motion and discovered that two different tapes, made about two weeks apart, had been spliced together and then identified as one film, allegedly taken at the later date after the change in U.S. policy. The telltale evidence lay in the height of the sandbag emplacements at the checkpoint: in the earlier sequence they were only five or six bags high; in the later one, ten to twelve. The earlier segment showed U.S. forces, in the person of an army major at the checkpoint, assisting the loyalists by allowing armed Dominican government soldiers to pass through the checkpoint. The added segment made it appear that the entire tape had been shot at the later date, after the U.S. policy of strict neutrality had gone into effect.

This deliberate distortion of the truth was a new experience for me, never having imagined that a responsible and respected network would stoop to such reprehensible trickery and deception. Later that year, when Eric Sevareid of CBS visited Santo Domingo, I showed him the evidence. Sevareid personally apologized, agreeing that it was unacceptable behavior on the part of the media, and indicated that the dirty work most likely had been done in New York, not in Santo Domingo. But CBS never made a public retraction.

On the other hand, an incident in Santo Domingo on the morning of 6 May caused much ill will toward the military on the part of the American press. Newsmen Alvin Burt and Douglas Kennedy, following prescribed procedures, had passed safely through a marine checkpoint on the southeast corner of the ISZ and had entered the rebel zone in a Dominican taxi clearly labeled as a press vehicle. Their purpose was to photograph a burning ship in the harbor a short distance away. After doing so, they retraced their route to the same checkpoint, where things were quiet at the time. But their Dominican driver, trying to obey hand signals from the marine noncommissioned officer at the checkpoint, became confused, stopped, and then started to back up. At this point the marines opened fire. Both newsmen were badly wounded and had to be evacuated, first to the hospital ship USS *Raleigh* offshore and then to Womack Hospital at Fort Bragg. It was a tragic episode that should never have happened and increased my determination to improve our fire discipline.

Kennedy and Burt survived but received permanent injuries and subsequently sued the United States for damages. In May 1971 the U.S. Court of Claims, after an exhaustive review of the evidence, found that the shooting was without sufficient provocation and that the firepower directed at the taxi was "grossly excessive." The Department of Defense declined to oppose the finding, and Kennedy and Burt were awarded $100,000 and $75,000 respectively.[9] I hasten to add that this was the only serious incident of this kind involving U.S. citizens in Santo Domingo, but its long-term adverse effects could not be undone.

Historically, a poor relationship between the military and the press has not been an unusual phenomenon in the United States, and the low points have generally (and naturally) occurred in wartime. But in World War II there seemed to be an unwritten agreement under which the press was granted access to the battlefield in exchange for a tacit understanding that it would comply with the military's ground rules, which sought to preserve the integrity of planned operations and to assure the safety and security of U.S. forces. With a few exceptions, this seemed to work reasonably well. Even Censorship (which can be imposed only by the president, was imposed in World War II, and has not been imposed since that time) caused no major problems. But this working military-press relationship has gone downhill since then, beginning in the 1950s in Korea and accelerating in the 1960s under the strains of Vietnam. The deterioration is perhaps only a reflection of more serious implications stemming from an increasing tendency of the press to pursue an aggressive, investigative style of reporting and apparently to assume the multiple roles of judge, jury, and executioner in examining major issues confronting the nation and presenting them to the public.

In mid-May 1965 in Santo Domingo, however, we were all preoccupied with the immediate problems of restoring law and order, establishing a climate of "peace and tranquility," defining our role, and trying to determine how best to perform it. I was grateful to have Creel and his JIB carrying out the difficult and sensitive job of handling public affairs.[10]

The JIB, operating as the Department of Defense (DOD) public affairs office, functioned until 4 June 1965, at which time the OAS/IAPF took over its facilities in the Embajador Hotel. Concurrently, HQ XVIII Airborne Corps/U.S. Forces Dominican Republic assumed the DOD's responsiblities for public affairs, and the JIB went out of business. For the duration of our mission my headquarters maintained liaison with both the OAS/IAPF public affairs office at the Embajador and its counterpart at the U.S. embassy. As far as I am aware, no joint public affairs office (combining the State, Defense, and USIS representatives located in Santo Domingo) was ever considered.

Creating the Inter-American Peace Force 6 May–15 June 1965

Almost from the beginning, when it appeared that the United States might become directly involved in the crisis, the Johnson administration was actively engaged in getting the OAS to focus on the potentially dangerous situation developing in the Dominican Republic. The State Department had been particularly busy, and Ellsworth Bunker, ambassador to the OAS, had vigorously taken the initiative to keep the other member states abreast of the fast-moving events and to enlist their support. Concurrently, the United States was pressing for the active participation of the OAS in an inter-American peacekeeping force in the Dominican Republic.

Not unexpectedly, given U.S. actions in the Caribbean in previous decades, other member states showed strong reluctance to approve such a proposal, fearing that it would lend legitimacy to a U.S. return to an interventionist policy and be interpreted as one Latin nation acting against another at the behest of the United States. OAS representatives in Santo Domingo, however, pointed out that the introduction of Latin American troops would provide a basis for the reduction or even total withdrawal of the U.S. forces present in the country. Moreover, many OAS states were ambivalent, publicly denouncing the U.S. unilateral intervention on the one hand but, on the other hand, showing their own shared concern about Com-

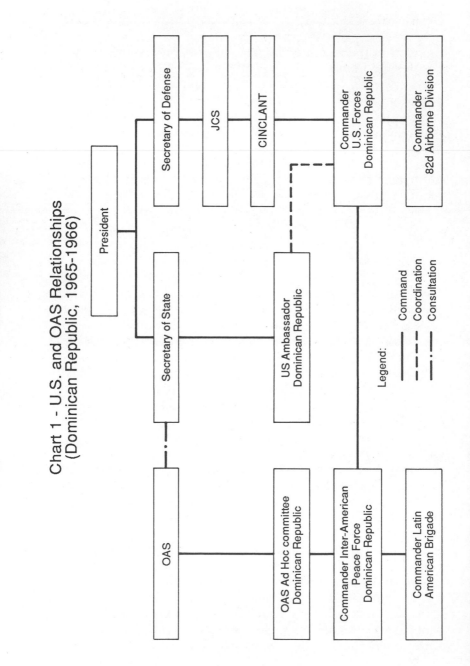

Chart 1 - U.S. and OAS Relationships
(Dominican Republic, 1965-1966)

President

Secretary of Defense

JCS

CINCLANT

Commander
U.S. Forces
Dominican Republic

Commander
82d Airborne Division

Secretary of State

US Ambassador
Dominican Republic

OAS

OAS Ad Hoc committee
Dominican Republic

Commander Inter-American
Peace Force
Dominican Republic

Commander Latin
American Brigade

Legend:

——— Command
- - - Coordination
—··— Consultation

munism in the region by private, discreet expressions of support for U.S. aims.[1]

At any rate, Bunker's persuasive diplomacy received swift attention, and on 6 May the OAS passed a historic resolution creating its first multinational force, initially called the Inter-American Force (IAF) and later redesignated the Inter-American Peace Force (IAPF). Fifteen member countries voted in favor, barely the required two-thirds majority; Venezuela abstained but agreed to support the majority decision; Chile, Ecuador, Peru, Mexico, and Uruguay voted against the resolution. The mission of the IAPF was defined as "cooperating in the restoration of normal conditions in the Dominican Republic, maintaining the security of its inhabitants and the inviolability of human rights, and the establishment of an atmosphere of peace and conciliation that will permit the functioning of democratic institutions." Major provisions of the resolution included the following:

—OAS Secretary General José Mora will request forces from the member states on a voluntary basis.

—Military forces assigned to the IAPF will remain under the control of their national armed services but will act under the operational command of the OAS Force Commander, who in turn will receive guidance and instructions from the OAS foreign ministers meeting in consultation. (In order to provide up-to-date guidance and to keep the United Nations informed of OAS actions, the OAS foreign ministers will remain in session.)

—Impartiality on the part of the IAPF in dealing with the two Dominican sides will be stressed.

—The OAS foreign ministers will have the power to withdraw the forces from the country as and when they see fit.[2]

On balance, the 6 May resolution was timely and useful. It clearly came as a relief to many nations of the hemisphere and provided the United States an umbrella of legitimacy until Latin American forces could be organized and sent to the Dominican Republic. The resolution also gave President Johnson a measure of multinational support for his strong anti-Communist position, at the same time providing the OAS an opportunity to demonstrate its willingness and ability to handle such a situation in a multinational manner.

All member nations with the exception of Haiti were asked to contribute to the IAPF, but only six responded. Brazil committed the largest contingent, including an infantry battalion, signal unit, and military police company, as well as a company of marines; Honduras, Nicaragua, and Paraguay each provided a rifle company; Costa Rica, which has no armed forces, committed a platoon of its Guardia Civil to be used as military police; and El Salvador provided several staff officers. The United States made available all its forces on Dominican soil but never committed any naval forces. (The U.S. Navy traditionally has resisted any attempt to place its forces under the direct operational command of a foreign national. It participates in combined maneuvers with naval forces of other nationalities but invariably under direct American command.) Rusk and McNamara had hoped that Argentina, Venezuela, and Colombia would also furnish contingents but were disappointed; the U.S. *fait accompli* in deploying troops before seeking OAS approval was too much for those governments to swallow. At this time, in early May 1965, large anti-American crowds in many Latin American capitals were demonstrating against the intervention, and in the great majority of Latin American newspapers anti-American editorials were running ahead of pro-U.S. ones about ten to one. Argentina, moreover, although willing to place its forces under a U.S. commander, would not accept another Latin American commander, particularly one from a traditional rival such as Brazil.[3]

Many OAS nations, however, including some who strongly opposed the IAPF, had responded to an OAS resolution of 3 May appealing for humanitarian aid to the Dominican Republic. Mexico, Venezuela, Colombia, Argentina, Brazil, Peru, Bolivia, Panama, and the United States contributed food, clothing, and medical supplies and sent doctors and nurses. An OAS relief coordination center, working with Dominican public health officials and agencies such as the Dominican and International Red Cross and USAID, was established in Santo

Domingo on 8 May and continued to operate throughout the IAPF presence.[4]

My headquarters, as well as the U.S. embassy, was given the opportunity in the first days of May 1965 to influence the formation of the IAPF when the Department of Defense sent a legal expert, Benjamin Foreman, to Santo Domingo for the purpose of drawing up proposals for the terms of reference to govern an international peacekeeping force. Foreman was especially helpful in sorting out the political and military ramifications of such a force, as well as the legal aspects.

Foreman was also involved in the discussion as to whether the IAPF commander should be a U.S. or a Latin American officer. On the grounds of preserving U.S. control and freedom of action, especially since the United States was footing the bill, both Tom Moorer (CINCLANT) and I recommended a U.S. commander to the JCS. But Chairman Wheeler agreed with the view that since the internationalization of the force had been devised to encourage OAS support for the intervention, endorsement of an overall American commander would be politically incompatible with that concept. Hence, on 22 May the OAS asked Brazil to name an IAPF commander, and the United States to designate his deputy. Brazil selected an army three-star general officer (equivalent to a U.S. two-star grade), Hugo Penasco Alvim, and the United States named me as his deputy. At the same time, I was to retain command of all U.S. forces in the Dominican Republic. Although it could be argued that by designating an overall U.S. commander the OAS might have ended up with a larger number of Latin American troops, in retrospect I conclude that the view our government took was a wise one, and the OAS made the right choice in deciding on a Latin American. At any rate, as the international deputy and the U.S. commander, I had sufficient leverage to get IAPF decisions that were compatible with U.S. desires.

In Santo Domingo we lost no time in preparing for an IAPF headquarters, forming a cadre staff of U.S. officers even before the headquarters was officially activated. We selected the Hotel Jaragua, located on the coast southwest of the embassy, as the

Chart 2 - Inter-American Peace Force
(Dominican Republic, 1965-1966)

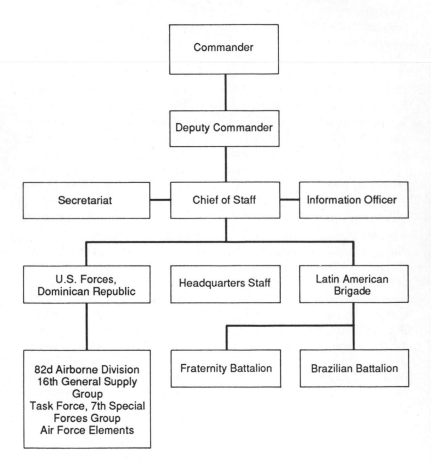

HQ site and began installing communications equipment. However, all the Latin American contingents except Paraguay's (which did not appear until late June) arrived in the Dominican Republic before the formal establishment of the IAPF, before the arrival of its designated commander, and before any modus operandi had been agreed upon. This made things a little awkward, but we made good use of the time to check the equipment and supply shortages of the incoming contingents and to brief the new troops on the peculiarities of the Dominican scene. Deploying Latin contingents were flown into San Isidro air base by U.S. Air Force C-130s except for the Brazilians, who were airlifted by the Brazilian Air Force in their own troop carrier aircraft. Some arriving troops had been assembled at home in such haste that they were literally without such basic items as boots and rifles; indeed, only the Brazilian forces arrived in a ready condition. Fortunately, our logisticians had done their planning well, and we had no problem in getting the new troops rapidly into shape. As a matter of fact, the United States continued to provide most of the logistic support for its Latin friends throughout the existence of the IAPF.

On 23 May in an impressive and emotional ceremony at the Embajador Hotel, the national commanders and Secretary General Mora of the OAS signed a formal document, "The Act Creating the Inter-American Force." After signing as the U.S. commander and concurrently as the acting commander of the whole force, I signed General Orders Number One, activating the unified command headquarters for operational command and control of the assigned national contingents. Thereafter, we habitually wore on our uniforms black armbands with the white letters "OEA" (Organizacion de Estados Americanos), the Spanish equivalent of OAS. Vice Adm. Jack McCain, the ebullient commander of the U.S. Amphibious Forces, Atlantic, attended the ceremony and joined in enthusiastically, putting on an OEA armband even though no U.S. naval forces had been assigned to the IAPF.[5]

The signing of this historic document, a unique experiment in OAS cooperation, produced a new organization and concept for collective action, the first time that sovereign states within the Americas had banded together to form a regional, multinational force. It also represented a fundamental change in the way the United States moved to influence events in Latin America.

The first combined IAPF operations involved MP patrols: Costa Rican, Honduran, and U.S. military police jointly patrolled the ISZ, beginning on 24 May. We also organized IAPF observer teams of Latin American (LA) personnel only, to investigate alleged cease-fire violations. These teams established liaison with Imbert's GNR, located in the fair grounds just west of the ISZ, and with Caamano's Constitutionalist Government in downtown Santo Domingo, something that could not be routinely accomplished by U.S. military personnel. Because it was simply too risky and incidents were too easily provoked, we did not permit U.S. citizens to enter the rebel sector.

The U.S. forces, which had been deployed very rapidly, had peaked in strength on 10 May with 22,500 troops in the country. This included most of the 82d Airborne Division and most of the 4th Marine Expeditionary Brigade. Feeling the pressure of much criticism at home and abroad for intervening and overreacting, President Johnson was eager to reduce the size of the U.S. force and ordered the withdrawal of 10,000 troops as soon as possible.

In my opinion, the hindsight judgment of too much force is neither fair nor accurate, because the use of overwhelming force, properly controlled, can save lives and reduce collateral material damage. Moreover, in the beginning no one was sure what the internal situation might bring, especially whether the revolt might spread throughout the countryside. It was clearly demonstrated that the rapid troop buildup in the Santo Domingo area allowed us to stabilize the situation on land quickly, which in turn permitted a significant and rapid phasedown of U.S. troop strength.

All concerned agreed that the withdrawal would begin with the marines because this would allow CINCLANT to reconstitute his marine and amphibious forces in their normal configuration, ready for the next contingency. It would also simplify the command and control structure ashore, as well as the logistic and administrative support of U.S. forces in the republic. A minor contretemps occurred after Bouker, the marine commander, and I had agreed on the order in which marine units would be withdrawn: Admiral McCain disapproved our plan, wanting to do it differently. But when I remonstrated with him over a cup of coffee in my office, McCain gave me an amiable grin and admitted that he had objected in order to "keep the marines in their place and remind them who was the boss!" We both laughed, and the upshot was that the withdrawal went according to the original plan. A reduction in U.S. forces, mostly marine, was well under way before the arrival of the IAPF commander, General Alvim. Later, Alvim agreed to the withdrawal of the remainder of the 4th MEB, and by 6 June no U.S. marines remained on the island, leaving elements of the 82d Airborne as the primary U.S. combat force. Total U.S. troop strength at this point was down to about 12,000.

General Alvim arrived on 29 May at San Isidro air base, where I met him at planeside and welcomed him to the Dominican Republic.[6] A short, rolypoly, bespectacled gentleman, he responded with the question "Habla espagñol, señor?"—to the great amusement of the reporters covering the occasion, because it did not take long to establish my lack of fluency. But he was an able, professional soldier, older that I, and we soon established a warm and close relationship. Likewise, the new IAPF staff and the U.S. staff established a mutually beneficial rapport, and there were enough Spanish- and Portuguese-speaking American officers and enlisted men on both staffs to make for a fairly smooth transition from U.S. to IAPF control of operations.

Officially, we published our written orders and other documents in three languages—English, Portuguese, and Spanish. We found that whereas we had no difficulty translating between Spanish and English, translating into Portuguese was another matter; there are Portuguese expressions that have no counterpart in either English or Spanish. We normally conducted our daily and special staff briefings in Spanish, which was good exercise for the weak linguists like me. It was also good for our Portuguese-speaking Brazilian colleagues, who tended to be a little overbearing toward their counterparts from the Spanish-speaking nations of Latin America, each dwarfed in area and population by immense Brazil.

To serve the new international command we organized a combined staff ("C staff," we called it) under Col. Julio Gutierrez, the commander of the Nicaraguan contingent, as chief of staff. Gutierrez was a competent officer with a talent for suave diplomacy and a spiritual streak; he became very popular with all nationalities and was much admired.[7] Brig. Gen. Henry J. Mueller, U.S. Army, was deputy chief of staff. Experienced in Latin American ways and fluent in Spanish, Mueller deserves much credit for the smoothly working IAPF staff team we developed; the fact that he was a "Master Blaster" (master parachutist) did not hurt his stature either. A Brazilian Army colonel had the key C-3 (operations, plans, and training) job, the army colonel commanding the Paraguayan contingent doubled as the C-2 (intelligence),[8] and a Honduran Army major had the C-1 (personnel) position. The C-4 (logistics), C-5 (civil affairs), and C-6 (communications) slots were filled by U.S. officers. Other staff positions too were held mostly by U.S. personnel because we had more people available, although the important job of provost marshal went to a Costa Rican, Lt. Col. Alvano Arias, who also commanded the "civilian guard" platoon from his country. Arias, outgoing and personable, soon became everyone's favorite.

Almost all the older Latin American officers were graduates of the U.S. Army's Command and General Staff College at Fort Leavenworth, Kansas; a few had attended the U.S. Army–operated School of the Americas located at that time in the Canal Zone, Panama.[9] This gave us a basis of common understanding with respect to military terms and procedures, and accelerated our progress as an effective and reliable staff that not only was responsive to its commander, Alvim, but also had the confidence of each national contingent.

One of Alvim's first decisions was to organize the Latin American troops, totaling about 1,800, into a separate brigade rather than comingling LA units among the more numerous U.S. forces. Although this approach had the disadvantage of presenting a more vulnerable target for rebel propaganda—one hostile objective being to drive a wedge between U.S. and Latin American forces—it had many overriding advantages. The decision preserved the integrity of LA troops as an entity, which was important psychologically and enhanced their pride and esprit. A combined force was also easier to support logistically and administratively. Formally designated the Latin American Brigade, it consisted of the Brazilian Army infantry battalion and the "Fraternity Battalion," as we named it, comprising the separate rifle companies from Honduras, Nicaragua, and Paraguay, the Brazilian marine company, and the Costa Rican platoon.

Colonel Carlos de Meira Mottos, Brazilian Army, commanded the Latin American Brigade and organized a small brigade staff made up primarily of Brazilian personnel and supported by a Brazilian Army signal detachment. Mottos was a cool and steady commander, well aware of the idiosyncrasies of his mixed force, and got the most out of them. He had a well-developed and sophisticated sense of humor that endeared him to most of his colleagues, but his political savvy was perhaps of greatest value to us.[10]

We sweated out the first few days of June when Brazilian Army soldiers, as an initial step, took over responsibility for the Presidential Palace, which had been a kind of neutral enclave within the constitutionalist sector. But the operation went well, and by 11 June the Latin American Brigade had taken over most of the ISZ as well, including the barricade line and check points facing the rebel zone, while U.S. troops manned the corridor.

During this period I kept General Wheeler and Admiral Moorer closely informed of the situation in Santo Domingo but received no specific guidance, being told simply to support U.S. policy. There was ample reason for this apparent lack of interest: Secretary McNamara and the Defense Department were absorbed with the worsening situation in Vietnam, where U.S. air and ground power had already been committed, and were content to let Secretary Rusk and the State Department handle the Dominican matter. Besides, it was now primarily a political problem. But what a tough problem! Twice, the United States government had tried to find a solution on its own; now it was the turn of the multinational OAS to negotiate a settlement between widely separated right and left poles with little maneuvering room between them.

I sensed that the majority view in both State and Defense was that, failing to find a solution acceptable to both sides, the United States should support Imbert's GNR and crush the rebellion, particularly the Communist elements in the constitutionalist faction. The OAS saw it differently, however, and deliberately selected a balanced Ad Hoc Committee of three: a conservative from Brazil, a liberal from El Salvador, and a de facto chairman from the United States who was considered to be fair and not committed to either side. Ellsworth Bunker was a fortunate choice. Not only was he U.S. ambassador to the OAS and, at the time, president of the OAS Council; he was President Johnson's personal representative. Finally, he had unequaled credentials as a successful negotiator.

Before Bunker's arrival in early June and before I got to know him, I was faced with my own ideological problems on the military side. Bob York, the 82d's commander, was conservative in his views, and to compromise with the left was not in his nature. Moreover, having his headquarters in San Isidro put him in ready contact with the hard right elements within the Dominican military, in particular, de Los Santos, the air force chief; Wessin y Wessin, the CEFA commander; and Martinez Arana, the army chief. Newly arrived IAPF commander General Alvim was likewise a rightist and viewed everyone on the rebel side as a card-carrying Communist. Alvim greatly admired York and his paratroopers, and the two commanders hit it off very well together. Ambassador Bennett also admired and liked York, who had his confidence. And so I had the additional burden, as both overall U.S. commander and Alvim's deputy, of establishing myself as the principal military adviser to the U.S. ambassador and at the same time keeping my military people in line and supporting the declared U.S. policy of neutrality between the Dominican factions. The difficulty became apparent during Imbert's drive to clear northern Santo Domingo while our military attachés in the embassy were still closely allied with the Dominican chiefs. Secretary Vance, who saw the problem without my having to spell it out for him, helped by bringing in some new, uncommitted attachés from the services. This situation eased still further in the summer of 1965 when York was reassigned to Fort Benning, Georgia.[11]

While the IAPF was getting established, the paratroopers in the corridor led a relatively quiet existence. A normal routine for a rifle company included a three- to four-mile morning run through the corridor, during which swarms of Dominican children would join them. The troopers then returned to a day of issuing food to the local population, maintaining equipment, attending unit schools on various military subjects, and standing inspections. They were never threatened from the GNR side but were often sniped at from the rebel sector. At the eastern end of the corridor, harassing fire was frequently directed against the vital city power plant from a tall hospital building, conspicuously draped in Red Cross flags, located in the rebel zone. At this time in early June, U.S. casualties stood at 18 men killed and 117 wounded in action, a grim reminder of the perils of peacekeeping.

Things got hotter in Santo Domingo with the arrival on 4 June of the OAS Ad Hoc Committee. Caamano and the constitutionalists opposed the dispatch of another OAS mission, preferring UN mediation because they believed the UN majority would more likely be partial to the constitutionalists than to Imbert's GNR. The United Nations had debated the Dominican crisis but had not come to a decision; in the absence of agreement in the Security Council, Secretary General U Thant had sent an observer team headed by José Mayobre, whose partiality toward the rebel faction has already been mentioned. In fact, shrill propaganda against the OAS presence emanated from both Dominican sides: the constitutionalists feared that Imbert would be favored and vowed to fight "to the last man," while Imbert and the GNR feared that a military solution would be ruled out and berated the OAS (and the United States) for "not accepting the necessity of wiping out this focus of Communism" in Santo Domingo.[12]

All things considered, then, it was no great surprise to anyone when the constitutionalists made one last effort to expand
out of the downtown section of the capital, known as Ciudad
Nueva. Because they must surely have realized that they were
far inferior in terms of military power, their real purpose was
probably political: to gain international sympathy for their en-
trapped position in Santo Domingo, as well as to inflict casualties on the IAPF and thus raise the cost of the U.S./OAS
intervention.

It was about 7:30 A.M., on 15 June, when the rebels suddenly
opened a series of sharp fire attacks ranging all around the land
perimeter of their zone, with the heaviest fire brought against
U.S. troops in the corridor. Our troops did not return the fire
initially, but as hostile fire became more intense and rebel
forces—supported by heavy machine guns, mortars, and even
a couple of light 37mm gun tanks—began to maneuver against
our positions, the 82d Airborne Division reacted. One result
was the heaviest single day of fighting recorded during the entire crisis. Although the American troops had not expected such
an offensive action and in fact were engaged in arms and equipment inspections, the paratroopers were soon in the thick of
things. By the time I had personally checked out the situation
with the Latin American Brigade and the 82d, they had moved
south from the eastern end of the corridor a good two blocks
and advanced even farther south of the power plant on the west
bank of the Ozama River.

At this point, I was concerned that a general advance of the
IAPF through downtown Santo Domingo, wiping out the rebel
zone, would leave the OAS and the United States open to the
charge of perpetrating "the Budapest of the Western Hemisphere." I knew that Bunker and the OAS Ad Hoc Committee
were counting on the IAPF to contain the constitutionalist
forces but not to eliminate them, because this would greatly
decrease the committee's leverage with Imbert and the GNR.
Moreover, I realized that Palmer and the U.S. forces would be
specifically blamed for the consequences.

After consulting briefly with General Alvim, therefore—
who reluctantly agreed—I jeeped directly to the 82d's brigade

headquarters in the corridor. There I found the whole chain of command in the eastern sector: division commander Bob York, brigade commander Col. George Viney, and Lt. Col. Rick Long, commanding the 1st Battalion, 508th Parachute Infantry. Confronting me was the most disagreeable task I ever had to do, to order that the successful operation under way be halted and that the 82d consolidate its position in the most defensible locations available. To their great credit, the division leaders understood and accepted the orders without complaint. But the attack was not easy to stop, because the men were aroused; comrades had been killed or badly hurt; and the momentum of the advance was not readily slowed in a short time.

By dusk, however, our forces had settled on their new positions, which were considerably more defensible than their previous ones—especially near the power plant, where for the first time we had good observation and could adequately secure the area. We also occupied the hospital building that had been such a thorn in our sides. A significant bonus was the securing of the world-famous Alcazar de Colon (Castle of Columbus), dating from the early 1500s and one of the oldest museums in the Western Hemisphere. Lawless elements had badly damaged the exterior, but inside, fortunately, damage was light. The 82d Airborne Division repaired the building, earning the deep gratitude of the Dominican curator and the GNR.

But these advantages were not achieved without cost; the eastern battalion in the corridor had an exposed flank during the operation and took more casualties even after we had tried to establish a new cease-fire. Mainly because of Caamano's inability to control his forces, the cease-fire was not fully restored until the evening of the next day, 16 June. U.S. casualties for the two-day period were five killed and thirty-six wounded. In the Latin American Brigade sector, where rebel fire had been returned but no advance had been undertaken, the Brazilians suffered five men wounded.

In all, it was a disaster for Caamano. His best troops had been badly mauled, and his casualties were estimated to be at least ten times greater than the IAPF's. He had lost not only some of his most experienced leaders, but also about fifty-six square city blocks. Militarily, this effort was Caamano's high-water mark; thereafter, he realized that he could not challenge the IAPF with force but would have to resort to other means to achieve his goals. Moreover, the actions of the IAPF demonstrated that it was responsive to OAS political guidance and control and that it would not take matters into its own hands. On balance, therefore, I believe we did the right thing. Caamano's hand was seriously weakened, and the negotiating position of the OAS Ad Hoc Committee was immeasurably strengthened.

Not long after the episode, both Bunker and Bennett at separate times half-jokingly remarked to me that it was too bad we had not gone all the way to the sea and crushed Caamano. I was a little taken aback and did not debate the question at either time, especially with Ambassador Bennett, who I suspected really wasn't joking. With Bunker's arrival on the scene as President Johnson's personal representative and as the recognized leader of the OAS committee charged with finding a political solution, Bennett was definitely playing second fiddle. His position was not an enviable one.

Immediately after their abortive attack of 15-16 June, the rebels concentrated their attention on the Latin American Brigade, particularly the Brazilian elements. There were rock-throwing incidents and some minor fire fights in the Latin American Brigade sector, but its troops had learned how to overcome trigger-happiness and kept their cool. My chief of staff, Bob Linvill, played a conspicuous role in achieving this fire discipline. Whenever a fire fight broke out, Linvill would take off for the area to help calm things down. Even when he was confronted with unusual problems—such as one outfit that preferred to toss hand grenades around like popcorn rather than firing their weapons—his steady demeanor was a big help.

Rebel propaganda hammered hard to drive a wedge between U.S. and LA forces, alleging that all the dirty work had been assigned to the undermanned and overworked Latin American Brigade. Vicious attacks were made on me personally as the "insanely brutal Pentagon ape," a white, Protestant "Nordic" who despised and spit on (the ultimate Latin insult) the "black,

Catholic Brazilian General Alvim" (actually, Alvim was Caucasian). We were vulnerable, however, to a charge of uneven division of labor because of the U.S.–Latin American troop ratio, so Alvim and I arranged to reduce the size of the Latin American Brigade sector to just the Presidential Palace and the southeastern part of the perimeter around the rebel zone. Nevertheless, we did not relax until early July, when the first "Brazilians Go Home" and "IAPF Go Home" signs were plastered up alongside the familiar "Yankee Go Home" ones. And thus the IAPF settled down for a "long, hot summer" of keeping the peace and holding the belligerents apart, while the protracted OAS negotiations continued.

CHAPTER 5

Establishing a Provisional Government 4 June–3 September 1965

Arriving in Santo Domingo on 4 June, the three-member OAS Ad Hoc Committee established itself in the Embajador Hotel and immediately went to work. Its recognized chairman, Ellsworth Bunker, made it clear from the outset that he was not an agent of the U.S. State Department but was his own man, devoting his full attention to the Dominican crisis even when his Brazilian and Salvadorean colleagues were attending to other OAS duties in Washington. Bunker had a personal staff of five bright, relatively young U.S. foreign service officers that gave him an organizational base independent of the U.S. embassy, though of course he relied on embassy support for such things as secure electronic communications to Washington.

Bunker's staff was headed by William A. Bowdler and Harry W. Shlaudeman, the latter having recently been State's desk officer for the Dominican Republic and having worked under McGeorge Bundy in Santo Domingo during the abortive May negotiations that advanced the "Guzman formula."[1] I had met Shlaudeman during that earlier period and found him very knowledgeable on Dominican affairs but standoffish and uninterested in military matters affecting the Inter-American Peace Force. Bowdler, on the other hand, was friendly and outgoing and did not miss a trick on anything of significance that might influence the activities of the Ad Hoc Committee.

As President Johnson's personal representative in Santo
Domingo, Bunker let it be known that he intended to tell Washington what should be done rather than the other way around.
At times, he would remind even the president that he had all
the advice he needed and would rely on his own best judgment
to achieve a solution in the Dominican Republic, adding point-
edly that this would take time. Characteristically, Bunker was
patient and unhurried even when under great stress and urgency, secure in the experience gained in two successful ca-
reers, one as a top executive in business and the other as a
diplomat. He had been U.S. ambassador to Argentina, Italy, and
India; he had settled the Dutch-Indonesian dispute in 1962 and
had negotiated the withdrawal of Egyptian troops from Yemen
in 1963; and now he was chairman of the OAS Council. So, he
could tell the president to "get off his back" and could, as one
analyst put it, "disdain deadlines, resist pressures, and ignore
the conventional wisdom about the Dominican situation."[2]

My first meeting with Ambassador Bunker was in Tap Bennett's office at the embassy not long after Bunker's arrival. I
was deeply impressed with this tall, spare man with snowwhite
hair and a patrician manner. He was courteous and even
courtly, taking the time to explain in a down-to-earth, low-key
way what he planned to do. As I was to find later, he deliberately eschewed the spectacular and played things straight
with all parties, refraining from glossing over the very real differences that existed but using a commonsense approach in
seeking simple ways to handle complicated problems. Urbane,
friendly, and often demonstrating a dry New England sense of
humor, he rarely showed any sign of emotion but maintained
a cool, detached attitude. What probably accounted for most
of his success as a negotiator was his integrity in dealing with
both sides; he was truthful, honest, devoid of any deception.
In the end, he was simply able to convince people that he was
uncommitted to either side and that he could be trusted.

During these extended negotiations in the Dominican Republic, I rarely received any information or guidance from the
secretary of defense or the JCS, who apparently were content
to let the White House and State Department handle the situa-

tion. Not being privy to the message traffic, much of it "Ex Dis" (extremely limited distribution), flowing between Bunker and Washington or separately between Bennett and Washington, I was often in the dark except for what Bunker or Bennett was willing to tell me. Bunker would discuss aspects of the situation that he felt I should know as U.S. commander or deputy IAPF commander, and he was always forthcoming and helpful on such occasions, but sometimes I had to "fly by the seat of my pants." Nor was Bennett, I suspect, privy to all Bunker's communications to Washington, and I am sure there were matters on which they did not see eye to eye. Still, their relations were generally close and cordial, and both treated me in a friendly, courteous, and understanding manner.

Over time, Bunker and I worked out a simple modus operandi in our relationships, the initiative coming from him, since he was calling the shots. Sometimes we would meet in Bennett's office, as at our first meeting, or occasionally in my headquarters when he wanted to discuss something privately with me. At those times when General Alvim was unhappy with the direction things were taking, Bunker and I would confer on the problem and then meet with Alvim at IAPF headquarters. Still later, after a provisional president was installed, Bunker would arrange for Alvim and me to meet with the president on a special problem. Being next door to the embassy, I also saw Bennett frequently and was always available—as was my staff—to meet with him or his staff as he desired. It was an easy relationship, especially after my staff and the embassy's got to know one another.

After being briefed by Bennett and other U.S. officials, the OAS Ad Hoc Committee began operation on its own, setting up channels for negotiating purposes with each of the two sides and holding discussions with Dominicans at various levels and of differing persuasions: military and civilian; loyalists and constitutionalists; businessmen, industrialists, the clergy, intellectuals; and both politically committed and noncommitted people. During its stay in the republic the Ad Hoc Committee met with Colonel Caamano and the constitutionalists forty-eight times and with Imbert of the loyalist military fifty-three

times, and held countless meetings with other Dominican individuals and groups—a remarkable performance. Meetings
with Caamano and his advisors were held at his office in the
constitutionalist zone in downtown Santo Domingo; meetings
with Imbert or the Dominican chiefs took place in the GNR
offices at the fair grounds, west of the city.

In only a few days the basic positions to the two sides became
clear to the committee. Caamano and his constitutionalists
reiterated their demands: restoration of the 1963 constitution
and the 1963 Congress associated with the regime of deposed
president Juan Bosch; formation of a "democratic" government; continued service of rebel soldiers in the regular armed
forces; and the immediate withdrawal of the IAPF. Imbert and
his loyalist military claimed that the GNR was the only rightful government and demanded that it continue to operate during any transition period.

Early in these consultations Bunker began to wonder
whether either of the two warring factions could really speak
for the Dominican people. To test his feelings, he visited Santiago de los Caballeros, the nation's second largest city, located
in the lush Cibao region, where he met with representative
groups of professionals, workers, students, farmers and ranch-
ers, businessmen, and others. This experience and other discussions convinced Bunker that the only way to overcome the
impasse between the two contending parties was to let the
people decide through early, free, and open elections supervised
by the OAS and a provisional government—operating under
an "institutional act" drawn up by eminent Dominican ju-
rists—that would temporarily represent an interim constitution. This approach, in the doctrine of the art and science of
negotiations, was in effect the "third force" formula but with
no individual or group as yet identified to represent that third
force. Two separate stages were visualized: first, establishing
a third-force government, and second, laying the foundation
for the electoral process. However, even before a provisional
government could be established, many of the same issues that
had doomed the earlier Guzman formula would have to be
settled, such as the timing of the elections, the form of the

interim constitution, what to do with the Communists in the constitutionalist camp, and how to deal with the military personnel in the rebel ranks.[3]

As has already been described (Chapter 4), heavy fighting broke out on 15 June between the 82d Airborne Division and the rebels in the eastern part of the corridor, and a new cease-fire was not established until 16 June. This episode, the "last hurrah" for the rebels, further complicated the negotiations. It seemed clear to me that the constitutionalists had deliberately started the fighting for political reasons—to support their desire for greater UN involvement, which would probably be in their favor, and to discredit the IAPF with the allegation that it was not neutral. At any rate, the outbreak of hostilities served to accelerate the Ad Hoc Committee's efforts, and on 18 June its proposals were first presented to the two sides and then publicly released, groundwork having been laid previously with the Brazilian and Salvadoran governments. Mayobre, the UN representative in Santo Domingo, who was not consulted in the preparation of the proposals, was given a special copy of the documents. Copies of the proposals also were provided to the press, and thousands were dropped over various areas of the countryside from U.S. Army helicopters or delivered by vehicle.

The first document involved, "Declaration to the Dominican People," was an appeal for support of a provisional government. The second, "Proposals for a Solution to the Dominican Crisis," presented general suggestions to resolve the most controversial issues with the expectation that both sides would contribute to their ultimate nature and form. These proposals called for a provisional government under a single, undesignated person; a general amnesty; a temporary constitution that would postpone controversial aspects but would ensure broad civil liberties; elections of both municipal and national leaders, to be held six to nine months after the installation of the provisional president; the preparation of a permanent constitution by a regular constituent assembly; and military reform. The last item was an especially difficult one because Bennett and the State Department wanted it high on the agenda, while Bunker wanted to take it on only in good time, arguing that amnesty was the crucial point in establishing a climate in which restructuring of the military could be achieved without explosive resistance from either or both sides.[4] Bunker was right.

The initial reactions of the two opposing leaders were interesting. Imbert praised the work of the Ad Hoc Committee and stated that he could accept most of the proposals. Caamano, on the other hand, withheld comments until he had time to review the documents. Bunker said later that Caamano was more relaxed than he had expected and even friendly, despite the recent drubbing his best soldiers had taken from the 82d. (This suggested to me that the outcome might have strengthened Caamano's control because the more radical elements of his motley force had been weakened. Bunker was inclined to agree.) Caamano had also asked that the IAPF be ordered to return to its pre–15 June positions in the city on the grounds that it would put him in a better position to control his forces and would improve the atmosphere for negotiations. My reaction to the proposal was negative because I felt that it would probably lead to renewed fighting and encourage the rebels to harden their line. Moreover, I told Bunker, since the 82d now had a much more secure position in the corridor and had lost some good men in attaining it, I could never satisfactorily explain to our troopers why they should withdraw. Bunker understood and accepted my views, which were later supported by General Alvim and Ambassador Bennett.

In fact, the results of the 15-16 June fight had given the Ad Hoc Committee a very high card—the IAPF—to use in the negotiations. The constitutionalists had a special incentive to talk with the committee because the recovery of the former rebel territory was important to them for military and morale reasons. The area seized by the 82d on 15 June had been one of their strongholds and had been defended by their toughest commandos. Rather than reject Caamano's request out of hand, however, Bunker simply responded in a letter stating that for reasons of security and the desire to preserve a state of calm in the city, the IAPF would temporarily maintain its present positions but that the matter was open to further discussion. Thus Caamano was disarmed on that particular question, and the committee still held a high card—the possible withdrawal of the IAPF to its previously held positions.

Other reactions to the committee's proposals were mixed in the beginning. Some member states within the OAS had doubts about the committee, feeling that it might have exceeded its mandate. The most common objections voiced by various sectors of the Dominican population were the absence of measures to control Communists in the country, and the length of the pre-election period; some wanted to wait for several years— rather than six to nine months—to provide enough time for the nation to cool off. Bunker and the committee declined to lengthen the period, although later the timetable for elections was modified to nine months after the establishment of the provisional government: an initial six-month political truce, followed by a three-month campaign period.

On 23 June Caamano presented the constitutionalists' formal reply to the committee's proposals, expressing basic accord but repeating demands along the lines of their original position. On the same day Imbert presented the GNR's counterproposals, still maintaining that the GNR was the rightful interim government. About the only thing the two sides appeared to agree on was the early departure of the IAPF and a general amnesty. With respect to the "institutional act," or interim constitution, Caamano wanted to include the liberal economic and social provisions of the 1963 constitution—the very provisions that had frightened the conservatives during the Bosch regime and had contributed to his overturn—whereas Imbert wanted a definitive constitution decided upon before an elected government took office, a proposition that Bunker and the committee were not likely to accept.

On the question of reintegrating the armed forces, specifically the army, the two sides were far apart: Caamano wanted to reinstate all the rebel military, including those purged by Reid Cabral just before the revolution; Imbert would permanently bar all constitutionalist officers from any military role. "Civilian-held" arms was another area of complete disagreement. Imbert thought they should be turned over to the IAPF and thence to the GNR; Caamano, unwilling to trust either, wanted the arms surrendered to the provisional government. Nevertheless, both sides appeared to be willing to negotiate, although the Ad Hoc Committee recognized that it was side-stepping for the moment the extremely sensitive issue of military reform: that is, gracefully easing out the hard-line regular Dominican military chiefs and replacing them with more moderate men who would nevertheless be acceptable to the conservative side. Such an action would also entail dealing with the radical military leaders in the rebel ranks and preventing their taking over the regular establishment.

The good news at this time was that Bunker and his colleagues had found a promising prospect for provisional president, Hector Garcia Godoy, an experienced diplomat and businessman who seemed to have no direct ties with either side and who was willing to serve. Godoy had been foreign minister under Bosch but professed no particular party allegiance. However, he had acted as vice-president of the Reformist Party (PR) of Dr. Joaquin Balaguer, a perennial political activist who was then in exile because of his previous association with the infamous Trujillo regime. On 28 June Balaguer returned to the Dominican Republic and announced that the 24 April 1965 revolution could have no other outcome than "the establishment of a provisional government [eventually] leading the nation to honest elections"—which, of course, he hoped to win. His statement endeared him to the committee but not to Imbert, who had no intention of stepping down as head of the GNR.[5]

Bunker had to find a graceful and face-saving means of persuading Imbert to make way for a new interim president. The United States achieved one form of leverage by assuming the payment (through the OAS) of GNR salaries in late June and arranging to finance most of the OAS emergency assistance for recovery programs in the Dominican Republic, which left the GNR completely dependent on OAS financial assistance. This leverage was not used until August, when payments were stopped, but in late June Bunker discovered another means to handle Imbert in the person of Rivera Caminero, Imbert's minister of the armed forces. Rivera confided to Bunker that the Dominican armed forces were not necessarily aligned with any particular individual but rather were concerned with what was best for the republic; he indicated that the military would be willing to cooperate if an acceptable nonpolitical candidate were chosen to head up the provisional government. This indeed was welcome news to Bunker and his committee, who saw it as an opening to persuade the Dominican military to adopt a moderate, middle-of-the road position.

By 9 July the rebels had agreed to Godoy's leadership of the provisional government, but not until after a bitter internal debate within the constitutionalist camp in which the left-wing groups opposed Godoy as a "reactionary" who was being imposed by the OAS Ad Hoc Committee. It now appeared that the extremist groups on both sides could be isolated from the moderates—a good sign for the future.[6] On 12 July Imbert also accepted Godoy's candidacy but only with the greatest reluctance, and it was obvious that he would stall as long as he could before stepping down. He no doubt felt secure because GNR security forces controlled the entire country except for downtown Santo Domingo, but he refused to recognize that the constitutionalist presence in the heart of the city made it impossible for the country to return to normalcy, especially in an economic and financial sense.

Alvim and I were formally introduced to Godoy on 13 July at Bunker's OAS headquarters in the Embajador Hotel. Alvim tried to give him a lecture on the Communist danger, but Bunker managed to get the subject changed; Alvim was right, but it was the wrong time and place for such a harangue, and I do not believe that it enhanced the standing of the IAPF with Godoy. My first impressions of Godoy were good. A middle-aged, balding, slim man sporting a moustache, he struck me as a nervous and high-strung individual who was sincere, intelligent, and straightforward with no illusions as to the difficulties he faced.

At U.S. headquarters we too had no illusions about the future, because it was obvious that both sides would maneuver for political, propaganda, and psychological (and, on Imbert's side, even military) advantage. The rebel side, for example, periodically tried to foment a general strike against the GNR and intensified its propaganda attacks, adding to its psychological arsenal a "yellow rag" newspaper, La Patria, a blatantly communist publication produced by the MPD (the Peiping-oriented Communist party in the Dominican Republic). Printed in the rebel zone, where the offices and presses of the leading reputable newspapers were also in rebel hands, La Patria had a wide underground circulation and did do some damage in the countryside. Communist-oriented political parties also began large-scale guerrilla training and political indoctrination in downtown rebel territory, giving three- to four-week courses to youths (mostly male) recruited all over the republic and bused into Santo Domingo. About 2,500 students graduated from these schools during July and August.[7]

On its part, the GNR maintained a constant stream of threats and rumors designed to make the rebels believe that GNR forces were about to attack the rebel zone with the support of the IAPF. Our close contacts with Rivera and the Dominican service chiefs, who convinced us that they had no such intentions and that the rumors originated with other GNR officials, enabled us to calm any resulting jitters. However, several night mortar attacks made in July against the rebel zone did result in some casualties among the innocent population and brought rebel accusations that the IAPF was the guilty party; the GNR also broadcast over Radio Santo Domingo, which it had controlled since Imbert's sweep, the IAPF was responsible. Fortunately, two countermortar radar units flown in from the United States soon pinpointed the mortar firing positions and exonerated the IAPF, at the same time supplying sufficient evidence to produce an admission by the GNR that CEFA troops from San Isidro had made the attacks.[8] These assaults on defenseless people further tarnished the reputation of Wessin y Wessin, still in command of CEFA, who was feared and hated in many quarters.

During this turbulent period IAPF headquarters, in conjunction with my U.S. headquarters, developed two basic military plans to be used in the event that negotiations failed and it became necessary to occupy the rebel zone. One plan, based on the use of military force against hostile resistance, was known as Operation Martillo. The other, visualizing a peaceful occupation with little or no resistance, was called Operation Suave. Extensive psychological and civil affairs activities were an integral part of both, and in each plan the basic scheme of maneuver involved a three-battalion brigade of the 82d Airborne Division moving south from the corridor, with the Latin American Brigade advancing east from the eastern edge of the ISZ. An initial buffer zone was provided between the two brigades to avoid their interfering with each other's actions. In early July we briefed the OAS Ad Hoc Committee on these plans at IAPF headquarters. Although its members were noncommittal, Bunker found it useful to keep those possible options in the back of his mind in case the situation demanded swift and decisive action. We also told the committee that, according to our current estimate, the rebel forces numbered some 1,000 to 2,000 "military" personnel (including 200-300 hard-core Communists and 400-500 ex-military who had rebelled), plus about 1,000 armed civilians. These forces were armed mostly with rifles, automatic rifles, submachine guns, or light machine guns, plus a few heavy machine guns, rocket launchers, and mortars. They also possessed a handful of very light tanks and armored cars.[9]

In private conversations, Bunker more than once told me that the Dominican negotiations were the most difficult he had experienced in his long career. He explained to me that in his judgment all of Latin America in a political sense was moving—some countries faster than others—inexorably to the left; that the nature of this move was probably unacceptable to the majority view in the United States but generally acceptable in Latin America; that there was virtually no chance to stop or block this movement, which was being generally adopted even by the Catholic Church in Latin America as the wave of the future; and that therefore our best bet was to try to moderate this movement and prevent it from going all the way left to Communism. Bunker's basic negotiating tactics reflected this philosophy. I believe too that Bunker thought a "just" settlement of the Dominican problem involved his personal conscience. He told me that his first job after graduation from Yale in 1912 concerned his family's sugar interests in the Dominican Republic; now, more than fifty years later, he was appalled to find that the lot of the *campesinos* working in the cane fields had not changed a bit—they were still poor, ragged, and uncared for.

Godoy, who lost no time in working closely with the committee and getting into the gut issues that separated the two sides, soon indicated that early military "reform" was critically important to him. Constitutionalists pressed hard for the removal of the senior loyalist officers and their replacement with more moderate and presumably pro-constitutionalist men. Rivera and the GNR military, on the other side, wanted assurances that they would continue in their jobs during the provisional government and that key rebel military leaders would be deported for at least five years once a settlement was achieved. While the loyalist chiefs seemed willing to compromise on the second point, they refused to budge on the first. Understandably, Godoy wanted this impasse resolved before he took office. Unfortunately, however, his frequent conferences with Caamano gave the impression that he was either favoring the rebels or afraid of crossing their leader. Contributing to this impression was the fact that Godoy also frequently consulted with Mayobre, head of the UN observer team, who was an old, close friend. On the other hand, he did not consult with Imbert—which was understandable, given Imbert's opposition to him. No doubt Godoy reckoned that since the United States had sponsored Imbert in the first place, removing him from his position of power was a U.S. problem.

Feeling that the pressure had built up long enough with no concrete results, Bunker and the OAS Ad Hoc Committee decided to present its proposals as a package representing the committee's views on a "final" solution. The two principal documents were "The Institutional Act," which called specifically for a provisional government headed by Godoy, spelled out the conditions for the elections, and described the power

and authority of elected officials; and "The Act of Reconciliation," which set out the actions to be taken by the provisional
government to achieve reconciliation. Article 3 of the latter
related to general amnesty; Article 4 concerned the demilitarization of Santo Domingo and elimination of the rebel zone;
Article 5 prescribed that public order would be maintained by
the provisional government, which could call on the IAPF if
necessary; Articles 6 and 7 pertained to the collection of civilian-held arms; Articles 8 and 9 called for the return of all
armed forces from both sides to their barracks and provided for
either the reintegration of ex-military rebels or their safe voluntary departure from the country; and Article 10 left the timing of the withdrawal of the IAPF to be negotiated by the
provisional government with the OAS.[10]

On 9 August the two new documents were presented to both
sides. Concurrently, a second "Declaration to the Dominican
People," summarizing the two acts, was publicly announced
in the press, on radio, and by special leaflets. Then the committee put additional pressure on the two sides by proposing
a signing ceremony in the Presidential Palace the following
week.

Agreement from Godoy and the two sides came relatively
easy on the Institutional Act, mostly because the constitutionalists had dropped their demand to reinstate the 1963 constitution and accepted the version that omitted controversial
aspects contained in both the 1962 and 1963 constitutions.
Final agreement on the Act of Reconciliation, however, took
three more weeks of hard bargaining, although considerable
progress was made after military representatives from both
sides began direct talks, at the suggestion of the Ad Hoc Committee. Agreement was reached on most issues, but on the
thorny questions of military reform, the shake-up of the military chiefs, and the reintegration of the rebels, the two factions
could agree only to postpone final decisions until after the provisional government was established. This was not what
Godoy wanted, but he reluctantly conceded.[11]

One issue not included in either act but discussed during
this stage of negotiations was the question of dealing with

Communists among the rebels. Rivera, supported by the GNR, wanted to deport all Communists and any other rebels considered to be "dangerous." The U.S. State Department, supported by Ambassador Bennett, held similar views. Godoy, however, refused to agree to deportation, and by mid-August the loyalist military dropped their demand. At this point, feeling that local Communists had been isolated and were relatively weak, Bunker persuaded State that Godoy could handle them. It was further agreed that the provisional government would assume responsibility for keeping them under surveillance and for taking necessary measures to deal with subversion. Later events demonstrated that Godoy was not as capable of dealing forcefully with this situation as Bunker had hoped. Moreover, the problem was exacerbated by the decision to let Godoy freely select his cabinet without consulting Bennett, Bunker, or the committee.

On the nights of 28 and 29 August, radical rebels tried to torpedo the talks by firing from the rebel zone on Latin American Brigade positions. The LA forces responded heavily in kind but did not move from their positions, and the U.S. troopers refused to be sucked into the fire fight. Thus, the rebel gambit failed, and the IAPF was able to keep the lid on hostilities in Santo Domingo until the talks could be consummated—though not entirely without casualties: a U.S. paratrooper in the corridor was killed by a rifle grenade fired from the rebel zone on the night of 2 September.

Meanwhile, Imbert stubbornly refused to sign any agreement, despite heavy U.S. and OAS pressure that included the cutting-off of all GNR salaries on 14 August. Not until 30 August did he finally capitulate and resign, following which Rivera and the other Dominican chiefs signed the agreement for the GNR. A slightly different agreement, which included a reservation about the final withdrawal of the IAPF, was signed by Caamano and his "foreign minister," Hector Aristy. Both documents were signed by the committee and Godoy.

On 2 September, Dominican Army troops were returned to the Presidential Palace, which had been demilitarized, to take over the internal security of the palace grounds, while the IAPF remained responsible for external security. Then, in a simple ceremony on 3 September, Godoy was installed as the provisional president. Although the ceremony itself went without a hitch, considerable firing occurred along the corridor on the rebel side as the rebels apparently celebrated (or protested) the occasion.

That same evening General Alvim and I met with the OAS Ad Hoc Committee to discuss the new situation. Committee members emphasized the point that the IAPF was no longer neutral but must now lend full support to the new provisional government. They urged us to establish close, friendly relations with the Dominican armed forces, pointing out that these forces had OAS support but making it very clear that the OAS did not expect any *golpes* (coups) during Godoy's regime before the elections. We were asked to lift immediately the restrictions on the Dominican Air Force and Navy, establishing a policy of not interfering unless we were specifically requested and authorized to do so. It was agreed that the old ISZ and corridor no longer existed and that all exit and entry checkpoints would be eliminated except for the one at the eastern end of the Duarte Bridge; it would remain in order to prevent CEFA troops from moving into the city from San Isidro without proper authority. Finally, it was agreed that the Dominican National Police now had full police powers under the authority of the new president.

Technically, the OAS Ad Hoc Committee had completed the negotiations, and it was now up to the provisional government to implement what had been agreed upon and to seek settlement on those matters that were still at issue. As it turned out, the continuing presence of not only the IAPF but also the committee was necessary to maintain the transitional government on an even keel and to keep the peace.

A very young Dominican watches action inside the corridor held by U.S. forces in the heart of Santo Domingo in early May 1965. The poster carrying a picture of President Johnson calls for "peace, justice, and a free government" in the Dominican Republic. U.S. Army photo.

Unless otherwise indicated, all photos are from the author's collection.

Above, on 30 April 1965, U.S. marines from the 3d Battalion, 6th Marine Regiment, assemble behind a landing vehicle in western Santo Domingo, where they are to establish an International Security Zone designated by the OAS. Below, the first Inter-American Peace Force MP patrols, made up of MPs from the U.S., Honduras, and Costa Rica, form up on 25 May 1965 in front of IAPF headquarters in the Hotel Jaragua, Santo Domingo. Note OEA (OAS) armbands.

Above, this building in downtown Santo Domingo was damaged during the first days of the Dominican revolution in late April and early May 1965. Below, Deputy Secretary of Defense Cyrus Vance, with his executive officer, Col. DeWitt Smith, and Lt. Gen. Bruce Palmer, Jr., commander of U.S. Forces Dominican Republic, in May 1965 pass through downtown Santo Domingo in a jeep driven by Sgt. Donald Lamm.

General Palmer stands beside the first HQ sign in early June 1965.

Dominican women took to the streets in several cities to demonstrate in favor of the loyalist "Government of National Reconstruction" and in opposition to the Constitutionalist followers of Juan Bosch. On 23 May 1965 these women march in western Santo Domingo.

Two paratroopers of the 82d Airborne Division man an elevated observation post along the corridor facing the center of the Constitutionalist (rebel) zone in Santo Domingo in early May 1965. U.S. Army photo.

Above, Col. Alvano Arias, Costa Rica, signs the historic OAS document establishing the Inter-American Peace Force on 21 May 1965 in the Embajador Hotel, Santo Domingo. Seated behind him are Gen. Palmer and Dr. José A. Mora, secretary general of the OAS. Below, gathered at the Embajador after the signing are IAPF contingent commanders. From left to right are Col. Arias; Col. Carlos de Meira Mottos, Brazil; Gen. Palmer; Maj. Hermano Paz, Honduras; and Col. Julio Gutierrez, Nicaragua.

The staff of the IAPF stand in front of their headquarters in the Hotel Jaragua, Santo Domingo, in mid-June 1965. At center is the IAPF commander, Gen. Hugo Penasco Alvim of the Brazilian Army. Chief of Staff Col. Julio Gutierrez is on Alvim's left. Gen. Palmer, deputy commander, is on Alvim's right; and Col. Henry J. Mueller, deputy chief of staff, is on Palmer's right. U.S. Army photo.

Above, William Tapley "Tap" Bennett, U.S. ambassador to the Dominican Republic, confers with Adm. Jack McCain, commanding the Amphibious Forces Atlantic, Gen. Robert H. York, commanding the 82d Airborne Division, Gen. John Bouker, commanding the 4th Marine Expeditionary Brigade, and Gen. Palmer aboard McCain's flagship off Santo Domingo in late May 1965. Below, in mid-June 1965 the rebel Constitutionalists launched an attack on IAPF forces in the ISZ. After two days of heavy fighting, a ceasefire was restored on 16 June. Here, Lt. Bernie Rethore, Gen. Palmer's junior aide, is in radio contact with 3d Brigade, 82d Airborne Division, headquarters.

Above, Gen. Robert C. Taber, 82d Airborne Division, Gen. Palmer, Col. Edward Mayer, commander, 7th Special Forces Group, and Gen. Robert R. Linvill, chief of staff at U.S. Forces HQ, stand in front of the commanding general's quarters in July 1965. Col. Mayer received an award for heroism in leading a dangerous night mission. Below, Ambassador Bennett offers traditional Independence Day remarks at a ceremony in front of his residence in Santo Domingo, 4 July 1965. Seated from left are Gen. Palmer, Col. Richard Bell, chaplain, XVIII Airborne Corps HQ, and Ellsworth Bunker, U.S. member of the OAS Ad Hoc Committee. U.S. Army photo.

An aerial view of the crowd gathered on 29 August 1965 at the fairgrounds west of Santo Domingo to show support for Antonio Imbert's loyalist Government of Reconstruction. The OAS Ad Hoc Committee was making intense efforts at this time to establish a provisional government under moderate García Godoy. Loyalists and Constitutionalists agreed the next day, and Godoy was installed on 3 September.

Above, President Godoy has lunch at the Dominican Mountain Training Center with Ambassador Bennett (back to camera), Gen. Palmer, and Col. Gorman Smith, a battalion commander of the 82d Airborne Division who escorted Godoy on an observation tour in September 1965. Dominican Army units were trained at the center by U.S. Army personnel. U.S. Army photo. Below, members of the Dominican Communist party await the return of former President Juan Bosch on 25 September 1965 after his "exile" in San Juan, Puerto Rico. The sign reads, "Let us organize to resist the Yankee invader."

Above, former President Juan Bosch is warmly welcomed by supporters as he arrives at Punta Caucedo International Airport on 25 September 1965, exactly two years after being deposed by a military coup.

Opposite: top, ex-Dominican Army rebels are escorted by U.S. MPs on 13 October 1965 from the former Constitutionalist zone of Santo Domingo to a neutral camp outside the city under the terms of the Act of Reconciliation signed by warring Dominican factions on 30 August. About 1,200 men were relocated in the move. Bottom, troopers of the 82d Airborne Division and a U.S. M-48 medium tank are in position in the Ciudad Nueva section of Santo Domingo on 25 October 1965 after a pre-dawn move by the IAPF. President Godoy had requested the movement after hard-core revolutionaries defied his order to demilitarize the city.

Brazilian soldiers pose on 25 October beside a light tank captured by Dominican rebels the previous April. This archway served as an entrance through the wall that once surrounded the historic capital city of Santo Domingo.

Above, a reception at IAPF headquarters on New Year's Day 1966. Left to right are Commodore Emilio Jimenez Reyes, chief of the Dominican Navy, Gen. Palmer, Gen. Alvim, and Commodore Francisco Rivera Caminero, Dominican minister of defense. Below, Gen. Palmer, with the XVIII Airborne Corps staff, which also functioned as the staff of the U.S. Forces Dominican Republic, pose in front of their headquarters in early December 1965. Front row, left to right, are Col. James Royalty, Col. John Foulk, Gen. Robert R. Linvill, Gen. Palmer, Col. Herbert Bowlby, Col. Jean Holstein, and Col. Robert Abraham. U.S. Army photo.

Above, in Santo Domingo, dignitaries watch a departure ceremony honoring Gen. Alvim on 17 January 1966. Left to right are John H. Crimmons, later U.S. ambassador to the Dominican Republic; Brazilian Ambassador Nasciemento; Ambassador Duenas, El Salvador; Ellsworth Bunker; Gen. Alvim; Gen. Palmer; Ambassador Bennett; Ambassador Penna Marinho, Brazil; an unidentified official; and Col. Julio Gutierrez, IAPF chief of staff. U.S. Army photo. Below, Gen. Palmer bids farewell to Gen. Alvim and his designated successor as IAPF commander, Gen. Alvaro Braga, at San Isidro Airbase on 17 January. The IAPF staff are on Gen. Braga's left and in the second row.

Return to Normalcy
4 September–25 October 1965

Originally, the Ad Hoc Committee had recommended its own dissolution once President Godoy was in office, but at Godoy's urgent insistence the OAS approved an extension of the committee's mandate to include the planned June 1966 elections. It was a sound decision because the road to the elections was a rocky one, and the committee's presence proved to be essential.[1]

By this time I had acquired an immense admiration for Ambassador Bunker, who single-mindedly refused to let any obstacle impede his steadfast path toward a negotiated settlement. Few people of any nationality would have had the courage and tenacity to persevere the way this man did. Time and again he would enter the rebel zone alone and confront a defiant, unstable, and undisciplined group who at times threatened his life and hurled vile insults at him. Usually, two of the three members of the committee were present in the Dominican Republic, but Bunker was always there. Often he was the only one at a meeting with Caamaño, the others sometimes becoming so turned off or so intimidated by the rebels' unruly conduct that they refused to go downtown. We became so concerned about Bunker's safety that we developed a contingency plan for his rescue, should that become necessary. We didn't tell him because, characteristically, he would have just shrugged his shoulders and asked us to belay such ideas. Nevertheless, we knew the danger was real because we experienced several incidents that did result in harm or death to the Americans involved.

In the IAPF the first task was to demilitarize Santo Domingo, as called for in the Act of Reconciliation. On 4 September we dismantled the IAPF entry and exit points in the ISZ and the corridor except for those protecting the Presidential Palace area, controlling the Duarte Bridge, and surrounding Ciudad Nueva, the former rebel zone. That evening Alvim and I met with Godoy in the presence of the Ad Hoc Committee to discuss how to go about completing the demilitarization of the city. We agreed that the national police should have no difficulty maintaining order in the former ISZ, which lay in the "better part" of the city, but would need the help of U.S. troops in the old corridor, which ran through a very poor and tough part of town, until things were stabilized. We also agreed that the IAPF would first remove all heavy weapons and sandbags around the perimeter of the old rebel zone, leaving only a lightly manned line of observation posts, barbed wire, and checkpoints; further progress in demilitarization would depend on steps taken on the old rebel side. The remaining IAPF checkpoints would be closed at night, and the government curfew during the night, which had been imposed within the former ISZ, would also continue. Godoy asked us to maintain full external security around the palace until further notice. He told us that he had brought the radio propaganda war under control by closing temporarily all radio stations, including the official Radio Santo Domingo, which would be transferred from military to civilian control.[2]

By 8 September these actions had been accomplished. Most of the Latin American troops formerly stationed along the perimeter returned to their base camps west of IAPF headquarters in the old ISZ, while most of the three U.S. battalions manning the old corridor remained in their billets within that area. But progress on the rebel side was much slower, and the original thought that the city could be demilitarized in thirty days was soon seen to have been completely unrealistic. Rightist coup plotting against Godoy was already evident on the one hand,

and on the other it was clear that the more extreme rebels did not intend to give up their "territory."

Godoy, meanwhile, sensing that he had to defuse the extreme right if he were to survive, made his move first against Gen. Elias Wessin y Wessin, the most feared of the Dominican military chiefs. Wessin's strength lay basically with CEFA, the autonomous armed force stationed at San Isidro, many of whose soldiers were almost fanatically loyal to him. When on 5 September Godoy abolished CEFA as a separate entity and directed that it be made an integral part of the Dominican Army, Wessin defied him. The next day Alvim and I conferred on the matter with the Ad Hoc Committee and concluded that Godoy should handle the problem within his own government, calling on the IAPF only as a last resort. We suggested that Godoy order Wessin at once to a post abroad and then, if he refused to obey, use government forces to remove him physically from his command.

The showdown occurred on 9 September. Wessin had met with Godoy, Rivera, the Dominican chiefs, and Bunker in the Palace, and had agreed to leave the country, but then he reneged and tried to rally his CEFA troops against Godoy. Rivera and the other Dominican chiefs, who feared Wessin and admitted that they could not handle CEFA, threw their support behind Godoy but only with the understanding that he would publicly confirm them in their positions once Wessin was gone. Consequently, Godoy asked the IAPF through the committee to perform the unpleasant but necessary task of getting Wessin out of the country and to the Panama Canal Zone that same day—a tall order, as the hour was already late.[3]

After consulting briefly with Alvim, I gave orders to Gen. Jack Deane, now commanding the 82d Airborne Division troops in the Dominican Republic, to blockade CEFA forces at San Isidro, neutralize the CEFA HQ *cuartel* (military barracks) there, and stand by in an area near Wessin's home with a reaction force—a reinforced rifle company of paratroopers— prepared to move quickly by helicopter to wherever they might be needed.[4]

Alvim and I, together with the Dominican chiefs, then proceeded in the late afternoon of 9 September to Wessin's home in Ensanche Ozama, east of the Ozama River, hoping to persuade the CEFA chief to leave peacefully. While Alvim and I traveled together in one radio jeep with an MP escort jeep, the Dominicans made up an impressive entourage, each traveling in a large limousine accompanied by a heavily armed bodyguard. It was quite a crowd. Wessin's home turned out to be a small fortress, a walled compound with heavy gates guarded by formidable-looking sentries with automatic weapons. Inside the compound was his home, appearing modest on the outside, as well as several smaller structures that apparently housed his security force and their families. The area was swarming with people; there were adults and children who seemed to be relatives or friends, and armed men of Wessin's bodyguard, most of them talking at once and furiously gesticulating.

Our meeting took place in a detached one-story, windowless building of obviously heavy construction, which appeared to be Wessin's alternate command post (the main one being at CEFA HQ in San Isidro). Only principals were present; all aides, guards, and the like were kept outside. General Alvim opened with a long, impassioned appeal to Wessin's patriotism, while Rivera Caminero and the other Dominican military chiefs sat impassively in a group, content to be witnesses only. By this time, I was acquainted with all the chiefs. Minister of the Armed Forces Rivera, a big, impressive-looking man, would listen but keep his own counsel. The air force chief, Gen. Jesus de Los Santos Cespedes, was intelligent but quick-tempered and therefore had to be watched. Commodore Ramon Emilio Jimenez Reyes, who had succeeded Rivera as navy chief, was a steady, cool individual who seemed to enjoy the other chiefs' trust and was intellectually a cut above the rest, while Gen. Martinez Arana, the army chief, was the most parochial of the group. All were staunch conservatives, de Los Santos and Arana more so than Rivera and Jimenez, whose outlook was relatively moderate.

In response to Alvim's appeal, Wessin tried to stall and temporize. Thereupon Alvim led him into a corner, where they engaged in an animated conversation for about twenty minutes, while I became more and more concerned about our lack of progress. Finally, I interrupted to tell General Wessin that he had no choice; he must leave that day for Panama to await whatever assignment President Godoy settled upon, and although we did not wish to use force, we were prepared to do so if necessary. Wessin caved in then and asked for the consul general job in Miami, the same job in New Orleans for an unnamed friend, and a job in Miami for his aide. Alvim committed Godoy on all three requests, and the meeting ended.

Outside, it had become quite dark, and there were some tense moments as Wessin said goodbye to his wife in the midst of a large and, by now, upset and unfriendly crowd that did not like what was going on; it was probably just as well that I understood little of what was being shouted in very excitable Spanish. I then made the almost fatal mistake of agreeing that Wessin could visit his troops at San Isidro to say farewell, and being completely inexperienced in the art of making a "snatch," I let him get away from us in the confusion and darkness. While the Dominican chiefs made their separate ways homeward, Alvim and I took off at high speed for San Isidro, hoping to catch up with Wessin en route; we did not, and so we went directly to the command post of the 82d Airborne Division located inside the cold brownstone walls of the Dominican Military Academy at San Isidro. On the way I briefly explained the situation to Deane by voice radio and told him to meet us at his headquarters.

In Deane's small office I described our problem in stark terms, concluding with the thought that if we failed in this mission, the IAPF's commitment to Godoy and his caretaking government would look suspect and we would probably be accused of collusion. I asked Deane to go to Wessin's headquarters, where we believed him to be—on the assumption that he was acting in good faith and had indeed gone there only to say goodbye to his men—and to bring him back to our location.

As Deane departed, we could hear the plaintive calypso beat of "Yellow Bird" from a radio several rooms away. Although the song is a favorite of mine, I thought sourly that this particular bird definitely did not want to fly away with us!

About an hour later, however, Deane arrived with Wessin and his deputy, Colonel Vicente Perdomo. Deane had entered Wessin's HQ *cuartel* accompanied only by his G-3, Lt. Col. Gene Forrester, and a Spanish-speaking U.S. Army lieutenant who was Cuban and a Bay of Pigs survivor. Through a mixture of luck and audacity they were able to persuade the reluctant Wessin to leave with them, despite the large group of Dominican soldiers who gathered around their jeep at the last moment.

Wessin looked haggard and disheveled, as well he might under the circumstances, while Perdomo seemed to be calm and cool. Both men were in simple khaki uniform, tieless in short-sleeved shirts, and wearing pistol belts with U.S. 45-caliber service pistols in the holsters. Wessin asked to keep his side-arm, and I readily assented. Then followed an emotional scene in which Wessin turned over his command to Perdomo, the ceremony consisting of Wessin's placing around Perdomo's neck, a leather necklace holding about half a dozen large keys, accompanied by a flood of tears and vigorous *embrazos*. Alvim got into the spirit of the occasion with a few tears of his own, and soon we were all embracing one another with great gusto. The ritual illustrated the Latin American military custom whereby the commanding officer is literally the keeper of the keys, receiving the pay and almost everything else provided for his troops by their government, keeping the money and supplies in his own custody, and distributing them to his men when and as he sees fit.

At last Wessin left quietly, and by 8:30 P.M. he was airborne in a U.S. Air Force C-130, heading for Howard Air Force Base in the Canal Zone, where he was met around midnight by Maj. Gen. James Alger, commanding U.S. Army forces in the area. According to Capt. Carl Hess, who at the time was assigned to HQ XVIII Airborne Corps, the USAF C-130 had stood for eight hours at the end of the runway at San Isidro air base, waiting for us to "produce" General Wessin. Hess tried to get Wessin to give up his pistol before he boarded, but he refused. En route to Panama Wessin traveled in the crew compartment, directly behind the pilot and flight crew, accompanied by Hess, who feared that Wessin might try to harm the pilot or his crew, but nothing happened. Wessin was quiet, although obviously his spirits were low, during the flight and behaved well upon debarking and meeting Gen. Alger; he perked up considerably when he found that Alger was fluent in Spanish.

Alger had had almost no warning but responded with characteristic aplomb and style. He put Wessin up in his VIP guest billets and took care of his personal needs the next day, including a trip to the local post exchange, where Wessin was provided with appropriate civilian garb before continuing his flight to Miami, courtesy of the U.S. Air Force.

Wessin's unceremonious removal was a severe and humiliating blow to Dominican rightists, especially the extremists, but on balance I felt that it was for the best. He had been the real locus of power in the country for more than four years, and his insubordination in defying President Godoy and Minister of the Armed Forces Rivera could not be tolerated. Still, the incident had caused considerable strain between Alvim as IAPF commander and the OAS Ad Hoc Committee, not to mention between Alvim and me, because Alvim took a dim view of forcibly removing such a strong anti-Communist as Wessin.

Meanwhile, there had been some favorable developments. The Dominican Navy had taken over the tasks of the U.S. naval task force temporarily operating off Santo Domingo, as well as the surveillance task along the northern coast. In the absence of any evidence of a threat from Cuba, CINCLANT also discontinued air surveillance of the area, though it would remain on call in case of necessity.[5]

On the assumption that progress toward a normal state of affairs would continue, albeit slowly, we did some force-structure planning for the IAPF over the long haul. By late July seven paratrooper battalions of the 82d remained in the country, and we visualized eventual reduction of U.S. forces to a reinforced brigade of three parachute infantry battalions and an airborne artillery battalion, with appropriate aviation, reconnaissance, engineer, signal, military police, and support elements. There would also be a special forces task force, civil affairs and psychological operations (PSYOPS) detachments, and a logistical support command. This brigade-size force would total about 6,700 men, all army (the support command accounting for about 1,600 of the total), plus an air force contingent of about 300. All told, counting the U.S. forces, the Latin American Brigade, and IAPF headquarters, the longer-term IAPF would total about 8,900 men.[6]

For psychological reasons Alvim had pushed hard for a U.S. tank company—which was not in the original troop list—arguing that its shock effect would, without its firing a shot, be valuable should we have to clear Santo Domingo. I agreed with him, but the State Department was understandably reluctant about the idea and did not approve the deployment until late September. The tanks arrived in the country in late October and subsequent events supported the wisdom of the decision. After their arrival Alvim, who had opposed any further reduction of the U.S. force, agreed to the withdrawal of another airborne infantry battalion, which brought the number then remaining in the country down to six battalions.[7]

Meanwhile, Godoy had been selecting members of his cabinet, including numerous loyalists but also several left-leaning constitutionalists, despite objections from the U.S. embassy that some were Marxists highly susceptible to outside influence or control. But Bunker believed that Godoy was an authentic Dominican nationalist who wanted to give such extreme elements a constructive role in the provisional government, hoping that this might keep them from going further left and might prevent the recurrence of hostilities.[8] It was a risky approach nevertheless and in fact precipitated a struggle for primacy within the provisional government between the regular Dominican military chiefs led by Rivera and the former rebel chieftains, military and civilian, led by Caamano and Aristy.

Alvim and I firmly supported the regular chiefs, feeling that they were the key to keeping the peace and maintaining Godoy in power—at least until some degree of normalcy had been restored in the downtown area, which the former rebels continued to treat as their own autonomous turf. Privately, I warned both Bunker and Bennett that although the IAPF had carried out Godoy's request to remove Wessin, neither Alvim nor any of the Latin American commanders would support any such precipitous moves against the other regular chiefs without specific instructions from their respective governments. Alvim and each national contingent commander maintained close contact via short-wave voice radio, usually in the clear, with high-level persons in their countries. President Stroessner of Paraguay, for example, held his commander on a short leash and spoke with him daily without fail. Moving too fast without the consent of our Latin American counterparts, I further warned, might well result in a split within the IAPF and the withdrawal of most, if not all, of the non-U.S. IAPF forces. Bennett supported my views, but Bunker, of course, had to deal with Godoy, who couldn't wait to replace the current chiefs.[9]

On 25 September, the second anniversary of the 1963 coup that deposed him from the presidency, Juan Bosch returned to the Dominican Republic. The chiefs had strongly opposed his return at such an early date, but Godoy had his way. National police escorted Bosch from the international airport, which had become operational in early June, to downtown Santo Domingo, where he gave an inflammatory, anti-U.S., anti-IAPF speech to a large cheering crowd. We then made certain that he went directly, and safely, to his home near the coast west of the capital, although he had his own bodyguard of ex-rebel Dominican Navy frogmen.[10]

Bosch was not a physically courageous man and rarely ever ventured from his home thereafter. In fact, even after the official electioneering began on 1 June of the following year, Bosch campaigned from his house, relying on personal radio broadcasts and the countrywide efforts of his supporters. In the interim, however, he remained very active behind the scenes and did all he could to stir up violence, to undermine Godoy's government, and in particular to weaken the regular Dominican security forces.

At this point, it was discouragingly apparent that Godoy was not making progress but steadily losing ground. His relations with the chiefs continued to deteriorate, especially after he transferred the national police from the control of the minister

of the armed forces to that of Minister of the Interior Ramon
A. Castillo, one of his leftist cabinet members. Ciudad Nueva
was still held by the former rebels. Godoy's efforts to collect
arms from various factions downtown had failed dismally, and
it was perfectly clear that neither the extremist factions nor
the relatively moderate groups in the former rebel zone had
any intention of turning in their arms. Because Despradel, the
national police chief, felt that restoring law and order in Ciudad
Nueva was beyond his capabilities, a climate of violence existed downtown, with extremists from both the right and the
left committing criminal acts. Godoy had allowed the University of Santo Domingo to be taken over by an illegal, leftist,
self-appointed council, and his official Radio Santo Domingo
was being run by Director Franklyn Dominguez, who slanted
all news reports and broadcast intemperate attacks on the IAPF.
Countrywide, as well as in the capital, there were rumors of
coup plotting and reports of violent acts implicating both Bosch
and well-known leftist leaders as well as right-wing leaders and
the regular military. Finally, no real progress had been made
in the disposition of those in the military who had joined the
rebellion.[11]

It was no wonder, then, that General Alvim, intensely concerned about the stalemated situation, submitted a written report to the Ad Hoc Committee pointing out the failure of
Godoy's provisional government to carry out the terms of the
Act of Reconciliation. He offered no solutions but asked for
guidance and requested that his report be submitted to the OAS
foreign ministers in Washington. The committee did not
choose to forward Alvim's report.[12] Alvim had originally intended to bypass the committee and appeal directly to the OAS
in Washington. He had discussed the matter with me, and I
had tried unsuccessfully to talk him out of making any such
report. His action hurt him in the eyes of the committee and
personally offended Bunker. To make these relations worse,
Alvim sent numerous messages to the president of Brazil, Castello Branco, that were highly uncomplimentary to Bunker;
indeed, in one he referred to the ambassador as a "sly, gray,
communist fox." What Alvim did not know was that we were

reading his mail and that Bunker was a personal friend of the Brazilian president.

To get things off dead center, I met with Bunker and Bennett on 6 October and proposed a new plan designed to demilitarize downtown Santo Domingo one way or another. The first step would be to organize a special element of the national police, equipped with helmets, armor vests, and heavier weapons on loan from U.S. forces, which would move gradually into Ciudad Nueva and take over police jurisdiction. To facilitate the plan, about half of this force was to come from the regular police and the other half from ex-rebels who either were former policemen or had been members of the irregular police organized earlier by Caamano. Back pay and a bonus were added incentives to serve in the force. (This worked pretty well, and later we used a similar formula to reintegrate the military rebels.) Concurrently with this police action, former military rebel forces with their arms would be moved under IAPF escort from Ciudad Nueva to a designated military camp outside the city, where they would be processed for reintegration or other disposition and arms turn-in. At about the same time the Dominican Navy, moving by sea, would secure the Santo Domingo port area with a small force of bluejackets; the part of the area already in U.S. hands would be turned over to the naval port authorities. A presidential decree would then declare the rebel zone demilitarized and outlaw the possession of weapons by unauthorized individuals. Thereafter, the IAPF would remove all vestiges of the old perimeter, and a gradual withdrawal of IAPF troops from the city would take place.[13]

Bunker liked the proposal, and that evening we presented it to Godoy, who likewise seemed to be in favor of it. Planning proceeded rapidly: on 9 October I met with Godoy, Bunker, Minister of the Interior Castillo, and Police Chief Despradel, and I held separate meetings with Rivera and Despradel; the latter were necessary because Godoy was not communicating well with Rivera, and Despradel was caught in the middle between the armed forces and Godoy's cabinet.

President Godoy held another planning meeting at the palace on 12 October to discuss the rebel move out of the city. Alvim was absent on leave in Puerto Rico, so I attended with Rivera and the regular military chiefs, Caamano, Castillo, Despradel, and Colonel Gutierrez, IAPF chief of staff.[14] It was my first and only meeting with Caamano. A moon-faced, pudgy man of medium build, he wore a khaki uniform with a short-sleeved shirt and a holstered U.S. 45-caliber pistol. I wore my customary combat-fatigue uniform with "bloused" parachute jump boots. Caamano was proper and courteous, but I could not get him to look me squarely in the eye. I got the worrisome impression that Godoy seemed to know Caamano well and treated him with considerable deference.[15]

Although the meeting was a little sticky, we did agree on a plan of action. Accordingly, on 13 and 14 October, U.S. troops escorted Caamano's former military rebels from Ciudad Nueva to the 27 February Camp outside the city on the east bank of the Ozama River, near its mouth. The U.S. 703d MP Battalion, which had been occupying the camp, moved to a tent camp not far away on the east bank at Sans Souci, site of the Dominican Naval Training Center. Ironically, having been put in tiptop condition with U.S. resources, the 27 February Camp was the best in the Dominican Army.

The operation went smoothly and was accomplished in three shuttles, each personally led by Colonel Caamano and using the rebels' own dilapidated transportation: a motley collection of buses, civilian cars, land rovers, jeeps, and the like. An estimated 1,200 men made the move with about 2,000 weapons, mostly rifles, automatic rifles, and light machine guns, plus a few heavy machine guns, rocket launchers, and mortars. Caamano ran the camp internally, but to forestall any hostilities we maintained a twenty-four-hour surveillance of the area and set up an arms control system worked out with Caamano. Armed body guards were allowed only for Caamano and two principal lieutenants, Manuel Ramon Montes Arache (before the rebellion, a captain in the Dominican Navy and head of the frogmen) and Col. Juan Lora Fernandez, Caamano's chief of staff. Officer leaders authenticated by Caamano could carry sidearms. All others could leave the camp only if unarmed.[16]

Planning for reintegration into the military of the former

rebels began immediately under a presidential joint commission charged with finalizing the arrangements. It took many weeks to settle on a system, because Caamano wanted to organize separate units made up of former rebels and bring them all back at the same time, whereas the regular military insisted on taking back only a few men at a time and assigning them to different units. There were other problems, such as identifying bona fide former military personnel and their true rank, but eventually an orderly, fair, and prudent process was agreed upon. The passing of time also helped, because many would-be reintegratees changed their minds and returned to civilian life.

On 15 October, according to plan, we completely eliminated the old IAPF perimeter and all checkpoints around the old rebel zone, and for the first time since the rebellion the city was open to free access from any direction. We also began withdrawing two of the three U.S. paratrooper battalions that had been controlling the old corridor, leaving only the eastern battalion near the Duarte Bridge and the power plant. This thinning-out was to take place over a period of about ten days.

About noon on 15 October, Alvim and I made a quick tour by jeep through part of the old rebel zone. Although the city was quiet, we were met by surprised stares and some hostility, and we observed several groups of armed civilians, obviously former rebels. There were only a few people in evidence, however, and traffic was light. The national police were conspicuous by their absence. Later, we learned that despite being more heavily armed than usual, the special police element that we had organized for the purpose of entering Ciudad Nueva had never really ventured beyond their line of departure along the eastern boundary of the old ISZ.

That afternoon we took Godoy on a helicopter inspection of the city and the 27 February Camp. Caamano's camp looked almost deserted, since most of the men had been given a forty-eight-hour pass to visit their families. Traffic was heavier downtown but normal for a Saturday afternoon. The city looked deceptively quiet; we were to learn that this was only a surface calm and that leftist extremists still ruled Ciudad

Nueva. One indication of this was the hostile reaction downtown when Alvim ordered in some IAPF patrols, mostly Brazilian. Hard-core extremist rebels had a particular dislike for the Brazilians. They didn't like Americans either, but we had made a point of keeping U.S. troopers away from the area. At Godoy's request we agreed not to send in any more IAPF patrols until things had settled down.[17]

By 17 October it was apparent that Godoy's control of his provisional government was rapidly weakening as the power struggle heightened. Balaguer became so alarmed that he temporarily withdrew his support of Godoy. And this time there was no stopping Alvim, who that day wrote and telephoned the OAS Council in Washington, bypassing the Ad Hoc Committee on the grounds that its members were not present at the time in the Dominican Republic (Bunker and the others were attending a meeting of the OAS foreign ministers in Washington). Alvim stated that he would not preside over a Communist takeover of the country and threatened to ask his government to withdraw the Brazilian contingent.[18]

Accepting the need to take action, Godoy allowed Rivera to move by water into the port area on 18 October, the Dominican Navy securing the area including the harbor entrance and blocking any reinforcements trying to cross the river from the 27 February Camp. Unfortunately, a fire fight broke out on the docks between rival—rightist and leftist—unions of longshoremen, and several workers, including the rightist union leader, were killed before the dock area was completely secured. A Canadian freighter, which had just docked, hastily departed. It was not an encouraging opening of the port.

That evening Godoy also allowed Rivera and a battalion of the Dominican Army to reoccupy Fortaleza Ozama (the oldest fortification in the Americas, begun in 1503), whose position dominated the port area. This triggered an immediate and violent reaction from the hard-core Communist groups, who on 19 October began to issue arms to civilians again and brought the Fortaleza under fire. We estimated the hostile strength downtown at this time at about 1,200 armed irregulars, including as many as half of the military rebels who had moved to the 27 February Camp but had since returned overland to the city.[19]

Rivera, as well as Alvim and I at separate meetings, urged Godoy to allow the regular Dominican forces to clear Ciudad Nueva at once, but Godoy vacillated and instead directed that Dominican troops remain in their barracks and asked Caamano to confine his forces to the 27 February Camp. And so on 21 October we found ourselves once again escorting Caamano, several of his main leaders, and a few hundred men from Ciudad Nueva back to the 27 February Camp. We recognized some of the men as original members of the groups escorted on 13-14 October, others were new. It was discouraging, to say the least. Nevertheless, we continued to thin down the U.S. forces in the city and redeployed another battalion back to Fort Bragg, leaving five airborne infantry battalions in the Dominican Republic.[20]

Over the next few days the situation worsened. Though they were unable to recapture it, Communist party–led forces in the city kept Fortaleza Ozama under fire. "Law and order" was ineffective in the old corridor and did not exist downtown. Leftists in Godoy's cabinet openly threatened strikes against government offices if the Dominican troops holding the Fortaleza were not withdrawn; they even planned a general strike if Godoy did not dismiss Rivera and the military chiefs. Rumors of coups abounded. Leftist groups in the Cibao and along the northern coast were engineering illegal land grabs by armed *campesinos*. The propaganda war broke out anew, with the Communist *La Patria* issuing a violent call to arms and Godoy's own Radio Santo Domingo, dominated by leftists, broadcasting barbs aimed at the Dominican military, the United States, and the OAS/IAPF. Beginning on 22 October, a clandestine station calling itself "Radio San Isidro" violently attacked Godoy and claimed that the end of his government was near. We were aware that the military-operated Radio San Isidro had been openly broadcasting inflammatory anti-Communist programs, and so we had asked Rivera to close this station down, which he did on 23 October. We also knew that a rightist, civilian-run station broadcasting clandestinely on

Radio San Isidro's traditional frequency was capable of such broadcasts. A few days later, however, we obtained indisputable evidence that a radio station operating under the personal direction of Hector Aristy, who had been Caamano's "prime minister" during his proclaimed constitutionalist presidency, was responsible for the virulent broadcasts against Godoy. But the damage was done—Godoy was unnerved, and it seemed clear that he could not bring himself to commit his own government forces again to clear the city.[21]

On 23 October there were disturbing reports of rightist plans to set up an autonomous government in Santiago, the country's second largest city and an important provincial capital in the north, and to denounce the provisional government on 25 October. Clearly, the time for action was at hand. Meeting with Ambassadors Bunker (who had just returned from Washington) and Bennett, I proposed a plan to clear the city and avoid a nationwide outbreak of violence. Specifically, IAPF forces—consisting of a U.S. brigade of three paratrooper battalions and a medium tank company, and the Latin American Brigade of two battalions—would move rapidly at first light with overwhelming force from positions in the old corridor and the old ISZ and seize Ciudad Nueva. Every effort would be made to move into position secretly and gain surprise. National police would follow behind IAPF forces. Dominican troops would be used to support the police only as a last resort, but this would probably not be necessary. Restraint would be the order of the day. Firing by IAPF troops would be limited to self-defense and even then restricted to small arms. In order to deter local coup attempts in outlying centers such as Santiago, other ready elements of the IAPF would be prepared to deploy outside the capital. The two ambassadors agreed with the proposal, and Bunker departed to see President Godoy and seek his approval while I tried to bring General Alvim aboard.

After a long discussion with me and his chief of staff, Alvim conceded that Godoy had gone about as far he dared in using Dominican forces to solve a Dominican problem, and he agreed with the concept of employing IAPF forces. We then put our various staffs to work preparing detailed operation orders while Alvim sought the support of the other Latin American national commanders, which did not take long. Late on 23 October we received Washington's approval of the plan, provided that President Godoy was in full agreement and with the admonishment that further Washington approval would be necessary for an IAPF operation that did not have Godoy's blessing. Godoy came through on 24 October and even obtained the agreement of Caamano in the hope that he would persuade the hard-core rebels remaining in the city to allow a bloodless IAPF entry.[22]

We set 4:30 A.M., twenty minutes before first light, on 25 October as the time for the IAPF to begin moving. The night of 24-25 October was hectic, with most of Godoy's cabinet trying to get the president to dismiss Rivera, threatening to call a general strike and to resign en masse if Godoy did not accede to their demands. Godoy wisely kept the timing and nature of the planned IAPF operations a secret from his cabinet, and even Caamano did not know exactly when it would start. All night long, with the OAS committeemen present and literally holding his hand, Godoy suffered an increasingly severe case of cold feet and several times threatened to resign, particularly if the plan turned sour. Both Godoy and Bunker were apprehensive about including the U.S. medium tanks in the operations, although we reassured them that no firing of any tank armament would be permitted. We held our ground on the matter, knowing what an invaluable psychological asset the tanks would be in a showdown in the city. At the very last minute Godoy tried to postpone the whole operation, but we informed him that it was too late—the troops were already committed, and it could be disastrous to call them off under the circumstances.

Luck was with us, and our careful planning—especially with respect to the coordination measures worked out between U.S. and Latin American formations—paid off. The operation went smoothly, and by 5:45 A.M. the entire downtown area had been secured with only very minor and scattered resistance. No fire was returned by IAPF troops, and there were no casualties in any quarter. Complete surprise had been achieved, and the shock caused by the sudden appearance of the tanks had a distinctly quieting effect.

Alvim and I called on the president in the palace to brief him, Rivera, and the Ad Hoc Committee on the initial outcome. Extremely hoarse and nervous, Godoy finally calmed down when we described how peaceful and bloodless the occupation of the city had been. Rivera was outgoing and cooperative, and the occasion served to improve communications between the president and his defense minister. We then drove Godoy and Bunker through Ciudad Nueva so that they could see the situation for themselves. The people seemed surprised and relieved, more curious than partisan, and many went out of their way to express their friendship and gratitude. Godoy was delighted and his morale visibly rose, although we all knew, without saying it aloud, that we still had a long, hard way to go.[23]

So ended the pretense of an autonomous constitutionalist government zone in Santo Domingo, which had persisted since the outbreak of the revolution in April. But it would take even more time before life in Santo Domingo would have some semblance of normalcy. By this time, however, I wasn't sure what "normal" meant in the Dominican Republic.

CHAPTER 7

The IAPF Completes Its Mission: 26 October 1965– 21 September 1966

With the Inter-American Peace Force in control of the old rebel zone, life in Santo Domingo began to improve steadily, though only gradually. On 26 October we withdrew all IAPF tanks from the city and by the end of the month had thinned out our troops in Ciudad Nueva and the old corridor. Police performance in the city was still disappointing, however, and tension still high, while outrages continued to occur in the countryside. In one instance the left-leaning governor of Van Verde Province was foully murdered near Santiago in late October, allegedly by regular Dominican military personnel. We assisted the provisional government and the Inter-American Commission on Human Rights in the investigation by escorting eyewitnesses, some of whom had also been attacked and had to be hospitalized, to Santo Domingo.

The human rights commission had been performing in a remarkable way since its arrival in the republic on 1 June. In contrast to the similar UN commission, the inter-American commission showed great courage in impartially investigating crimes reportedly committed by rightists *or* leftists. With its constant scrutiny and widely known public presence, the commission kept the pressure on both sides and in a few short months dramatically brought down the number of reported violations and reduced the number of political prisoners from an estimated 4,000 in early June to about 700 in August.[1]

One of the remunerative results of clearing Ciudad Nueva was the closing of the headquarters of three Communist parties that had been conducting illegal activities in the country. Many incriminating documents were found in two of these offices—those of the Castro-oriented IJ4 (Movimiento 14 Junio) and the more Chinese-oriented MPD (Movimiento Popular Dominicano); the offices of the smaller PCD (Partido Comunista Dominicano) were found abandoned and empty. These leftist parties had placed huge anti-U.S. and anti-IAPF signs at key locations in Ciudad Nueva such as Independence Plaza; their favorite one read "Fuera Yanquis de Quisqueya," meaning "Yankees begone from Quisqueya" (the old Dominican name for the country). Our forces also put the MPD newspaper *La Patria* out of business, Godoy directing that it be permanently closed and the premises turned back to the rightful owners.

On 2 November, a red-letter day, all the major banks reopened in Santo Domingo for the first time since the rebellion. A short time later the old reliable and more moderate, conservative newspapers *El Caribe* and *Listin Diario* returned to print. On 11 November Godoy felt confident enough to lift the government curfew, but in mid-November leftist demonstrations, during one of which a U.S. flag was burned, were allowed in front of the palace without any interference—a poor performance by the police and Chief Despradel, as well as Interior Minister Castillo and the president himself. Santo Domingo was having its ups and downs.[2]

One important factor in bringing a measure of stability to the Dominican Republic was the relatively moderate line taken by the two major political parties, Balaguer's PR (Reformist party) and Bosch's PRD (Dominican Revolutionary party), in support of Godoy's provisional government. Balaguer was particularly constructive in this regard, putting pressure on Bosch to follow suit and refusing to go along with Bosch on a "United Front" general strike against the government. The bona fide Radio Santo Domingo, however, continued to be a major problem for Godoy; he could not achieve a general housecleaning until mid-December, when a more moderate and neutral director and staff were installed.[3]

In the more prosperous residential and international part of Santo Domingo, the national police were more in evidence than they were downtown, and a relatively tranquil climate prevailed. The U.S. embassy had ended its self-imposed blackout, and both Dominicans and foreigners—including American families—began to return to their homes in the city. Among the first to come back were Margaret Bennett, wife of the U.S. ambassador, and her redheaded teenage daughter Victoria. Morale in the embassy immediately picked up with their arrival, and it was not long before the grand ballroom of the residence came to life again with music and lively guests. Indeed, more than one romance blossomed among the larger American "family" as a result of the revolution.

One of the more pleasant diversions within the U.S. military was maintaining our proficiency as paratroopers. Using hueys, we regularly conducted static line jumps with individual weapons and full field gear onto drop zones in the vicinity of San Isidro air base. (Troopers consider jumps from a helicopter as "Hollywood" jumps—a cinch, compared to jumps from regular troop carrier aircraft such as the C-130 or C-141.) Our favorite DZ (drop zone) was a large, unharvested sugarcane field because it provided a soft landing—that is, until some of us landed on coral outcroppings that could not be seen from the air, being completely hidden by the luxuriant growth. These caused some injuries, and we soon devised ways of avoiding those particular spots. We also befriended some young *campesinos* in the fields, whose poverty-stricken tatters-and-rags appearance shocked us. They were eager to make friends and voluntarily helped us roll up our chutes, while the young American soldiers responded with kindness and generosity.

We also sent some members of the Inter-American Peace Force to Puerto Rico for a few days of R&R (rest and recreation)—San Juan is a congenial place for both North Americans and Latin Americans—though only the Brazilians, some Costa Ricans, and a few Nicaraguans could afford it. Another worthwhile achievement was the establishment of U.S. Armed

Forces Radio in Santo Domingo, which became operational in mid-August. Although it lacked the talent to broadcast in Spanish or Portuguese, the station featured contemporary American music and domestic news—for example, the major league baseball scores—that avoided political issues. The program became popular not only with U.S. personnel but with Latin American soldiers in the IAPF and especially with Dominican youths in the city. When the rebels tried to sell "Yankee Go Home" T-shirts to the Dominicans, our troops bought them all up; the T-shirts that became local best-sellers had "Yankee Go Home" on one side and "Take me with you" on the other.

My senior aide, Maj. William E. Klein and I found some other diversions. Klein, who came from a brigade S-3 job (plans, operations, and training) in the 82d Airborne, was a livewire who kept everyone's spirits up and was idolized by his paratroopers.[4] He discovered the national police stables on the old Haina road a short distance west of the Hotel Embajador and arranged to let me ride from there. Some fine horseflesh resided in these stables, including a beautiful gray Arabian stallion who stood almost sixteen hands high and could run like the wind. El Diablo had belonged to the eldest daughter of the hated dictator Trujillo, who owned many valuable horses before they were seized by the government that succeeded him. Alone and unarmed, I rode in my uniform and jump boots, my normal route taking me back toward the Embajador, moving up to the old polo grounds via a dirt road going through a narrow defile. Once on more open ground, I could let out El Diablo, riding him on a loose rein with a plain snaffle bit and without a martingale. One day on the way back to the stable, as I was taking him at a walk through the defile, a rifle shot rang out from close by; El Diablo shied violently, and we departed for the stable at a fast clip, not bothering to investigate. The rifleman could have killed either or both of us, and I took it as a warning. That was my last ride in the Dominican Republic and the last time I saw El Diablo.

Another short-lived diversion was playing golf at Santo Domingo's only (at that time) country club. It was a sporty course, located up on the coral coastal escarpment west of the city. The rough was impossible: a golf ball hit into the coral rocks below the fairways simply could not be found. One day Klein and I were walking along a fairway some distance from the clubhouse, where we had left our radio jeep and Sgt. Donald Lamm, our faithful driver. The fairway, bounded by a low chickenwire fence, paralleled a dirt road only a few feet away. Suddenly, a rickety old flatbed truck came barreling down the road toward us, the back crowded with standing Dominican civilians yelling, "Jeneral Palmaire go home!" Klein had his 45-caliber pistol in his golf bag, but otherwise we were pretty vulnerable, and it was a long way to the clubhouse. If they had wanted to start something, the men in the truck had us at a disadvantage. But they continued on their way, while we beat a retreat back to our jeep and went home without finishing the game. Thus ended my brief golf career in the Dominican Republic, although Klein and Col. Robert Abraham—an outstanding staff troubleshooter and our liaison officer with the air force[5]—and a few other U.S. military men continued to enjoy some Sunday golf interludes.

By now we had learned that U.S. troops generally got along better with Dominican citizens than did the Latin Americans, especially in downtown Santo Domingo. Our men had their share of unpleasant and dangerous incidents, but at times the Latins would overreact and make more trouble than was necessary in situations that our soldiers handled with more finesse. The Brazilians particularly tended to be overbearing toward Dominicans and even at times toward their fellow soldiers from other Latin American countries.

A disparity in pay among the various LA soldiers, especially between the Brazilians and the others, who were paid far less, was also a source of irritation. But by and large, they could all relax off duty and enjoy each other's company. The Paraguayans, unsophisticated young men from the countryside of a landlocked nation, were enchanted with the sea when they first arrived and stayed up all night just watching the waters of the Caribbean; they never tired of this simple diversion. Like all the others, they also loved music and liked to dance, although there was a difference in the kind of music they preferred. Paraguayans could listen for hours to bittersweet love songs accompanied by the famous Paraguayan harp, while the Brazilians with their omnipresent steel drum bands could create a kind of instant Rio carnival atmosphere, complete with the rumba, the merengue (a Dominican dance), and the cha-cha-chas. But none were more fun-loving than the friendly *soldados* from Central America, who liked to go around together, regional bonds seemingly to be compatible with love of individual native lands. We found Latin American amateur troop shows remarkable and their huge pit barbecues irresistible.

During the summer and fall of 1965 I got to know some of the Brazilian military men pretty well—especially Alvim and Meira Mottos. They talked at length about what they felt to be their country's "manifest destiny": becoming a world power, dominant in the southern part of the hemisphere. Geopolitically minded and well aware of Brazil's immense land area, large population, and strategic location, they were sure the inherent Brazilian potential would sooner or later be felt in the world. Their contribution to the Vietnam War, in their words, was their presence in the Dominican Republic, and they were proud of this effort. They were likewise proud of Brazil's military contribution to the Western allies in World War II. Within the Western Hemisphere, Alvim often remarked, the United States should "take care" of the northern half and let Brazil worry about the southern part.[6]

As relatively stable conditions allowed the redeployment of more forces back to the United States, by early December the headquarters of the 82d Airborne Division had returned to Fort Bragg, and the U.S. force level was down to the approved structure: one reinforced brigade of three airborne infantry battalions. For the remainder of its mission, then, the IAPF consisted basically of a Latin American brigade of about 1,800 and a U.S. brigade of about 5,400 men. (These figures are based on authorized, not actual, strength, and the U.S. figure includes logistic elements that supported the entire force. Losses and normal attrition, along with a shortage of infantry replacements, had resulted in U.S. battalions' averaging only 50 percent of authorized strength during the summer, a trend that was not reversed until late fall.)

In Ciudad Nueva IAPF troops had been thinned down to a minimum, with one reinforced U.S. paratrooper company in the Duarte Bridge–power plant area and two Latin American infantry companies in the vicinity of Independencia Plaza. All other IAPF troops were normally located in their semipermanent base camps outside the city. We also kept a bobtailed battalion of U.S. troopers in what was called the Mountain Training Area, located off the Santiago highway about twenty miles northwest of Santo Domingo. This had been a field training center for the Dominican Army; we used it to conduct U.S. sponsored basic and small-unit training for selected Dominican personnel and units. Our logistic command and complex were located near the fair grounds west of the capital except for our 15th Field Hospital, which moved from Sans Souci east of the city to its final site at a former Dominican nurses' training center west of Santo Domingo about halfway to Haina. This not only placed the hospital nearer the IAPF camps but also gave it a better position from which to carry out the substantial health care program that our medical people devised for needy Dominicans.[7]

Before 1965 came to an end, however, some unsettling events occurred that required intervention by IAPF forces. By 21 November rightist agitation in Santiago (about 125 road miles from Santo Domingo) and in Barahona (a coastal city about 175 miles by road west of the capital), coupled with rumors of coup planning against the provisional government, had reached the point where Godoy asked the OAS Ad Hoc Committee for support. As a result, company-size IAPF patrols were sent by vehicle to each city as a show of force to scare off the plotters. Imbert and other well-known rightists were apparently involved, and Wessin from his exile in Miami helped stir the pot. But the public announcement of Rivera and the Dominican military chiefs in support of Godoy, plus the presence of IAPF troops, quashed the effort. Nothing really happened in Barahona, and only a feeble, short-lived attempt to set up a new government occurred in Santiago. And so our IAPF troops returned to their bases on 22 November. On the same day Alvim and I carried out a previously scheduled air reconnaissance of the western part of the Dominican Republic, generally along the Haitian Border. On the way back we landed at Santiago in the early afternoon and conferred briefly with the local police chief and air base commander, as well as the U.S. consul, who confirmed that the city was quiet and the situation well in hand.[8]

The November threat had some good consequences that greatly strengthened Godoy's position. One was the marked improvement of relations between the president and Rivera, as well as his military chiefs. Other encouraging events were Godoy's replacement of his left-wing attorney general with a moderate of good reputation, and a reorganization of the palace staff that placed important and sensitive functions in more prudent hands.

Unfortunately, a far more serious incident in Santiago in mid-December was to undo much of the progress made and undermine relations between Godoy and his military leaders. A preview occurred in Santo Domingo on 16 and 17 December, when the spirit of Christmas, which had prevailed since the first of the month, was damaged by riots in the city. The instigators were apparently left-wing extremists who had tried to revive the revolution; it took extra police and some Dominican troops to restore order downtown.

On Sunday, 19 December, in what appeared to be a deliberately planned provocation, Caamano led an automobile caravan, carrying about 150 former military rebels armed with rifles and machine guns, from Santo Domingo to Santiago, arriving there about 8:00 A.M. Rivera had alerted Godoy to the trouble that the trek might cause, but nothing was done to stop it. Caamano's destination was the city cemetery, where he held a memorial service for fallen comrades. Details are not known, but apparently the local police and military authorities converged on the cemetery, where inevitably a fire fight broke out. This was about 9:00 A.M. Caamano retreated to the Matum, the main hotel in town, where the fight continued after the building had been surrounded by some 300 Dominican troops and police. Trapped in the hotel were about fifteen U.S. citizens and later the U.S. consul in Santiago, Leslie A. Scott, who had gone there in an attempt to get the others released. We learned thereafter that the Americans were being held hostage by Caamano.

It was a tense and delicate moment because blood had been shed on both sides, and it seemed to have been the intention of the local Dominican forces to exterminate Caamano and his rebel band. Caamano got word of his predicament to President Godoy; Consul Scott likewise informed the U.S. embassy in Santo Domingo. By then it was 11:00 A.M. It took Godoy some time to locate Bunker and the OAS committee, and to ask that the IAPF intercede; word of Caamano's plight and Godoy's request did not reach my headquarters until after twelve noon, although a little earlier I had received some fragmentary bits of information through the embassy.

Another half-hour went by before I could consult with Alvim, who would have preferred to let Caamano sweat it out but conceded that the IAPF would be blamed if we did not go to his rescue. Alvim also agreed that we should use U.S. troops. I had already alerted the U.S. airborne brigade, and we had decided to assign the mission to Lt. Col. John J. Costa, commanding the 2d Battalion, 508th Airborne Infantry, based near San Isidro airfield.

Accordingly, we airlifted a reinforced U.S. airborne rifle company to the airfield at Santiago, closing there at about 2:30 P.M. and arriving at the Matum Hotel just before three o'clock.

Costa, meanwhile, had flown ahead to make a personal reconnaissance of the situation while his executive officer brought up the troops. Arriving at the hotel in the early afternoon, he found that the Dominican Red Cross was already attempting to arrange a cease-fire in order to evacuate the dead and wounded, and that the Dominican government forces were willing to respect a cease-fire but intended to take Caamano, dead or alive. Costa then went inside the hotel and after a long palaver came out, bringing Consul Scott with him, just after the U.S. paratrooper company arrived on the scene. At that moment, about 3:00 P.M., a fire fight broke out again, and Costa deployed his men between the two belligerent groups. This quieted things down, neither side being willing to take on the paratroopers. After some intense negotiating, Costa managed to gain the release of the other U.S. citizens in the hotel and to achieve an unconditional cease-fire. He also persuaded the Dominican officials to withdraw their forces from the area, while he arranged to take Caamano and his men out of the hotel the next morning for air evacuation to Santo Domingo.[9] It was an impressive demonstration of personal courage and professional skill on the part of Costa and his paratroopers.

On 20 December Caamano's band was flown to San Isidro air base and escorted back to the 27 February Camp; at the president's request Caamano himself was escorted to Godoy's home. It had been a costly fight for the Dominicans: Caamano's group suffered four killed (including Lora, chief of staff of the former rebels) and six wounded; the police and military casualties were eleven dead and eleven wounded. There were no U.S. casualties, either civilian or military.

For years after the affair, various writers and commentators alleged that the IAPF or the U.S. embassy, or both, dragged their feet in reacting to the Santiago fight. In my opinion there is no hard evidence to support this claim. It is true that many North Americans and Latin Americans in the IAPF, as well as Americans in the U.S. embassy, had no use for Caamano and would have liked to see him wiped out, but not one shirked his or her duty in carrying out the request of the OAS Ad Hoc Committee to intercede. As I have pointed out, the time and space factors involved were complicated and difficult. No one analyzing the actual sequence of events can make a persuasive case for deliberate stalling or delay in reacting.

Concurrently with the fight in Santiago, well-organized disorders—obviously coordinated with Caamano's actions—took place in Santo Domingo, the overall objective apparently being to create chaos all over the city, particularly in the center of town. Because it was Sunday, and recognizing how long it would take to get the Dominican military and police to react, we took the temporary measure of moving a U.S. paratrooper battalion into the city to restore order. General Alvim and the OAS committee were simultaneously informed of the action and made no objection. The troopers acted with speed and restraint; the crowds were dispersed without casualties; and the city calmed down without further incident.

Several adverse results grew out of the December Santiago affair. Bosch, who had heretofore walked a tight rope, decided to exploit it and threatened a general strike unless the Dominican military and national police were punished. Once again he called for the immediate removal of the Dominican military chiefs. Workers in the sugar industry, the mainstay of the slowly reviving economy, likewise threatened to strike if Rivera, the three service chiefs, and the police chief were not removed at once. Godoy too blamed the incident on the Dominican chiefs, alleging that they had overreacted; he apparently absolved Caamano of any blame. In fact, there was blame on both sides, but the initial provocation was Caamano's sortie into the upper Cibao Valley. Regrettably, the good relations that had been building between Godoy and his military chiefs were dissipated by suspicion and distrust on both sides.[10]

Christmas passed without untoward incidents in Santo Domingo. I received Christmas cards from several former rebels, one signed by Colonel Francisco Caamano as "Presidente Constitucional de la Republica" and another by Montes Arache as Caamano's "secretary for external affairs." The gist of the greetings was that while "you Yankees" are despoiling and plundering our country, we (the *constitucionalistas*) are peacefully celebrating a happy Christmas.

But after the New Year began, tensions rose quickly to new heights. Godoy insisted that the regular military chiefs must depart and announced that he and his cabinet were ready to resign if some action was not forthcoming. Bunker, who had held out for gradual military reform, then agreed to a joint effort with Godoy that would bring about the departure of the leading military figures from both sides: Caamano was to leave first, with the understanding that Rivera would soon follow.

Thereupon, Godoy jumped the gun: on 6 January 1966 he issued a decree removing Rivera and all the service chiefs and

Caamano and his lieutenants, all simultaneously, and posting them abroad. Fearing betrayal, Rivera and the military chiefs responded by defying Godoy and seizing Radio Santo Domingo and the telecommunications center in the city. At this juncture Godoy called on the IAPF via the OAS Ad Hoc Committee for support, but Alvim flatly refused. After some difficulty in getting Alvim to confer with us, Bunker and I together finally persuaded him to comply with Godoy's request. IAPF Chief of Staff Gutierrez and I then went to see Rivera, and after we assured him that we would not permit any precipitous actions endangering the security or integrity of the Dominican armed forces, Rivera agreed to relinquish control of the station, and that particular crisis was over.

Bunker and I had for some time been discussing the implications of General Alvim's increasing resistance to political guidance from the OAS Ad Hoc Committee. Alvim saw things as either black or white and could not appreciate that much of what we confronted in the Dominican Republic was in an ill-defined gray area. To compromise with the left was simply not in his makeup, despite the fact that the average Brazilian military officer seemed to have superb political instincts. Colonel Gutierrez and I spent many hours trying to persuade the stubborn commander that our guidance from the OAS committee was not only reasonable but also, more to the point, unique to the situation facing us. At any rate, Bunker had privately proposed to me that both Alvim and I be replaced with officers of lesser rank, using the rationale that this would be appropriate to the decreased size of the IAPF and would recognize the improved state of affairs in the country. We had agreed that this was a desirable move and that it should be carried out early in 1966.

Ambassador Bunker, attending an OAS conference in Rio in late November 1965, took the opportunity to raise the matter with President Branco of Brazil, who readily assented. In the meantime, I had informed General Johnson, the U.S. Army chief, who also agreed and so informed the JCS and the civilian side of the Pentagon. Johnson told me that he planned to have Bob Linvill, my chief of staff, replace me as U.S. commander in the Dominican Republic. Linvill was both the logical and the best man for the job, and I heartily concurred. Johnson also told me that I would probably pick up my original assignment as the commander at Fort Bragg.

When informed by his government of the change in commanders, Alvim too responded positively, and in fact I believe he was glad to leave the Dominican pressure cooker and return to his native land. On 15 January 1966 Ambassador Bennett awarded him the U.S. Legion of Merit at a colorful ceremony held at the polo grounds, and on 17 January Alvim turned over command of the IAPF to a fellow Brazilian, Maj. Gen. Alvaro Braga. At the same time I turned over command of the U.S. forces and deputy command of the IAPF to Linvill, an outstanding leader and paratrooper, who handled the final difficult stages of the Dominican mission with fortitude, skill, and determination. Braga, a diminutive, friendly, and quiet man, turned out to be another excellent Brazilian commander, and he and Linvill hit it off well from the outset. This marked the end of XVIII Airborne Corps's dual role in the Dominican Republic, and that morning the corps staff and I departed San Isidro air base.

Every effort was then made to persuade the Dominican military leaders of the crisis period, loyalist and constitutionalist, to leave the country voluntarily for an indefinite period of time as a patriotic act. Some lesser rebel leaders had already left on 11 January, but a breakthrough occurred when Caamano and his three principal lieutenants departed on 22 January. The key factor was Bosch and Caamano's agreement that the move would help Bosch in his coming campaign for the presidency. Godoy, meanwhile, had appointed Caamano military attaché in London; Montes Arache, in Ottawa; Hector La Chapelle Diaz, in Brussels; and Pena Taveras in Santiago, Chile. U.S. troops escorted them and their families, using helicopter transportation, to the Punta Caucedo International Airport not far from San Isidro.[11]

But it was some time before agreement could be reached on the departure of the loyalist chiefs, Rivera steadfastly refusing to leave until he was satisfied with the men selected as replacements. On 9 February a Communist-led student demonstration at the Presidential Palace brought on a violent clash with police, resulting in the death of several students. This triggered a general strike on 10 February—supported by labor, government workers, and Bosch's PRD—that threatened to cripple the country and cause disturbances countrywide. In Santo Domingo, atrocities against the national police and hostile demonstrations against both Dominican and IAPF military personnel led CINCLANT to order an amphibious force with marines aboard to move toward Santo Domingo in case reinforcements should be needed ashore. (CINCLANT had taken similar action when the IAPF occupied Ciudad Nueva in October 1965.) Finally, upon agreement from Godoy that the army and air force chiefs would not be replaced, Commodore Rivera Caminero agreed to accept the defense attaché post in Washington and to be replaced as minister of the armed forces by the army deputy chief of staff, General Eduardo Perez y Perez. But even though Rivera departed quietly late on 11 February, tension continued high in the city.

Godoy had requested the IAPF to take over responsibility for the security of the entire Ciudad Nueva sector of town, which the national police had been forced to abandon because of heavy fire from suspected former rebel and radical elements. This was accomplished without incident, for the most part by U.S. troops, during the night of 12-13 February. At Bosch's request, the strike was called off on 17 February after Godoy had appointed the army and air force chiefs, Martinez Arana and de Los Santos, as deputy ministers of the armed forces and had replaced them with Colonel Perdomo (who had commanded the newly formed 4th Brigade, formerly CEFA) and Colonel Folch-Perez, respectively. Commodore Jimenez, the navy chief, who had not become a target of the malcontents, was allowed to remain in his post. Although this was not the widespread reform that the OAS Ad Hoc Committee had envisaged and that Godoy had wanted, it was about all that could be accomplished under the circumstances, and it did serve to defuse an explosive situation before the presidential political campaign began.

Godoy appeared confident that with the lessening of the immediate political-military impasse the Dominican armed forces would be impartial during the elections and therefore that the electoral campaign could safely begin. On 2 March the provisional government issued a decree setting 1 June 1966 as the date for the elections. This allowed planning to go forward with respect to OAS, UN, and U.S. measures to bring about a climate conducive to free and fair elections.[12]

As the anniversary of the initial U.S. unilateral intervention (late April) approached, the U.S. government decided that it was the appropriate time to replace Tap Bennett as ambassador in Santo Domingo. And so on 11 April the American and Dominican political and military community in the capital turned out to bid farewell to Ambassador Bennett, who had tenaciously and skillfully guided U.S. efforts in the country since the beginning of the revolution. His post was filled by John H. Crimmins, another experienced U.S. diplomat.

Likewise, it seemed only prudent to withdraw all IAPF elements from the capital before the anniversary. To minimize adverse incidents, IAPF troops had already changed their tactics to an observation-post system, using rooftops and strong points, that made their presence much less visible and generally kept the soldiers off the streets. In the meantime, national policemen had gradually returned to Ciudad Nueva, and IAPF troops were withdrawn from the area on the night of 23-24 April. Nevertheless, extreme left-wing groups increased their hostile activities, culminating in a protest march against the U.S. embassy on the morning of 28 April. The crowd was frustrated by a cordon of U.S. paratroopers ringing the area, however, and after a noisy hour or so it dissipated peacefully. Thereafter, IAPF troops remained out of sight and as inconspicuous as possible in their camps.[13]

Both principal candidates for the presidency and their parties, Bosch and the PRD, and Balaguer and the PR, campaigned hard. Balaguer stumped throughout the countryside, however, whereas Bosch remained mostly at home, relying on the radio—which was no doubt a significant factor in the outcome. Charges and countercharges were hurled, and acts of violence did occur, but the long-awaited elections were held on schedule on 1 June with a record voter turnout and a minimum of untoward incidents.

Rarely has any election been so closely covered by so many official observers: the UN, OAS, United States, and many Latin American countries as well as the Dominican Republic itself were represented, not to mention unofficial American groups. The overwhelming consensus was that a truly honest election had been achieved. Even Dr. Mayobre from the UN, who had not been particularly helpful in the early days of the crisis, publicly expressed his praise for the electoral process.[14]

Election results were a surprise to many who had thought that Bosch, for whom the rebellion had presumably been fought, would emerge as the clear victor. In the final count, concerning which no evidence of fraud ever surfaced, Balaguer received almost 57 percent of the vote to Bosch's 39 percent, with splinter groups from the far right gathering about 3.5 percent, and from the extreme left about 1 percent.[15] Clearly, it was a decisive victory for Balaguer and Dominican moderates, and just as clearly it showed that Bosch's strength had been overestimated.

These results came as no surprise to Bunker, who in June 1965, during his discussions with numerous Dominican citizens throughout the country, had learned that public support for the constitutionalists was not as strong as commonly believed. Nor was it a surprise to me, because in the fall of 1965 Bunker had told me confidentially that he had asked the State Department (with CIA assistance) to conduct a quiet unofficial poll both in Santo Domingo and in various other sections of the country; the results showed Balaguer an overwhelming favorite. The principal reason appeared to be that Dominican women judged Bosch a coward who had been afraid to return to his country until months after the rebellion started. Thus it appeared that the Latin American macho male image was important and, in this instance, decisive to the outcome. I have no objective way to judge how pertinent this factor is today in Latin America, but I suspect that in many areas it is still a matter to be reckoned with.

Even before Balaguer's inauguration, renewed agitation for the withdrawal of the Inter-American Peace Force had begun, and in mid-June, confident of the legitimacy and fairness of the elections, Godoy, Balaguer, and the OAS Ad Hoc Committee had agreed on the timing. Accordingly, the OAS announced on 24 June that the withdrawal would begin before 1 July and that it would be completed within ninety days. Concurrently, the Ad Hoc Committee would cease to exist.[16]

Despite rumors of plans to harm or assassinate Balaguer, he was inaugurated on schedule on 1 July 1966 without incident. Vice-President Hubert Humphrey of the United States represented President Johnson at the well-attended ceremony. Balaguer lost no time in organizing a new government, in which he was clearly the leader, and boldly initiated an austerity program for the country. All government salaries were lowered, unnecessary government positions both at home and abroad were eliminated, and a general belt-tightening was put into effect. It was not a popular move, and many Dominicans—particularly members of Bosch's party—complained vehemently, but Balaguer got away with it.

The new president also made some immediate changes in the security forces. One was to depose Chief José de Jésus Morillo Lopez of the national police, whom Godoy had appointed in the aftermath of the December 1965 Santiago affair to succeed Despradel. Morillo, who was believed to be corrupt and unduly harsh, was replaced by a veteran policeman, Gen. Luis Neit Tejeda Alvarez. Balaguer also replaced the air force chief, having good reason to suspect that Folch-Perez was in sympathy with right-wing extremists who never stopped planning coups; his choice for the job was Col. Alvaro Alvarez. These were the last top personnel changes among the Dominican military leaders before the withdrawal of the IAPF. Significantly, the peacekeeping force was never committed again in support of the Dominican government, although Dominican security forces and the Dominican people remained well aware that it was present if needed.[17]

On 9 August Ambassador Bunker departed Santo Domingo amid resounding farewells that reflected the respect he commanded from all Dominicans who were familiar with the truly historic role he had played in their country. Most of the newspapers and other media treated him as a national hero. A few disparaged him as an "operator" who got his own way in resolving the crisis, but none could deny that he had accomplished an unparalleled feat of diplomacy in bringing about a peaceful and democratic resolution of the conflict. As the late Ambassador Martin F. Herz said, "Bunker brought off one of those rare events in the history of revolutions and civil wars, an end on the basis of compromise and an orderly and peaceful transition to democratic majority rule."[18] Bunker himself knew, more than anyone else involved, that his feat would not have been possible without the presence of the Inter-American Peace Force.

Withdrawal of the IAPF proceeded smoothly and on schedule. The single artillery battalion of the 82d Airborne had departed in June; the U.S. tank company and the Paraguayan contingent left in July. In August the Central American troops departed, followed in early September by the Brazilians and the bulk of the U.S. airborne brigade and its logistic support group. In mid-September the 2d Battalion, 508th Airborne, was withdrawn, the last major combat unit to leave the Dominican Republic. And on 21 September the last of the IAPF departed in the person of General Linvill and a small security group. With outstanding interservice coordination and cooperation, redeployment of troops was accomplished in essentially the same way they had been brought in: U.S. Air Force C-130s airlifted most of the U.S. troops and all the Latin American forces— except the Brazilians, who returned home in their own aircraft—and some of the heavier U.S. vehicles and equipment were redeployed by navy LSTs.[19]

And thus ended the IAPF presence in the Dominican Republic, a success story by any reasonable and objective standards in the limited context of the country itself (although admittedly a different story with respect to the damage done to U.S.-Latin American relations). Its stay had lasted for almost seventeen months, but it had accomplished its mission. It had stopped the Dominican civil war, provided a measure of security and tranquility to the country, brought the republic safely through honest, free, and fair presidential elections a little more than one year after the intervention, and assured the safe transition to a legally constituted government. Significantly, the new government assumed power under a constitution and electoral process that had not been imposed from without but had been drawn up by Dominicans.

Certainly the Dominican affair was not without its cost in human lives and suffering. On the military side, U.S. casualties were 44 dead (27 killed in action), 172 wounded in action, and 111 injured—the bulk of these suffered by the 82d Airborne Division. Some of the non-battle casualties were caused by terrorist-style actions. Latin American casualties within the IAPF were 6 Brazilians and 5 Paraguayans wounded in action.

Dominican casualties were more difficult to quantify, particularly given the difficulty of distinguishing "loyalist" from "constitutionalist"—that is, regular military from rebel military—or military from civilian when irregulars are involved. The best U.S. estimate of losses among the "regular" Dominican military and national police was about 500 killed or missing in action for the armed forces and 325 for the national police, for a total of 825 dead plus an undetermined number of wounded. Among the rebel military the best estimate was about 600 dead and again an undetermined number of wounded. The Dominican Red Cross estimates, which excluded regular (loyalist) military and police but covered civilians (not necessarily noncombatants) and apparently included rebel military, were approximately 2,000 dead and 3,000 wounded. Thus, a reasonable estimate of total Dominican casualties (both sides, civilian and military) attributable to the rebellion is about 6,000 people. The great bulk of these occurred in the early fighting in late April and early May 1965. No one can take any consolation from this toll of human lives and suffering; nevertheless, it can be safely said, that had the civil war continued, Dominican casualties without a doubt would have been far greater.[20]

President Johnson, incidentally, in his book *The Vantage Point* (1971), makes only a passing reference to the U.S. and

Latin American troops in the Dominican Republic during the
1965 crisis, and then in the limited context of the initial commitment and movement to the island of Hispaniola. Missing
is any mention of the continuing actions of the IAPF that made
the peaceful resolution of the conflict possible. Nor is there
any mention of the personal sacrifices of the American soldiers
and marines—with some 350 dead, wounded, or injured—or
their extensive humanitarian activities and exemplary conduct. Presumably writing for posterity, the president naturally
stressed the diplomatic and political aspects of the episode. As
a career soldier of long service, I can understand and accept
such apparent oversight, but the rank and file, who took the
brunt of the consequences of intervention, would have appre-
ciated a pat on the back from their commander-in-chief.

CHAPTER 8

An Assessment

What are the major lessons of the 1965 Dominican crisis? The political-military issues raised by the intervention, the overall effectiveness of the Organization of American States, the operational performance of U.S. forces and agencies need to be examined so that conclusions and judgments may be drawn from this experience. Because nearly a quarter-century has passed since the intervention, hindsight will no doubt color some judgments, although I feel that the passage of time has not substantially altered my own views.

Two related issues dominated the debates at the time and continue today: the legitimacy and legality of the intervention, and the seriousness of the Communist threat in the Dominican Republic in April 1965. With respect to these issues, Senator J. William Fulbright, chairman of the Senate Committee on Foreign Relations during the period, was probably the most vocal, articulate, and severe U.S. critic of the Johnson administration's actions. His views, coinciding with those of most Latin American nations at the time, are clearly enunciated in his book *The Arrogance of Power*, published in 1966 after the crisis had been resolved.

Fulbright concedes that the intervention restored a degree of stability in the Dominican Republic more quickly than seemed likely in the spring of 1965 and that U.S. diplomacy, the OAS, and the IAPF share with the Dominican provisional government the credit for bringing about the "fair and free" June 1966 election of Joaquin Balaguer as president. Fulbright also admits that the election was widely interpreted in some quarters as vindication of the intervention: that is, as proof that the action was "necessary, justified, and wise." But that is all Fulbright concedes. As he puts it, "The fact remains that the United States engaged in a unilateral military intervention in violation of inter-American law [and contrary to] the good neighbor policy of thirty years; that the OAS was gravely weakened as the result of its use—with its own consent—as an instrument of the policy of the United States"; and the "confidence in the word and in the intentions of the United States Government has been severely shaken."[1]

Fulbright's legal argument rests on Article 15 of the OAS Charter, which states that "no State or group of States has the right to intervene, directly or indirectly, for any reason whatever, in the internal or external affairs of any other State"; and Article 17, which states that "the territory of a State is inviolable; it may not be the object, even temporarily, of military occupation or of other measures of force taken by another State, directly or indirectly, on any grounds whatever." Fulbright points out that the charter admits one sole exception to the foregoing articles: Article 19 states that "measures adopted for the maintenance of peace and security in accordance with existing treaties do not constitute a violation of the principles set forth in Articles 15 and 17." Accordingly, he argues, the United States could have called for an urgent session of the OAS Council to invoke the Rio Treaty, Article 6 of which provides that if any American nation is affected by an aggression that is not an armed attack or by any other circumstance that might endanger the peace of the Americas, the OAS Council shall meet immediately to consider what measures should be taken for the common defense and maintenance of peace. But, Fulbright adds, the United States did not call such a session, on the grounds that the urgency of the situation did not permit time to consult the OAS—an excuse that he rejects. Thus, he concludes, the United States intervened in the Dominican Republic unilaterally and illegally. He acknowledges that had the OAS Council been consulted, it might have delayed a decision or refused to authorize any collective action, but, he argues, this still does not justify U.S. military action except for the limited purpose of evacuating U.S. and other foreign nationals. In any event, he insists, the United States should not have intervened without the advance consent of our OAS allies.[2]

With respect to the second issue, Fulbright contends that the United States ignored the causes and legitimacy of the Dominican revolution, judging that the involvement of an undetermined number of Communists discredited "the entire reformist movement" and thereby giving credence to the notion that "the United States is the enemy of social revolution, and therefore the enemy of social justice, in Latin America." Thus, he concludes, the U.S. government "acted impetuously and unwisely in unseemly fear of an indigenous revolution in the Dominican Republic."[3]

Fulbright is particularly hard on Ambassador Bennett, contending that he lost a "great opportunity" on 27 April to mediate a "democratic solution" when PRD leader Molina Urena, head of the constitutionalist government, and rebel military commander Colonel Caamano called on Bennett at the U.S. embassy and requested that the United States side with the constitutionalists. Fulbright calls Bennett's refusal to help Urena a mistake based primarily on the embassy's estimate, at the time, that Communists were in the ascendancy within the revolutionary leadership, an estimate with which Fulbright disagrees.[4]

But the fact is that no one, including Bennett, knew who really controlled the rebels, and it would have been a rash act to support the PRD, which might well have been only a temporary front—however well-intentioned—preceding a Communist takeover. After meeting with Bennett, Urena took asylum in the Colombian embassy, his behavior seeming to indicate that he was abandoning the revolution, possibly even in fear for his life or of serious injury at the hands of the extreme leftists in the movement. Caamano, however, apparently with Urena's consent, returned to the rebel side and became titular head of the constitutionalists. This would indicate that the rebels intended to continue the fight, which they did, apparently hoping to seize power by military force before the United States could act to prevent it. The possibility of such an outcome was precisely why President Johnson decided to intervene without further delay—he feared a creeping coup by Communists using the PRD as a screen to disguise their intentions.

I find it difficult, therefore, to fault Ambassador Bennett under the circumstances. Senator Fulbright was not at the scene and was hardly in a position to judge conditions at the time in Santo Domingo. Law and order had disappeared; the national police had simply melted away, and the so-called loyalist forces were not to be seen in the city either. Downtown Santo Domingo was in utter chaos, and even in the relatively quieter part of town the U.S. embassy found itself frequently under direct hostile small-arms fire. It was truly a touch-and-go situation, with no one seeming to be in charge on either side of the civil war. The senator's notion that anyone would be able to mediate a peaceful and democratic solution in such a turbulent environment of violence does not hold water.

Nevertheless, Fulbright is right about the devastating effect of the Dominican intervention on United States–Latin American relations, not to mention the strong adverse reactions that occurred at home in the United States. Historian Frederico G. Gil calls the intervention a "serious setback to the regional system, as well as a demeaning episode for Latin Americans," pointing out that the United States could retain a military emphasis on its policies to deal with Communism in the Western Hemisphere only at the cost of further deterioration in U.S.–Latin American relations.[5] John W. Ford, another scholar and a historian of the State Department, in 1986 cited the Dominican crisis of 1965 as no doubt "the most damaging to the OAS and its #1 crisis in its institutional history," particularly because it diminished the potential for strengthening the authority of the OAS and improving its modus operandi in handling disputes. In the mid-1960s, Ford states, there was some movement toward revising the OAS Charter, one objective being to make the organization a more effective instrument for dealing with serious quarrels among member states, but dissension over the Dominican crisis prevented any progress in this direction. Indeed, the affair had loud repercussions not only within the OAS but also worldwide.[6]

I cannot quarrel, then, with Senator Fulbright's harsh criticism of the U.S. failure to consult its OAS allies; consultation in advance of intervention would certainly have modified Latin American reactions. However, expert consensus seems to have been that there was virtually no chance that the OAS would sanction intervention, even though the objectives of the majority of American nations coincided with those of the United States: namely, to end the bloodshed and to allow the Dominicans to choose their own government freely.[7] The prospect of failing to persuade the OAS to act may thus have been the prime motivation for President Johnson's decision to intervene first and consult later. Even so, at least informing the OAS in advance and *then* promptly intervening might have been a wiser course of action. But this is judgment made in hindsight, and one must recall that the president and his advisers were faced with what seemed a "no win" situation, that the hour was late, and that reliable information on the situation in Santo Domingo was scarce. All the close presidential advisers at the hour of decision reportedly pleaded for more time to "get the OAS aboard," but the president was unwilling to risk further delay. For this, I cannot fault President Johnson.

As for the nature and magnitude of the Communist presence in Santo Domingo at the time of the rebellion, proof or hard evidence in any such situation is difficult if not impossible to produce, particularly at the beginning of a revolution when the situation is likely to be chaotic. Communist leaders are adept at concealing their role, remaining in the shadows and not revealing their hand until success is assured. Their doctrine stresses this practice and warns against surfacing prematurely, especially if doing so might trigger a forceful response from "imperialist" or "reactionary" governments. In the Dominican instance, Senator Fulbright admits that the Communists were present and that "they very rapidly began to try to take advantage of it [the revolution] and to seize control of it." He acknowledges that there is "little doubt that they had influence within the revolutionary movement," but, he adds, evidence to show that they were in actual control of the revolution is lacking. Finally, he calls intervention on the grounds of Communist participation, as distinguished from Communist control, "a mistake of panic and timidity which also reflects a grievous misreading of contemporary Latin American politics."[8] But he does not consider the potentially grave consequences had Communist involvement proved to be underestimated.

In the early days of the revolution, when the Congress, the press, and critics of the intervention pressed for proof of Communist influence, President Johnson asked his new CIA director, Admiral William F. Raborn, to produce evidence of a Communist link. Raborn, lacking any background in national intelligence, responded hurriedly and apparently without a thorough review of the known facts; he produced two CIA lists of Communists or Communist supporters within the rebel movement, which were released to the press. One list was called "Current Rebels Who Had Cuban Training"; the other, "Rebels Who Are Known Leftist Activists." Unfortunately, the lists included several individuals only loosely associated with the Communist cause, as well as two or three deceased persons, and several names were listed twice—inaccuracies that damaged the credibility of the CIA documents.[9] As a result, the CIA effort left much of the press and many among the U.S. and Latin American public unimpressed with the urgency of the Communist threat and probably did more harm than good. It might have been better to avoid going public on a matter of such sensitivity and ambiguity.

In Santo Domingo during this period, the Communist connection seemed ominous to us on the ground. There was ample evidence that the major Communist parties had been secretly organizing for an attack against the Reid government, if and when an opportunity arose, and that when hostilities did break out on 24 April, these parties had in fact rapidly mobilized and in less than an hour had put large numbers of armed civilians into the streets, inciting them into mob violence, killing police, looting, and burning.[10] Later, it became clear to our intelligence people that a tightly controlled cell-by-cell, block-by-block organization had been developed in downtown Santo Domingo. Still later, Communist party officials openly conducted Marxist political indoctrination classes and guerrilla training for Dominican youths recruited in the rebel sector and bused into the city from the countryside.

As more and more evidence accumulated, by midsummer 1965 there was little if any doubt within the intelligence community, including State, Defense, and CIA elements in Santo Domingo, that the Communist presence was substantial, pervasive, and dangerous. Although Caamano was the titular head, it had become clear on several occasions that his authority and control over the revolution was limited, primarily confined to the military rebels, and that the Communists and radical leftists were the dominant force in the movement and probably calling the shots.

The most convincing evidence, perhaps, was produced by the Communists themselves in a critique of the revolution—"Revolutionary Struggle in the Dominican Republic and Its Lessons"—that was published in two parts in the December 1965 and January 1966 issues of the authoritative Communist publication *World Marxist Review* (English version). Written by two leading members of the PCD (Dominican Communist party), J.I. Quello and N. Isa Conde, this two-part exposé is remarkably candid in its admission that Dominican Communists were deeply involved in the revolt, that their aim was to take over the country, and that it was only armed intervention by the United States that stopped them. The authors describe a city-oriented doctrine of armed uprisings by the people, preferably starting in the large, important urban areas, as the way to overthrow Western democratic governments; they emphasize the necessity, after first mobilizing "the revolutionary spirit of the people," to arm and train them in taking to the streets, seizing key locations, and organizing their defenses with the intent of permanently holding these areas. The authors express their opposition to the notion of organizing free elections, implying that this is the way imperialist democracies retain their power over the people. They admit that their leaders were not as well prepared for the revolution as they should have been and that by the time they corrected their initial mistakes it was too late. A fundamental error in the beginning, they conclude, was to concentrate the best leaders and fighters in a single *commando*. Belatedly, these elite Communists were distributed throughout the revolutionary forces with the intent not just to influence the direction of the revolution but to guide and control it.[11]

How effective was the Organization of American States during the crisis? From an objective, overall viewpoint, its performance was nothing less than extraordinary. Informed of the U.S. intervention after the fact, the OAS could have "sulked in its tent" and done nothing. Instead, it acted swiftly, wisely, and decisively. This is one of the untold stories of the 1965 crisis, a noteworthy performance that has never been recognized but, rather, scarcely noticed and largely overlooked. In the course of the crisis the OAS became more deeply involved than in any other case before or since. In early May 1965 it sent a senior committee to the Dominican Republic to achieve an effective cease-fire and report on the situation, and for the first time in its history it dispatched the secretary general himself to the scene of trouble. In May it succeeded in creating the Inter-American Peace Force as a multinational instrument to keep the peace in the republic, even though most major Latin American countries remained aloof, regarding the IAPF as a cover for the U.S. unilateral intervention. In late May, the OAS also sent its Inter-American Human Rights Commission to Santo Domingo. Then in early June it sent the distinguished Ad Hoc Committee to find a political solution and pave the way to the election of a new government. With the Dominican economy at a standstill, the OAS acted as the agency for paying civil servants and keeping the de facto government operating. The funds for doing so were mostly provided by the United States, which also undertook, with OAS sanction, a massive economic aid program.

All these activities inevitably involved the OAS in complex

political negotiations with the two Dominican factions and other groups, much to the displeasure of strict noninterventionists. Another source of unhappiness within the organization was the dubious legality of some OAS actions from a narrowly constructed point of view. However legitimate the ultimate goal, the prolonged negotiations leading to the establishment of a provisional, caretaking government did in reality constitute intervention into domestic Dominican politics. The duration of the OAS presence, extending to over a year, also had a negative influence, presenting abundant opportunities for personal friction and bitter debates within the organization. Finally, the victory of the more conservative presidential candidate, although the 1 June 1966 election was conceded to be a fair and honest contest, was a deep disappointment to many people and the highly vocal press throughout Latin America.[12]

Although the foregoing goes a long way toward explaining why the role played by the OAS in the Dominican Republic has been largely ignored, it still cannot gainsay the fact that the OAS played a crucial role, one that history, at least, should recognize. In short, though faced with an almost impossible situation in April 1965—a full-scale civil war in Santo Domingo, complicated by the unilateral intervention of a member state—the OAS responded to the crisis without undue delay and found solutions that have contributed to longer-term stability in the Dominican Republic and throughout the hemisphere. Two names stand out in this chronicle—those of José Mora of Costa Rica, the secretary general of the OAS, and Ellsworth Bunker, the U.S. representative to the OAS and recognized leader of its Ad Hoc Committee in the Dominican Republic. Their personal courage, professional skill, and devotion to duty in a cause that transcended national boundaries and considerations were truly remarkable.

How effective was U.S. operational performance? My judgment is that on balance it was generally good. Given little warning and with the growing Vietnam problem absorbing most of their attention, U.S. forces and agencies responded quickly and effectively to an ambiguous situation of unknown dimensions, rapidly overcoming some minor difficulties that surfaced in the beginning and later on working smoothly with the Latin American contingent of the IAPF.

First of all, *movement to the Dominican Republic* was accomplished efficiently with no major problems. U.S. naval amphibious forces, marines, army airborne troops, and the air force TAC are all accustomed to rapid deployment with little warning and know how to handle several missions concurrently. Three marine battalions, totaling about 2,500 men, landed on Dominican soil and remained a little over one month, the last marines being withdrawn on 6 June 1965. Army elements constituted about 90 percent of the force deployed (frequent press references to "25,000 marines" notwithstanding), arriving by U.S. Air Force aircraft: in six-plus days almost 16,000 troops and about 14,000 tons of materiel and supplies were airlifted between the United States and the Dominican Republic—the largest sustained U.S. troop airlift ever accomplished up to that time. Almost 1,500 sorties involving 181 C-130s and twenty-three C-124s were flown under difficult weather and airfield conditions without a single mishap. In mid-May U.S. force strength peaked at some 22,500 troops but was rapidly reduced during the following weeks, reaching about 10,000 men in late July. Army elements were present for the duration, the last trooper coming out on 21 September 1966. Latin American troop deployment was also by air, all except the Brazilian contingent using C-130s flown by the U.S. Air Force between mid-May and late June 1965—again, without any major problems. Lifting ground forces over a considerably longer distance, the Brazilian Air Force likewise did a commendable job.

Next, command and control on the U.S. side were hampered in the beginning by lack of adequate strategic, long-line *communications* from the United States to the Dominican Republic, a problem made even more stringent by the rebel hold on major telecommunications centers and equipment, including the undersea cable links to Puerto Rico. The senior land force headquarters in the republic, that of the U.S. Army's XVIII Airborne Corps, possessed only relatively short-range tactical communications equipment completely inadequate for the long-range job, and other than the Brazilians, the Latin American units had virtually no modern communications capabilities beyond short-wave radio contact with their governments— and even the Brazilian Army communications element present had only a limited capability.

The suitable, jointly manned strategic communications units available at U.S. STRICOM headquarters were never released for the Dominican Republic mission. Eventually, other long-line army communications equipment was sent, but much valuable time had already been lost. ·

Obviously, communications planning for contingencies should include strategic communications units with long-range capability. Moreover, such planning should take into account the communications capabilities of other U.S. agencies that may be involved in a contingency operation, such as the State Department, the CIA, the Defense Communications Agency, the unified command concerned, and even the White House Communications Agency. In the Dominican affair, all of these ultimately became involved and worked closely and harmoniously together to find solutions to the communications problems.

At the beginning, the Department of Defense had scanty *intelligence* with respect to the national leadership, major personalities, political parties, fronts and movements, and military forces in the Dominican Republic, despite a long history of U.S.–Dominican Republic relations and the strategic importance of the Caribbean to the United States. Whatever additional information State and the CIA had was apparently not available to Defense before the intervention was launched. Because a lack of suitable targets made technical methods such as signal intercept and overhead reconnaissance of very limited value in the Dominican Republic, it took some time to collect pertinent intelligence and develop an adequate data base.

Nevertheless, the cooperation and team spirit among the

various intelligence agencies in Santo Domingo were remarkable. The CIA, State, Defense, all the services, the National Security Agency (NSA) and all the service cryptological security agencies, and the FBI (which had excellent sources in Puerto Rico) together achieved a first-rate intelligence effort (although with no love lost between J. Edgar Hoover and the CIA, it took President Johnson's personal orders to direct that the FBI assist the agency with security and intelligence collection in the Dominican Republic).[13] David A. Philips, the CIA chief of station in Santo Domingo, and my corps G-2, Col. John Foulk, deserve much credit for this outstanding accomplishment. On the Latin American side, the IAPF and the intelligence section of its headquarters added a new dimension and flavor as well as considerably more substance to our intelligence effort.

A vital part of intelligence for this kind of mission concerns the location of important political and economic, as well as military, places and facilities in a nation's capital. Examples in Santo Domingo included the U.S. and other foreign embassies, government offices, military and police headquarters, national radio and other broadcasting stations, telecommunications centers, news centers and press offices, banks, customs and port offices. As a result, maps are of critical importance both for planning and for operations involving such installations. But until the Army Map Service delivered updated tactical maps—well after the intervention—road maps of Santo Domingo and the Dominican Republic issued by the oil companies were our primary sources of current information.

The *troop performance* of the marines and army paratroopers, both elite elements of the U.S. armed services, was commendable—as expected. Marines, however, trained and indoctrinated to be an all-out assault force, find it difficult to adjust to a peacekeeping role. The 82d Airborne Division, whose troopers carried the brunt of the mission, was singled out for high praise by distinguished visitors, civilian and military, U.S. and foreign. Admirals Moorer and McCain separately told me that they had never seen troops anywhere of any nationality with comparable qualities. Their appearance, self-assurance, discipline, esprit, grasp of their mission, and obvious readiness for action were often the subject of uninvited comment.

The army's special forces unit, a reinforced company of the 7th Special Forces Group, deserves separate mention. Highly professional and possessing many skills—among them, language fluency—its members carried out highly unusual, sensitive, and dangerous missions with distinction, including several covert and clandestine operations, both with and without the help of Dominican personnel. Even lacking such items as civilian garb, or weapons and equipment not readily attributable to U.S. sources, the special forces troopers proved to be highly flexible and adaptable to the various kinds of operations assigned to them.

The Latin American troops too carried out their assigned missions successfully, even though they did not have the background, training, or experience of their American counterparts and were usually a little tentative in reacting to a new situation. With the exception of the Brazilian marines, a company entirely composed of professional soldiers and, not surprisingly, the outstanding unit, the enlisted men of all nationalities were draftees with terms of one to two years. Noncommissioned officers of all contingents were career soldiers, but with some exceptions the LA officers and staffs were not up to U.S. professional standards. Nevertheless, IAPF headquarters, a mixed U.S.–Latin American organization that had to overcome language, cultural, and doctrinal differences, managed to function in a reasonably good fashion. Despite obvious problems, the U.S. forces were happy to have the Latin American contingents on our side, and they were a definite morale booster during the long, arduous, and often frustrating peacekeeping chore.

In Santo Domingo the welfare, as well as the control, of the people was a prime consideration; hence, the *civil affairs and psychological operations* (PSYOPS) units were extremely useful in accomplishing our mission. Our G-5, civil affairs officer, became a key and busy member of the U.S. staff, working closely with the embassy staff, which came to rely heavily on him. In addition, the military police were worth their weight in gold. Early in the intervention we found that a major weakness in the initial troop lists was a shortage of MP units, and we soon had to give them a priority on a par with combat units.

The United States did not establish a joint *public affairs* setup in Santo Domingo; State, Defense, and the USIS each handled its own press responsibilities, each doing its best to present U.S. policies and actions in the best possible light. There were no doubt inconsistencies in the story, but since the United States had intervened unilaterally and surprised both its Latin American and other Western allies, it may have been impossible to present a consistent, credible explanation. On balance and in light of such difficult circumstances, the public affairs people performed pretty well, although a joint State-Defense organization in Santo Domingo might have improved the results.

Finally, in an assessment of performance, there is the matter of *logistics*. U.S. marine units going ashore normally take only minimum ammunition, rations, fuel, and other supplies, relying on the sea line of communications back to their amphibious force afloat for resupply. In the Dominican Republic, U.S. army and air force units, deploying by air, likewise took in only a few days of supplies but required resupply by air until a sea line could be established from U.S. bases in Puerto Rico. Resupply by ship was established on 10 May, about ten days after the arrival of the first troops. Logistic support included food and medical supplies for civilian relief, not to mention a large humanitarian, civic-action effort for the benefit of the Dominican population. U.S. engineers, as examples, erected temporary bridges during heavy flood and storm conditions, and maintained the main Dominican fuel supply system. In short, our logisticians performed in an outstanding way, providing not only all necessary support and medical care for U.S. forces but also the great bulk of the support required by the Latin American troop contingents and IAPF headquarters.

The Puerto Rican base was used as a staging and holding area for aircraft during the deployment, a safe haven for thousands of civilians evacuated by sea and air from the Dominican

Republic, a supply base for U.S. and Latin American forces, a communications outlet and gateway, an asylum for political refugees, and later as a troop rest-and-recreation area. It would have been considerably more difficult to operate without this important base (although U.S. bases in Panama and Guantánamo Bay, Cuba, were also available for the operation).

In an overall sense, what conclusions can be drawn about the 1965 Dominican affair? At the outset, in the narrow context of just the Dominican Republic, an objective examination of the U.S.-OAS intervention would have to conclude that the outcome was favorable. True, there was a decided element of luck from the beginning and throughout; for example, the intervention was fortunate in being able to confine the rebellion essentially to the capital city and prevent its taking hold in the countryside. Nevertheless, since the June 1966 elections and the withdrawal of the Inter-American Peace Force, the Dominicans have held free elections every four years, and although its economy has had frequent ups and downs, the republic has enjoyed a political stability rarely equaled in its history.

President Balaguer held power for twelve years, until the May 1978 elections, in which both the favored Balaguer and opposition candidate Antonio Guzman claimed victory. (This was the same Guzman who was seriously considered as an interim president during the initial days of the 1965 crisis but rejected as being too far to the left politically.) After a tense ten days, during which the Carter administration in the United States expressed its deep concern that the electoral process might be violated, Balaguer conceded defeat and accepted Guzman as the victor; the Dominican Minister of the armed forces too vowed to respect the election results. In 1982 another liberal won the election: Dr. Jorge Blanco, who had been a representative of the constitutionalist side during the OAS negotiations that resulted in a provisional government in 1965. Ellsworth Bunker, incidentally, headed the U.S. delegation at Blanco's inauguration in August 1982. In May 1986 three candidates made strong showings: Balaguer, seventy-eight years old and blind, ran for the Social Christian Reform party (successor to his old Reformist party); Jacobo Majluta, age fifty-two, ran for the governing Dominican Revolutionary party (PRD); and Juan Bosch, at seventy-six, ran for the newly formed leftist Dominican Liberation party. In a close contest Balaguer won with 41 percent of the vote, Majluta received about 39 percent, and Bosch about 20 percent. Surely these events show that democracy in at least one important sense is alive and well in the Dominican Republic.

The Dominican affair demonstrated that the United States can move rapidly, decisively, and in a timely manner when its national interests in the hemisphere are believed to be jeopardized. Moreover, although large and powerful forces were deployed to the region, the United States showed great restraint, using only the minimum force appropriate to the situation—a basic principle in dealing with a problem such as the 1965 Dominican case. Yet even though the United States showed that it can orchestrate with finesse the political, economic, and military actions required in a complex, sensitive situation, the nation fell far short of developing a convincing psychological climate within which its public affairs efforts could bear fruit. Although both the United States and the OAS were technically proficient in the science of disseminating their sides of the Dominican story, neither demonstrated a sufficient grasp of the intricacies and subtleties of such matters.

The IAPF, a historical first, demonstrated the feasibility of organizing and actually committing an inter-American force on a peacekeeping, stability-maintaining mission within the territory of a member state. Moreover, the IAPF demonstrated that such multinational force can work effectively and harmoniously in consonance with political guidance from the OAS.

From President Johnson's point of view, the Dominican intervention essentially achieved his strategic objectives: preserving the integrity of the fundamentally important Caribbean region, positively discouraging the export of Castro-style Communism from Cuba to other nations in the region, and freeing the United States to commit its power in southeast Asia without having to worry about the security of the Western Hemisphere.

What significant lessons, then, should be drawn from the Dominican experience that might be relevant to other real world situations? Perhaps the most profound overall lesson of such an undertaking is the necessity for a complete integration of effort: political, military, psychological, socioeconomic, public affairs, and information—an extremely difficult challenge. Marxist Communists are masters at making the political-psychological aspects dominant but not hesitating to employ force, or the threat of force, so long as it is subordinated to and in consonance with the unifying political purpose. Western democracies such as the United States, regrettably, are amateurs in this business—but perhaps a fully integrated effort is not feasible in so open a democratic society.

Among other things, an integration of effort means that there must be close civilian-military relations at high decision-making levels. For example, the senior U.S. commander must establish close relationships with the U.S. ambassador or other political representative on the spot, so that together they can consider the appropriate political-military moves to be made. In Santo Domingo we were blessed with two outstanding American ambassadors, William Tapley Bennett and Ellsworth Bunker, who not only were superb diplomats but also grasped the true relationship of diplomacy and military force, understanding that in order to achieve success, the two had to work in tandem. In this connection, the Dominican experience demonstrated the wisdom of keeping the senior military headquarters separate from the tactical commander directing operations. Doing so allows a smoother transmission of political-military guidance and relieves the tactical commander of the onus for decisions dictated by political considerations and having to explain them to his troops. In the Dominican case, HQ XVIII Airborne Corps played the senior military role of HQ U.S. Forces Dominican Republic, while HQ 82d Airborne Division played the tactical role.

From the very beginning of such crises, military advice is essential to top civilian leaders if they are to avoid misjudgments with respect to the use of force. In this instance, no military person was present during the almost continuous conferences held in the White House between 24 April 1965, when the Dominican revolution began, and late on 29 April, five days later, when the JCS chairman was invited to join the presidential group. By that time, decisions had been made and actions taken that involved military matters. It seems obvious that a responsible senior military individual should have participated in those earlier decisions.

Planners for an operation like the Dominican one must ensure that adequate long-line communications are provided for the designated overall commander. It is almost a foregone conclusion that Washington will take direct control of the action and that direct, preferably secure, voice communications with the commander on the ground will be required. In Santo Domingo, although CINCLANT was nominally in the chain of command, the de facto chain did run directly to Washington.

Adequate intelligence for such a mission is so obviously essential that it is sometimes neglected in the planning phase. The collection and analysis of intelligence is relatively uncomplicated in a conventional war against regular military forces but can be more complex and difficult in a civil war (such as the Dominican one) involving both military forces and armed civilians, and even more so in a conflict (such as in Vietnam) involving the whole spectrum of unconventional as well as conventional warfare. Contingency planners must develop at least some idea of the range of probable missions that might confront the assigned forces so that the intelligence people can gather relevant information about not only the political situation but also key locations and facilities that might be useful military objectives to seize in support of the political objective. Moreover, since commanders start more or less from scratch, with little in the way of an intelligence data base, planners must include appropriate intelligence units on early arriving troop lists.

In a civil war, propaganda is a deadly weapon, and words can at times be more effective than bullets. After the United States intervened, psychological warfare became the Dominican rebels' principal weapon, and for a while Radio Santo Domingo in constitutionalist hands appeared to be our Achilles heel. The dictator Trujillo had developed an extensive and sophisticated telecommunications and radio broadcasting system that could easily reach every corner of the republic; Radio Santo Domingo, with its numerous alternative transmitter and antenna field sites and relay stations, was almost invulnerable. The constitutionalist rebels used this radio capability skillfully, not only in attempts to incite the entire population to revolt but also as an effective means of communication with their own forces. U.S. forces in the area had a powerful electronic warfare capability that could be employed in a jamming mode from navy ships, air force aircraft, and army ground units, but these systems were designed for use against military targets; as we soon discovered, they had only a limited effect against commercial transmitting systems. Hence, we were unable to deny the rebels' use of this propaganda weapon until the main Radio Santo Domingo facility was physically put out of operation. In a positive vein, however, we established our own commercial transmitters and broadcast radio programs not only for our own troops but for anyone else wanting to tune in. The lesson would appear to be that military jamming against commercial systems is not an effective denial means and that a positive approach of getting out one's own "friendly information" is a better way to go.

No matter how foresighted the plans or how skillful the operations, there are limits to military intervention of this nature. Military action can stabilize conditions but cannot alone solve political problems, much less basic social and economic inequities; indeed, military efforts can make matters worse. Foreign forces, sooner or later, are singled out by all local factions and blamed for anything that goes wrong. Although foreign troops may conduct themselves in an exemplary manner and favorably impress the population, even the youth, those troops will remain the target of virulent propaganda and provocative actions designed to cause an overreaction. Intervention, therefore, should be used only as a last resort and, if at all possible, only on an international (preferably regional) basis. There are many benefits stemming from sharing the onus of intervention with one's allies.

Once intervention on the ground is decided upon, however, it is well to heed the old adage "Don't send a boy to do a man's work." Sending too small a force can backfire by accomplishing only a stalemate or, worse, failing the mission entirely. Political, psychological, and military advantages outweigh the disadvantages of overwhelming force deployed to the crisis area as rapidly as possible. The presence of ample force is more likely in the end to result in fewer human casualties, combatant and noncombatant, and less material damage as well; sending an inadequate force is more likely to have the opposite result.

The intervening forces should get in and get out as soon as possible. Stability operations of this nature are, in a sense, dead-end situations: the longer the forces stay, the worse things are likely to become. To emphasize the temporary nature of our presence in the Dominican Republic and to remind ourselves, as well as anyone who saw us, why we were there, all U.S. military personnel habitually wore working field combat uniforms.

Strategic air and sea mobility are the keys to any successful quick-reaction force. In the Dominican case the initial U.S. ground force, a marine battalion, came in over the beach, their timely arrival having been possible because the amphibious task force transporting them had been positioned over the horizon from Santo Domingo several days in advance. The other two marine battalions went in by air, as did the bulk of the U.S. force, including the 82d Airborne Division, other army troops, and air force personnel. Likewise, resupply depended on air transport until a sea line of communications was established from bases in Puerto Rico. In a conventional conflict of any duration, the sinews of war—heavy tonnage items such as the ammunition, fuel, and rations that make up more than 90 per cent of the total supplies required—must come by sea; in less conventional stability operations of the Dominican type, the premium will normally be on rapid initial movement by air.

The basic troop requirement on the ground is for infantry, preferably light infantry but highly disciplined and skilled; troops of poor quality are a liability. Other combat and combat support units—field artillery, armor, attack aviation, engineers, and so on—must also be available, while the necessity of troop-carrying, scout, and utility helicopter units is a given. Military police are particularly useful and should be deployed in early echelons. Special forces, with their great versatility and high skill levels, are needed for the unconventional and unexpected tasks that are bound to arise in such undertakings. Civil affairs and psychological operations units are valuable; such activities should become second nature and an integral part of operational planning.

What I am addressing is simply the time-honored principle of tailoring a force for its anticipated mission. One of the basic reasons the U.S. Army maintains a unit such as the 82d Airborne Division is that it is basically a light infantry division, easily and readily adaptable to a variety of missions.

Preparing troops for a peacekeeping mission calls for a particular approach. Time permitting, the special preparation they should receive is not training so much as indoctrination. "Training" implies that peacekeeping requires qualities and abilities different from those demanded in battle. On the contrary, peacekeeping demands the same disciplined, skilled troops as does combat—troops with high morale and such soldierly qualities as courage, patience, endurance, vigilance, initiative, and leadership ability. In addition, however, all involved—officers, noncommissioned officers, and private soldiers—must understand the political objectives sought and the mission of the force. Everyone must be conditioned to expect the extraordinary rather than the ordinary and routine, particularly the strong likelihood of facing chaos in the early stages of any crisis. Ad hoc, quickly improvised operations are often necessary, and these require well-trained soldiers and units. The art of soldiering involves remaining flexible in mind and actions, staying alert and watchful, and being skilled in the crafts of the observer scout and small reconnaissance patrol. These characteristics are at a premium.

Troops must also be willing and ready to undertake unusual tasks with little relevance to normal military duties. In Santo Domingo, for example, the IAPF assumed responsibility for emergency relief operations for a large segment of the city's population: distributing food and water, providing medical care, and ensuring the uninterrupted operation of the city's utilities. In other words, they were called upon to meet the basic needs of the people, to perform tasks that do not come naturally to the armed forces of some nations. Unintentionally, U.S. forces also provided some amusement for the Dominican people. Armed Forces Radio in Santo Domingo, which played music designed for the ears of U.S. troops and provided news from home (deliberately refraining from any political comment on Dominican affairs), became by far the most popular radio station among Dominicans of all ages throughout the republic. The lesson here is that contingency planners might do well to provide for the early introduction of such radio and television capability in the objective area.

Perhaps the oddest task assigned to the 82d Airborne Division was temporarily taking over the Santo Domingo Zoo, which was full of starving creatures of many species. Abandoned by their keepers, the animals, birds, reptiles, and other zoo inhabitants were hungry and letting the world know about it. To make matters worse, many Americans and other foreign nationals, departing the country hastily at the beginning of the revolution had left their pets in the zoo in the belief that there they would get some modicum of care. The 82d showed considerable ingenuity in meeting the wide variety of food needs at the zoo, even the huge requirements of such large carnivores as lions and tigers.[14]

Of particular interest in the Dominican affair was the fact that without any previous experience or prior knowledge with respect to peacekeeping, we discovered two of the most important principles involved in such an undertaking. One involves interposing the peacekeeping force between hostile parties, a difficult operation at best. The other is avoiding the firing of weapons whenever possible and shooting only in self-defense: that is, when the peacekeepers' lives are in jeopardy or their positions in danger of being overrun—not always easy judgments to make, particularly under unfriendly fire![15]

As we discovered in Santo Domingo, however, such "rules of engagement" can be a double-edged sword. Soldiers must not become so imbued with the principles of restraint and use of minimum force that they are reluctant to act when hostile locals try to take advantage of the situation and do serious harm. Large mobs bent on violence in Santo Domingo could be dispersed without casualties, using familiar wedge formations of soldiers with bayonets fixed. But Dominican trouble-makers would often try to isolate and hurt a soldier on sentry duty, throwing garbage, large rocks, and other objects, all the while yelling the vilest of epithets and, if they succeeded in knocking him down, doing all the damage they could to him. In fact, the 82d took some severe casualties in this manner. So there comes a time when peacekeepers are justified in using force under sufficient provocation, and their chain of command must support them. Discipline is a two-way street: leaders must swiftly punish a soldier guilty of deliberate, unprovoked assault on a local citizen but must also back up a soldier doing what he believes is necessary to protect himself or a fellow soldier thought to be in imminent danger.

Every American—North, Central, or South—has his or her own views, but in my own admittedly subjective opinion the United States can, on balance, be proud of what was ultimately accomplished in ending the Dominican crisis. Moreover, I believe that the Dominican experience, although now dated and overtaken by events in many ways, taught lessons that may still be pertinent in the event of a similar situation in the future. The concluding chapter explores further the question of whether the United States has really profited from the past experience of the Dominican affair of 1965.

CHAPTER 9

Caribbean Realities for the United States Today

Twenty-four years have gone by since the 1965 intervention in the Dominican Republic, and many significant developments have taken place in the Caribbean region that affect the future of Americans. Five U.S. presidents—Johnson, Nixon, Ford, Carter, and Reagan—served during those years, and Central America and Caribbean island nations often required their close attention. Given the enduring importance of the Caribbean Basin to U.S. national interests, did the Dominican experience teach the United States anything of lasting value?

A look at the Dominican Republic today shows not only the remarkable political stability outlined in the preceding chapter—both conservative and liberal presidents have been elected and have served out their terms—but some encouraging improvement in the nation's economy. There have been setbacks as well: economic growth has not been able to keep up with population growth, and so per capita income has remained at about $1,250 for several years—very low in comparison with more highly developed countries in the world but about average for the Caribbean region. Nevertheless, Dominican industrial development has progressed, and jobs have been created by innovative manufacturing programs. The labor force in both urban and rural areas has increased in size; increases in both absolute number and percentage have been much greater in the urban areas, but agriculture remains important in the Dominican economy and continues to be the major source of foreign exchange. Tourism has also increased with the building of fine hotels and other facilities that attract affluent travelers. And aid from the United States, other foreign countries, and international agencies has helped enormously, though it also leaves the republic vulnerable to any reduction of such outside assistance. Education prospects, too, have improved for the less privileged; literacy has increased to 77 percent; and the middle class continues to grow in numbers and influence.

Yet social and racial inequities still exist today—inequities that do not stem from Dominican law but have come about through centuries-old tradition and custom. Whatever the country's progress, the hard fact remains that Dominicans, like many other Caribbean peoples, continue to migrate north to the United States in large numbers: about 400,000 Dominicans reside abroad, the great majority in Puerto Rico and the continental United States. The civil war endemic to many countries is one cause, but the basic reason for such migration is a simple desire to find a better life—to escape hunger, poverty, and oppression, real or perceived. Thus, it seems in the selfish interest of the United States to do all that it can reasonably afford to improve the quality of life in the Caribbean, as well as in the best interests of the Caribbeans themselves, who, despite their admiration for their northern neighbor, would much prefer to remain in their own homelands.

In the broader picture, what has happened to United States–Latin American relations in the Caribbean Basin during the period following the 1965 Dominican episode? In the Johnson-Nixon-Ford years, Vietnam preempted U.S. attention at the expense of Latin America, and near the end of that era Watergate paralyzed the presidency. Meanwhile, in Nicaragua during the early 1970s, Somoza and his infamous National Guard had become so corrupt and brutally oppressive that the left, led by the Sandinista Front, began to win not only popular support but also the backing of the Church, moderate Nicaraguan leaders, and businessmen. By the end of the Nixon-Ford years virtually all Caribbean Basin states had condemned the Somoza regime and sharply disagreed with the U.S. policy of continued military and economic aid to Somoza. The dilemma facing the

United States was that Soviet-Cuban arms and economic aid
were being supplied in increasing amounts not only to the Sandinistas in Nicaragua but also to insurgents in El Salvador,
Guatemala, and Honduras. Moreover, the Sandinista leadership
was undeniably Marxist in nature.

Things went from bad to worse in Nicaragua in 1977 and
1978, all efforts to find an acceptable political solution coming
to naught. Then, in the spring of 1979, too late to avoid a Sandinista victory in the field and having eschewed intervention
up to that time, President Carter called an emergency meeting
of the OAS Council to consider a U.S. proposal for an inter-
American peacekeeping force to stop the fighting and establish
an acceptable regime, as had been done in the Dominican Republic in 1965. It was the idea of Cyrus Vance, Carter's secretary of state, who had been President Johnson's deputy
secretary of defense at the time of the Dominican crisis. Re-
calling that experience, Vance had advised against unilateral
action but waited too long to propose OAS action. Predictably,
the other OAS nations unanimously and flatly rejected the
belated proposal, recognizing that the Nicaraguan case was
much different from the earlier Dominican one, where the rebellion was confined to the capital city and widespread resistance against the government did not exist. The Dominican
rebels, moreover, were poorly organized and had no equivalent
to the Sandinista Front, whereas in Nicaragua the Sandinista
movement was well organized and widely based, extending into
the countryside as well as the capital, Managua. So the inevitable occurred, and the Somoza dynasty was overthrown in
mid-July 1979.[1]

Another significant Caribbean development during Carter's
term was the signing of the Panama Canal treaties, negotiated
in 1978 by Ambassadors Ellsworth Bunker and Sol Linowitz
but not ratified by the Senate until a clause was added speci-
fying the U.S. right to intervene militarily should the canal
be obstructed for any reason. Under the reversion treaty the
United States will turn over control of the canal to Panama,
relinquish sovereignty in the former Canal Zone, and withdraw
all its forces without any residual base rights at the end of 1999;

under the other treaty the United States assumes responsibility for guaranteeing the neutrality of the canal as an international waterway. But it has no way of enforcing neutrality, short of invading the sovereign territory of Panama. These conditions were negotiated on the assumption that Panama would remain a stable, friendly country—an assumption that recent events have shown to be flawed.

When Ronald Reagan assumed the presidency in January 1981, his administration recognized from the start the central strategic importance of the Caribbean region and focused on Central America. It seemed abundantly clear that the new regime in Managua was a self-avowed Marxist government that made little pretense of being democratic. Accordingly, President Reagan suspended all U.S. aid to the Sandinista regime on 23 January 1981. Then Secretary of State Alexander Haig made the point that the only way to stop Communist/Marxist subversion in the Western Hemisphere, particularly in the Caribbean region, was to go to the "source"—apparently a reference to Cuba, although Haig recognized that the primary source was the Soviet Union.

Among the courses of action considered was to use U.S. naval forces to interdict Cuban, Soviet, or other foreign ships introducing weapons and equipment into Nicaragua, as well as to stop the infiltration by sea of such materials from Nicaragua or other sources to insurgents operating in El Salvador and Honduras—a course similar to the naval quarantine imposed on Cuba by President Kennedy during the 1962 missile crisis. Defense Department and U.S. Navy officials, however, opposed the idea on the grounds that the navy was already overcommitted, and the proposal was dropped. This significant decision showed that the Reagan administration was unwilling to confront the Soviet Union and its proxy, Cuba, even where the United States enjoys an enormous advantage over any potential adversary. Thereafter, Reagan chose a less effective way to oppose the Sandinista government: namely, to support the Nicaraguan counterrevolutionaries. U.S. aid to the "contras" has been a controversial issue ever since.

But in another part of the Caribbean the United States was

presented with an opportunity to take swift and decisive action—with relatively little risk of escalation or involvement in prolonged conflict—to eliminate a clear Marxist/Communist threat to the hemisphere. That, of course, was on Grenada, the largest island in the Grenadines and a former British crown colony with a population of about 100,000 English-speaking people, where a U.S. *coup de main* occurred in October 1983.

Striking similarities and several differences between the Grenadian and Dominican interventions invite a comparison of the two operations. First, in both instances, U.S. action to protect the safe evacuation of endangered Americans and other foreign nationals was founded on well-established principles of international law and thus went unquestioned. But because the United States intervened unilaterally in the Dominican Republic before proposing that the OAS take over, the legitimacy and legality of its subsequent actions were severely questioned. (Ironically, U.S. support of the United Kingdom in the April 1982 Anglo-Argentine conflict over sovereign rights in the Falklands—Islas Malvinas—has since overtaken the 1965 Dominican crisis as the most controversial in the history of the OAS.) In Grenada, however, although the OAS declined to support an intervention, members of the Organization of Eastern Caribbean States (OCES) agreed among themselves to intervene, provided the United States would assist, and then urgently requested U.S. participation in a collective military intervention.[2] Two non-OCES states, Jamaica and Barbados, joined in the request, and the British governor general on Grenada appealed for OCES action to restore order on the island. Thus, the Grenada intervention had an aura of legitimacy with substantive legal foundation that the Dominican Republic action lacked. In consequence, whereas the Dominican action badly damaged United States–Latin American relations, Grenada escaped such a fate.

Indeed, the Grenadian affair clearly demonstrated the need for an effective inter-American organization in the Caribbean to handle such emergencies—and both interventions had substantive inter-American participation, although no inter-

American political effort to negotiate a settlement like that performed by the OAS and the IAPF in the Dominican Republic was undertaken in Grenada. The United States and the OCES simply agreed to commit a combined U.S.-Caribbean force in a collective effort to restore order, and to withdraw their forces as soon as circumstances permitted. The Caribbean nations visualized the restoration of a constitutional government, albeit initially a provisional one, to be determined by the Grenadians themselves. Six Caribbean states contributed troops totaling about 400 and collectively called the Caribbean Peacekeeping Force.

In the Dominican Republic the extent of the Communist/Marxist threat was a major and contentious issue that is still being debated today. In Grenada, on the other hand, the early seizure of extensive stores of Soviet and Czech arms and ammunition, the discovery of elaborate military facilities controlled by non-Grenadians, and the uncovering of numerous documents detailing Soviet-Cuban-Nicaraguan plans to subvert nations in the Caribbean left no doubt as to the gravity of the threat.[3]

In both instances, that perceived Communist threat plus instability, rising tensions, and a rapidly escalating series of events served to convince the president that decisive action could no longer be delayed. In Santo Domingo the situation deteriorated so badly in just five days, 24-29 April 1965, that President Johnson and his top advisers agreed that drastic measures were necessary, even though his advisers wanted time to consult with the OAS. A military voice in these deliberations was absent, however, until the day of decision, 29 April, when the JCS chairman was included in the high-level White House meetings for the first time. Johnson was slow in seeking congressional support as well, but on 28 April he did gain the approval of the majority and minority leaders in both the Senate and the House—including Senator Fulbright, who later became a highly vocal critic of the intervention.[4]

In Grenada, a particularly bloody and brutal coup had taken place on 19 October 1983, and a Revolutionary Military Council had taken over the government. The OCES appeal for U.S.

action was received in Washington on 22 October, and two days later President Reagan gave the order to intervene. Again, although Secretary of State George Schultz favored intervention, some administration officials were concerned about another wave of anti-U.S. feelings in Latin America, while Secretary of Defense Caspar Weinberger and General John Vessey, the JCS chairman (who this time had been included in the high-level councils of government from the beginning) wanted more time to assess the situation. On the congressional side, leaders of both parties were briefed at the White House on 24 October, the day before troops began to land in Grenada. Questions were asked, but no objections were raised. In fact, House Speaker Thomas O'Neill, a veteran critic of Reagan, reportedly said that he had no intention of being "critical of my Government at this time."[5]

However hastily the decisions to intervene were taken, the United States had had ample strategic warning of trouble in both countries. The Dominican Republic entered an unstable state after Trujillo's assassination in 1961, and when President Juan Bosch was exiled to Puerto Rico after a bloodless coup in 1963, it was apparent that serious civil conflict was inevitable. So the April 1965 rebellion came as no real surprise—it simply came a little earlier than expected. The United States was also well aware of Soviet-Cuban intentions and Cuban activities in Grenada. Indeed, President Reagan, in a televised speech as early as 23 March 1983, had displayed an aerial photograph of a large military-style airfield being constructed on the island by Cuban engineers and warned of Soviet-Cuban subversion and militarization.

Nevertheless, advance preparation was minimal. U.S. contingency planning for the Caribbean Sea area is a responsibility of the Commander in Chief, Atlantic Command, a U.S. unified commander. CINCLANT's contingency plans for the Dominican Republic, though more advanced than those for Grenada, were still little more than an outline for the initial movement of U.S. forces to the republic, and intelligence concerning the overall political situation—internal conditions within the Dominican government and the strength of organized opposition—was inadequate prior to the intervention. As for Grenada, because only about forty-eight hours were available to update CINCLANT's very sketchy contingency plans and to ready the forces involved, a U.S. amphibious force, including a marine battalion, en route to Lebanon at the time, was diverted to Barbados, where it staged for Grenada. Complicating matters further, special forces from the various services, tasked to carry out specific missions prior to the arrival of the main forces, were added to the troop list late in the hour. On balance, CINCLANT and the major units concerned did a remarkable job of executing a difficult and complex assignment in an extremely short time, but more than one adverse consequence stemmed from this lack of time. Among other things, it precluded the development of a joint communications plan providing such essential information as the radio frequencies and call signs of all units involved in the operation. Again, the intelligence available was inadequate, particularly with regard to the size and capabilities of the Cuban force present and the number and location of U.S. citizens involved, most of them medical students; fortunately, all the students were found unharmed, even though only one of the three locations where they lived was known in advance of the U.S. landing. And again, as in the Dominican situation, no suitable maps were immediately available; the 82d Airborne Division in Grenada devised some, based on tourist maps.

Tactical communications between units of different services, always difficult even when adequate time for planning and rehearsal is available, were a special problem in Grenada, owing in part to the lack of a joint communications plan. Army rangers and paratroopers had difficulty calling for close air support from carrier aircraft; a similar problem arose between army rangers and air force gunships. In a tragic accident one U.S. paratrooper was killed and fifteen wounded by a navy carrier aircraft on a close air support mission. However, GI resourcefulness usually found a way around communication obstacles, and successful interservice operations included the teaming up of marine helicopters and army rangers, after the initial landings, to carry out a successful air assult against stubborn Cuban resistance.

The scheme of employment of assigned forces in Grenada was similar to that in the Dominican Republic, with marines and army troops landing at widely separated points and linking up on the ground later. In Grenada, navy SEALS and the army's Delta Force were introduced in advance for such tasks as securing the governor general's residence and a prison for political prisoners, but they were unable to accomplish all assigned tasks alone. Then, early on 25 October, U.S. marines landed in the eastern part of the island, securing the civilian Pearls airport and meeting little resistance, while army rangers made a low-level parachute assault to seize the uncompleted Point Salines military airfield under construction in the western part of the island, where the heaviest fighting occurred. That afternoon, lead elements of the two brigades of the 82d Airborne Division committed to the action began landing on the airfield. On 27 October the paratroopers secured the capital, Saint George's, and captured the last defended position on the island, ending all resistance. Cuban casualties were 24 killed, 59 wounded, and about 600 captured; U.S. casualties among a force of approximately 6,000 were 18 killed and 119 wounded—about half the number suffered in the Dominican Republic.

As in the Dominican case, deployment of U.S. forces to Grenada went smoothly, by both sea and air, while the great advantages of strategic air mobility for the movement of troops and initial supplies by air were again dramatically demonstrated. The forces selected for the operation were suitable for the tasks visualized and were generally deployed in the optimum sequence. In both cases, army civil affairs and psychological operations units proved invaluable in critical nonmilitary aspects of the situation. One failure to learn from the Dominican experience, however, was that military police units were not given priority of movement to Grenada; hence, infantry troops had to handle captured Cubans and help Grenadian authorities control the populace, predictable tasks for which MPs are far more suited.

Command of the U.S. forces ashore was handled differently in the two cases. In the Dominican Republic, a commander of all U.S. forces ashore was designated shortly after the intervention began. A logical and sensible arrangement, this worked well. In Grenada, in contrast, no overall commander ashore was designated; instead, the joint task force commander, a vice admiral, U.S. Navy, whose headquarters was afloat, retained operational control of all forces in the operational area, including all ground forces ashore. Moreover, differing views arose with respect to the timing, sequence, and relative urgency of subsequent operations after the landings on the island. This led to some confusion as to who was in charge on the ground, as well as delay in carrying out the mission—a situation that would have been avoided had a commander ashore been designated.

In both interventions the U.S. armed forces performed exceptionally well. Despite some shortcomings of the Grenada operation singled out by critics and armchair strategists, the fundamental fact is that the overall mission was accomplished successfully. Moreover, throughout their stay, U.S. forces conducted themselves in such an exemplary manner that the Grenadian people simply begged the United States to let the troops stay.[6]

In both instances, too, the size of the force committed was adequate to carry out the job visualized and confirmed the wisdom of not sending a boy to do a man's job. Moreover, the number of troops was reduced as rapidly as circumstances would allow, marines being withdrawn first and army troops left to complete the job. In Grenada, all combat forces were withdrawn by December 1983; a small U.S. military support group remained until mid-June 1985, when the U.S. military presence on Grenada was terminated. Concurrently, the Caribbean Peacekeeping Force departed the island. In both interventions, the U.S. and inter-American presence lasted about a year and a half.

With respect to Grenada, one major controversy—and a bona fide one—was the decision to exclude the press at the beginning of the operation. In 1965, as already chronicled above, journalists had arrived in Santo Domingo days ahead of U.S. troops, and relations between the press and U.S. forces during the Dominican affair were, at best, strained. A primary reason for the prohibition in Grenada, however, was to preserve secrecy. But on the day before the invasion the Grenadian press reported that the OCES, plus Jamaica and Barbados, were preparing for such an action; likewise, the diversion of U.S. marines en route to Lebanon and their arrival in Barbados had been widely reported. Surprise was not achieved—Cuban and Grenadian troops on the island were forewarned and ready[7]— and scores of journalists descended on Barbados beforehand.

Although U.S. uniformed personnel had heartily applauded the decision to shut out the press, TV networks and other national media denounced it. Secretary of Defense Weinberger tried to persuade the world that it was the doing of the JCS— but such a decision is a highly charged political one and is not the prerogative of the military, especially in the United States. Some time later the Department of Defense acknowledged that it had been a mistake, and appointed a distinguished group of Americans to study the issue. Defense accepted the panel's recommendation that in future operations a small group of selected press representatives be allowed to accompany U.S. forces and share the news stories on a pool basis. More significantly, the panel noted the deep division and mistrust existing between the military and the media, urging that both sides take steps to foster better mutual understanding and improved relations. I heartily second that motion. But the unhappy memories of Vietnam run deep within the armed forces, and it may take years to overcome old animosities that have a life of their own.

Be that as it may, in a political-military sense, the two island interventions have much in common. Both presidents acted to preempt an undesirable takeover that might cause further instability in the critical Caribbean region. Each decision was aided by the estimate that the political-economic-military costs would probably be outweighed by the favorable effects of the intervention. Both presidents were also motivated by personal nightmares: Johnson by the fear of a second Cuba; Reagan by the fear of another Iranian hostage situation. In both instances the rush of events forced the executive branch to reach a timely decision and not allow enough time for congressional opposition to build. Legitimacy was a problem in both cases, but agile diplomacy limited the damage, and the presence of endangered Americans made intervention easier to defend, especially at home.

Another significant event in the Caribbean during Reagan's tenure was the downfall of the last of the old-time dictatorial dynasties when president-for-life Jean-Claude Duvalier ("Baby Doc") fled Port-Au-Prince, Haiti, in February 1986. Violent and disputed elections have been held since, but a civilian government has yet to take over and survive. To date, an unstable political climate and a deplorable economy remain in Haiti.

United States interests in the Caribbean Basin today go beyond the question of the country's participation in the specific events outlined here. The Caribbean region is truly vital to the U.S. economy and defense because through it pass many of the lifelines that sustain the nation in peace and would be essential to any prosecution of war. Through the Gulf of Mexico and the Caribbean Sea pass 55 percent of the crude oil the United States uses and 45 percent of its imports and exports; in the event of hostilities in NATO Europe or the Persian Gulf, 60 percent of reinforcements and supplies needed to conduct operations would transit these waters. In addition to crude oil, the United States is also heavily dependent on the Caribbean Basin for refined petroleum products, especially from the Dutch Antilles, Trinidad, Venezuela, and the Bahamas. Moreover, the Caribbean is important as either a source or a transit route for such vital minerals as manganese, nickel, bauxite, and iron ore.[8]

Traditionally, the United States has been the major trading partner of the nations of the Caribbean and all of Latin America, and that trade has been growing rapidly, even though the U.S. share—particularly in South America—has been declining steadily. And as the United States consumes its own natural resources, it needs not only raw materials but also finished and manufactured goods and even foodstuffs from Latin America. The complex interdependence developing between the United States and the nations of the Caribbean Basin involves not only trade policy but such related matters as energy policy, problems of environmental pollution, immigration and migrant worker policies, and the international battle against the organized drug traffic between continents.[9]

In addition, there are political-military matters that affect the hemisphere strategically. The Panama Canal, for example, although not as important to commerce as it has been in the past, remains one of the world's major maritime choke points, and in the context of its relationship to the Caribbean Basin it must still be considered to be of overall vital concern to the United States.

On the economic side, the United States is still the major user; Japan is next, and the largest single trade route through the canal is that between Japan and the U.S. east coast. The canal is also of major importance to the trade of Latin American countries, and about 5 percent of all international trade uses it. If it were closed the effect on Panama's economy and future would be disastrous because steady income from the canal is essential to Panama's economic existence. But markets, routes, and trading partners would adjust over time without any severe effect on the United States; therefore, in a strictly economic sense, the canal is by no means vital to the United States.

Militarily, the canal was important through World War II because all U.S. warships could pass through it. But with the advent of aircraft carriers that are too wide for the locks, although all other classes of U.S. naval vessels still travel the waterway, the canal has lost much of its usefulness. Moreover, its three sets of locks are vulnerable to air or missile attack and, to a lesser extent, sabotage, especially in times of civil unrest. Given its vulnerability and inability to handle the big carriers, then, the canal in its present state is not vital to U.S. defense.[10]

In a broader context, however, the area formerly called the Canal Zone continues to serve as an important strategic forward site for the support of U.S. activities in any crisis affecting national interest anywhere in the Caribbean Basin or South America. U.S. activities and facilities within the canal area have been much reduced in recent years; the navy possesses only limited facilities and the air force maintains a presence at Howard Air Force Base, leaving only the army with any sizable force—a reinforced infantry brigade. There is also the headquarters of U.S. Southern Command, the unified command responsible for the planning and supervision of U.S. security assistance to all the nations of mainland Latin America.[11] But by the end of 1999 this headquarters, all U.S. forces, and all U.S. military activities in the canal area will have been withdrawn and relocated elsewhere because under the Panama Canal treaty the United States will then cease to have any base rights within the area—a parlous prospect, I believe, given the situation in Panama today. Clearly, the United States could not, upon its withdrawal, tolerate the entry of Soviet/Cuban forces or significant numbers of Soviet/Cuban advisers, or the establishment of Soviet/Cuban bases.

In sum, while the canal's economic importance, its military utility, and the usefulness of the readily available base complex in the area taken singly may not be critical to the United States, these factors in the aggregate constitute a valuable asset that could not be replaced without significant tangible and intangible costs that might not be acceptable to the United States.

Within the broader perspective of worldwide realities, although the United States is still the number-one superpower in an overall sense, other power centers are gaining in an economic sense: Japan is clearly number two; western Europe, led by West Germany, is number three. No longer can the United States conduct such great and noble undertakings as the Marshall Plan; it simply lacks the resources, having squandered them over the years—the readiest evidence being the present enormous budget and trade deficits. The country has no choice but to restore its economic health at home and reorder its priorities of effort abroad.[12]

Others have emphasized the point that national security can be no stronger than a nation's economy. Walt W. Rostow, President Johnson's national security adviser in the 1960s, was recently asked what he would do differently now in that position. His reply in part was, "I would try to assure that the state of the domestic economy and the nation's economic position on the world scene were treated as the single most important aspect of national security policy, both within the government and in expositions to the Congress and the public." He held this view, he added, because he "had no faith that over time a democracy such as ours would be able to protect its vital interests and meet its responsibilities in the world scene if we [the United States] did not pay our way in the world."[13]

There is increasing recognition, too, of a growing economic and environmental interdependence among the nations of the world that is eroding national autonomy. One result is the intertwining of the foreign and domestic affairs of nation-states as their private sectors become more and more internationalized in order to survive in a global commercial and financial marketplace. As the dean of Georgetown University's School of Foreign Service, Peter F. Krogh, put it, "To a degree unprecedented in world history, businessmen, by decisions of where to locate, and financiers, by decisions of where to place money, are shaping national economic destinies independent of national dictates. . . . A profound and promising development is the recognition in the world's power centers that a country's fortunes in the 21st century will depend on domestic reforms in the balance of the 20th century. This recognition has been accompanied by an unprecedented acceptance of interdependence . . . [that] requires a new brand of international relations. . . . It might be labeled 'pursuing national interests through international cooperation.' "[14]

Within the Communist world, the Soviet Union, China, and other nations have openly questioned their own state-run, tightly closed economic systems and are not only experimenting with various aspects of western capitalism, but also seeking large amounts of capital from the West to shore up their stagnated economies. In addition, Soviet leader Mikhail Gorbachev has launched a political offensive, announcing unilateral reductions in Soviet armed forces, making proposals to reduce East-West tensions, and proposing specific, phased reductions in the forces of both sides in the NATO-Warsaw Pact area. Coupled with American pressures for more NATO "burden-sharing" and unilateral U.S. troop withdrawals from Europe, Gorbachev's challenges have captured the attention of governments and peoples alike on both sides of the East-West confrontation. Some, such as the renowned scholar George F. Kennan, have concluded that Gorbachev's bold and embattled policies, both internal and external, are ending the revolutionary epoch in Russia that began in 1917 and that the Cold War is dead. Although he recognizes that the situation in Moscow is unstable and in some ways dangerous, Kennan believes that it is "quite impossible" for the Soviet Union to turn back to previous policies. In sum, he believes that a breakup of the Soviet system of power is taking place and that the Soviet Union should no longer be regarded primarily as a possible, if not probable, military opponent. Rather, he feels, the Soviet Union should now be treated essentially as another great power whose differences with the United States should be adjusted through normal peaceful processes.[15]

Be that as it may, it seems clear that Gorbachev's initiatives, both foreign and domestic, as set forth in his concepts of *glasnost* and *perestroika*, are largely motivated by the realization that the Communist/Marxist economic system is not working in the Soviet Union or anywhere else. The system cannot compete with the West's major economic power centers and has failed to better the lot of the peoples involved.

In the next few years, assuming that Gorbachev and his "new broom" survive, extraordinary opportunities may allow the United States, among other things, to reduce its defense burden and rationalize its regional priorities abroad, steps that should help in a major way to restore its national economic health. By far the largest U.S. commitment worldwide is to NATO, involving forward deployed U.S. forces in the North Atlantic, Europe, and the Mediterranean, as well as backup forces in the United States. Although all U.S. services are concerned, the largest elements are army and tactical air elements of the air force.

A former supreme commander of NATO forces (1969-1974),

retired U.S. Army General Andrew J. Goodpaster, has recently proposed bringing half of the U.S. forces home from Europe by the mid-1990s under a negotiated cutback of NATO and Warsaw Pact military strength.[16] If major reductions in NATO force levels can be negotiated with the Soviets, Goodpaster noted in the Atlantic Council study, it could be an opportunity to turn over greater, if not primary, responsibility to Western Europe for its defense, and allow the United States to assume more of a supporting role "as was envisaged by Gen. Eisenhower and others at NATO's beginning."[17]

Recognizing that current NATO proposals to cut force levels and the numbers of major weapons categories in both NATO and Warsaw Pact forces did not take into account a rapidly changing East-West situation,[18] President George Bush in May 1989 proposed a reduction of 30,000 U.S. combat forces in Europe, bringing the U.S. total down to 275,000, while the Soviet Union would have to reduce its forces in Europe to the same figure. He further proposed specific lower ceilings for the numbers of conventional weapons on each side in such categories as tanks and combat aircraft. These proposals were generally well received at the May NATO summit and were welcomed by the Soviet leader, Gorbachev.[19]

For many years, in lists of areas in the western world considered most important to the national interests of the United States, the NATO region—the North Atlantic, Western Europe, and the Mediterranean—has retained top priority. Latin America and the rest of the Third World, with a few exceptions, have generally placed last. In between, generally in a descending order of regional priority, have been Northeast Asia, including Japan and South Korea, and the western Pacific; the Arab-Israeli confrontation area, including North Africa; the Persian Gulf, the Horn of Africa, the eastern Indian Ocean, and the subcontinent of Asia; Taiwan; and Southeast Asia, including the Philippines and Indonesia.[20]

In my view, the United States should make a fundamental and major change in its evaluation of which regions of the West are most important to its national interests. Because of its overall stature and relative worth in the Western Hemisphere, the

NATO area should continue to enjoy the highest support and interest of the United States, particularly in light of possibly momentuous change in Eastern Europe. In the Far East and western Pacific, the East-West situation seems to be stabilizing, but the conflict areas of the Middle East, the Persian Gulf, and the Near East will continue to require close attention. The Western Hemisphere, however, is of even more direct, basic interest to the United States; clearly, setbacks in this region affect the status of the United States as a great power far more than in some other parts of the globe. In its own self-interest the United States must preserve the strategic integrity of the Western Hemisphere and cannot afford to allow further unfriendly penetration of the region. The hour is late in Latin America, especially in the Caribbean Basin, where many Western-oriented nations are struggling for their very survival. South America, on the other hand, is more remote from the United States and with such well-endowed countries as Brazil, Argentina, and Chile, is in a more self-sufficient position.

For these and other reasons already presented, the Caribbean Basin, in my opinion, should be considered second to none as a regional priority for U.S. attention, at least on a par with Western Europe. This reordering of regional priorities can and should start immediately and is not dependent on developments affecting U.S. interests in other regions of the world. The resources required are very small compared with what the United States devotes to other regions.[21]

Yet in this hemisphere the United States is in a weaker position today than it was in the 1960s when U.S. dominance—political, economic, cultural, and military—was overwhelming. U.S. foreign assistance has declined; USAID, military, and other missions have been drastically reduced; and American businesses have cut back their activities. Although the United States is still the dominant military power in the hemisphere, its overall presence has decreased. The one major foreign aid program for the area, the Caribbean Basin Initiative, has been badly hurt by its trade provisions, as protectionist sentiments rise in the United States.[22]

Concurrently, some Latin American countries have increasingly perceived a need to diversify their trade partners and to seek non-U.S. ties. This new assertiveness is found in Central America—witness the current peace plan developed by Latin American leaders—and is especially pertinent in the case of Mexico. A political dynamism, motivated by a nationalistic spirit, not heretofore seen to such a degree now exists in the Caribbean.[23] The political nonalignment movement among Third World nations has also affected inter-American relations, especially since Caribbean states such as Cuba, Mexico, and Venezuela each considers itself a leader in the movement, not just one among many.

Regrettably, the stature, role, and level of activity of the OAS have changed for the worse since the 1960s. In the 1980s the organization has had to reduce its budget, staff, and functions. The once almost exclusively Hispanic OAS is being joined by more English-speaking countries, which has broadened the OAS base but has also weakened the unity of its voice, because Spanish-speaking and English-speaking members do not always agree.[24] From the U.S. point of view, however, the OAS is still important because such a regional institution is far more amenable to friendly persuasion than is a global institution like the UN, where the United States now represents a lonely minority in the General Assembly.

While U.S. leverage and presence have noticeably decreased in the Caribbean Basin, the entry into the area of other foreign nations to fill the vacuum is even more evident. Japan, western European nations, Canada, and Israel are prominent new "players."[25] But the most ominous reality for the United States is the penetration of the Soviet Union into this hemisphere, particularly in Cuba and Nicaragua in the Caribbean Basin.

Cuba is a major Soviet military base with extensive air and naval facilities, powerful communications installations, the largest Soviet electronic intercept station in the world outside the Soviet Union, and a combat brigade to protect Soviet equities. Long-range Soviet military aircraft can gather sensitive intelligence concerning vital U.S. installations located along the Atlantic and Gulf coasts and can land in Cuba without overflying U.S. airspace.

On the mainland the Soviets have made Nicaragua the dominant military power in Central America, turning Corinto on the Pacific coast into a modern naval base and building a similar one on the Atlantic coast. From a major military airbase, near the Pacific side, now under construction, Soviet long-range aircraft will be able to fly intelligence missions against sensitive U.S. installations on the Pacific coast without over-flying U.S. airspace.

Finally, Nicaragua, like Cuba, serves as a base for organizing, training, and supplying insurgents to be introduced secretly into Caribbean countries from Guatemala to Columbia for the purpose of subverting constitutionally elected governments. Mexico, apparently because of its strong support for the Sandinista government in Nicaragua, has not as yet become a target of such hostile intent but might well be so in the future. Moreover, Mexico's political climate, stable over the last six decades, now faces an uncertain future.

It seems clear that if the United States as a nation and a people wants to remain a respected superpower and an admired leader of the free world, North Americans can no longer think that "it can't happen here," that the United States is too strong to be bothered with the petty problems caused by small-time dictators in the Caribbean. The Caribbean is not only very close but also of vital importance, and conditions within many Caribbean countries both threaten the stability of their own region and affect U.S. "domestic tranquillity" in a profound way. Surely it is in the best interest of the United States to do everything it can to improve the political, economic, and social well-being of its southern neighbors. A fresh look at U.S. policies in the Caribbean is urgently needed, giving special consideration to Latin American views and sensibilities.

Interrelated problem areas must be reexamined together: for example, Hispanic immigration to and migrant workers in the United States. As a matter of practicality, how much control can the United States exercise over such movements of people? Since the late 1970s a rapid and massive flow of Central American peoples to the United States has been under way, hundreds of thousands each year fleeing Nicaragua, El Salvador, Honduras, and Guatemala, and seeking refuge in the United States. Although many are trying to escape civil war and repression, the basic and enduring cause for the flight is overpopulation and poverty. Caribbean nations such as Jamaica, Puerto Rico, the Dominican Republic, and Haiti have long experienced a similar loss of population to the United States.[26]

Along the roughly 2,000-mile border that separates the United States and Mexico, a remarkable process of local economic and social integration between the two countries has been going on for many years. About ten million Mexicans reside in the United States, while large numbers of retired Americans live in Mexico, and hundreds of thousands of people on each side of the border have relatives on the other side. Daily many thousands of Mexicans cross legally to work on jobs on the U.S. side, the busiest crossing being between San Ysidro, California, and Tiajuana, Mexico, where 50,000 pass every day, with the El Paso, Texas–Juarez, Mexico, crossing a close second. In addition, an unknown number, believed to be considerable, daily cross illegally. A strip on the U.S. side is being gradually "Mexicanized," giving rise to the slang expression "Tex-Mex." Some commentators call the border area "Mex-America," one writer predicting that by the year 2000 Mex-America could become the dominant and most populous region on the North American continent. Another scholar predicts that if the American fertility rate remains low and immigration remains high, all population growth in the United States will soon come from immigration and that within twenty years California and Texas will no longer have majority populations, while "Anglos," Hispanics (the most rapidly growing ethnic group in the United States), blacks, and Asians will all be minorities.[27] Such possible developments pose some basic questions: What are the implications for the future? What is being done in the way of planning for the resulting Mex-America?

An even more far-reaching problem for the United States and its southern neighbors is the international drug trade that originates in the Caribbean Basin: current measures are failing; destroying drug-producing crops is counterproductive; and all the police and armed forces of the world could not stop the flow of drugs across U.S. borders. Are there any solutions other than the education of future generations?

Obviously, these direct sociological connections between the United States and countries of the Caribbean Basin have enormous significance for the future of all the nations concerned. Likewise, the geopolitical aims of the Soviet Union with respect to the Basin and the entire Western Hemisphere are of great import. Gorbachev's unprecedented visit to Cuba in early April 1989 and his discussions with Cuban leader Fidel Castro, the substance of which has become publicly known, throw new light on this question.

In overall terms, Gorbachev indicated his support for détente with the West, including reducing tensions and armaments in Europe as well as continuing to pursue negotiations on strategic nuclear weapons. He regarded the resolution of regional conflicts as the "most immediate task" facing the two superpowers. Castro, on the other hand, bluntly informed Gorbachev of his doubts about Moscow's détente with Washington and said he would continue to take a hard line with the United States.[28]

Speaking of the Western Hemisphere, Gorbachev said that the Soviets are "not seeking political or military advantages in this hemisphere," while Castro emphasized that he directed Cuba's foreign policy, independently of the Soviet Union, and did not necessarily follow Moscow's lead. Gorbachev implicitly played down Cuba's importance in the overall Soviet scheme of things by looking forward to new relations with what he called the "giants of the future" on the continent, such as Brazil and Argentina, where good trade prospects lie.[29]

Gorbachev also tried hard to persuade Castro to embrace *glasnost* and *perestroika*, but Castro rejected both concepts out of hand, emphasizing that what was good for the Soviet Union might not be appropriate for Cuba. Although other Soviet officials stated that Gorbachev would not reduce Soviet aid to Cuba (estimated at $6 billion a year), they said that Moscow seeks a "gradual balance of its economic ties with Cuba."[30]

Although he praised Castro as a great revolutionary hero, Gorbachev spoke forcefully about his opposition to the export of revolution, saying, "We are against doctrines that endorse the export of revolution or counterrevolution." (Other Soviet officials pointed out that the Cuban revolution had its own local roots.) Castro, however, restated Cuba's right to support revolutionary movements in the region because the United States supports counterrevolutionaries, specifically in Nicaragua.[31]

With respect to Nicaragua, Gorbachev reiterated his support of Esquipulas II, the Central American peace plan authored by President Oscar Arias of Costa Rica, and denounced the recently approved $40 million nonmilitary U.S. aid package for Nicaraguan contras. He emphasized that he would not halt military aid to Nicaragua so long as the United States continues to supply military aid to its allies in the region. On 29 March 1989, before the Havana Summit, President George Bush in a letter had urged Gorbachev to end aid for the Sandinista regime in Managua—roughly $1 billion annually, half in arms and half in economic aid—and cooperate with Central American peace efforts. President Arias hailed Bush's action and challenged both Gorbachev and Castro to abandon support of guerrilla insurgencies in Central America in favor of diplomacy and negotiation.[32]

Where does the United States stand with regard to Nicaragua and the Central American peace plan? Although the United States does not intend to let the present impasse affect U.S.-Soviet relations in other matters, the prospects for improving U.S. relations with Cuba and Nicaragua are not good. The United States has pointed out that there are no legitimate security issues for the Soviets in the Western Hemisphere as there are for the United States. Rejecting "the idea of equivalence between legitimate U.S. interests and Soviet presence" in the region, the United States has held that U.S. aid to democratic governments is not in the same category as Soviet aid because the democratic nations, unlike Nicaragua and Cuba, are "not involved in subversion of their neighbors."[33]

The fact remains, however, that Nicaragua is the dominant military power in Central America, its modern armed forces larger than those of all the other countries in the area combined, and continues to receive $500 million in arms annually from the Soviet Union. The contra military threat to the Sandinista government no longer exists, and it is extremely doubtful that the United States will resurrect it, the Bush administration and the Congress having agreed to humanitarian aid only. On the other hand, both Nicaragua and Cuba continue to provide military aid to the rebels fighting against the government of El Salvador, and Nicaragua substantially increased its direct aid to insurgents in El Salvador after the United States stopped military aid to the contras—one major reason why the situation in El Salvador deteriorated in 1988-1989. Thus, President Daniel Ortega of Nicaragua holds a strong political and military position, albeit a desperate economic one, and has no need to "democratize" Nicaragua, other than through lip service, but can look forward to the promised "free" elections in 1990.

What can the United States do? For the time being at least, it is committed to support Esquipulus II and can only hope for the best, having apparently ruled out any use, or threat of use, of force against the Sandinista regime. One great advantage of the Central American peace plan is that it is a Latin American one, rather than one imposed by North American *Yanquis*, thus enhancing political, psychological, and moral support for the position taken by the United States. But if the peace plan fails, the situation deteriorates further, and severe civil disorders occur in Nicaragua, the United States must consider other measures.

The American people have no enthusiasm for a U.S. invasion, which would no doubt be denounced by friends and foes alike and would play into the hands of Ortega, who would say that this was the U.S. intention in the first place. But there is another military option that might be considered if all else fails: a U.S. naval quarantine of Nicaragua, physically preventing the delivery of more arms from the Soviet Union or Cuba, similar to the quarantine of Cuba imposed by President Kennedy in October 1962. It would involve U.S. naval and air forces operating on both the Atlantic and the Pacific side of Nicaragua. This move would also help in the interdiction of military aid flowing from Nicaragua and Cuba to insurgents operating in

El Salvador. U.S. aims would be to stabilize the situation in Central America, put a cap on Nicaragua's military capabilities, and discourage Nicaraguan and Cuban export of aid to insurgent forces operating against other Central American countries. Such a quarantine runs little risk of escalation. The United States can still dominate the sea and air space in the region, Cuba lacks the capability to oppose our operations, and the Soviet Union is not in a position to challenge the United States in the Caribbean, the "American Mediterranean." Moreover, it would not be in the Soviet Union's interest to do anything more than protest for fear of jeopardizing more urgent and important things on its agenda. Such a U.S. action, openly announced to the world in advance, should finally convince Gorbachev and other Soviet leaders that the United States will no longer tolerate Soviet meddling in the Western Hemisphere.

Another potentially intolerable situation for the United States in the Caribbean concerns Panama, where U.S. governmental blunders of the recent past have weakened the U.S. position, have placed U.S. forces and citizens in the Canal area in harm's way, have hurt the Panamanian economy and American businessmen there, and have been costly to the Panamanian people. Unfortunately, despite U.S. economic sanctions, Panama's military strongman, General Manuel Antonio Noriega, together with his government and his power base, the Panamanian Defense Forces (PDF), became stronger than ever. Violence against American military personnel, their families, and other U.S. citizens escalated during 1988 and early 1989—harassment, intimidation, detention without charge, interference with school buses carrying American children, interference with U.S. troop movements, and outright physical assaults were committed by the PDF, which functions as both uniformed military and police. Employees, both U.S. and Panamanian, of the Panama Canal Commission, which operates the Canal, were also victims of such abuse.[34]

Recognizing that its options were limited, the Bush administration decided to wait for the outcome of the 7 May Panamanian elections. Even before the event, numerous indications pointed to a rigged campaign of massive electoral fraud directed by Noriega's government with the aim of installing his hand-picked candidate for a five-year term.[35] After the election, the Panamanian government on 9 May began releasing election results based on returns described by foreign observers as fakes. On the same day, returning American observers, including former President Carter and a bipartisan congressional group, reported that the opposition had won by a three-to-one margin but that an enormous election "steal" was being manufactured by Noriega's forces. President Bush then promptly denounced the election and called on Gen. Noriega to resign.[36] The next day the Noriega-controlled Electoral Tribunal nullified the election, while Noriega's troops and paramilitary thugs brutally beat the opposition presidential candidate, Guillermo Endera, and an opposition vice presidential candidate, Guillermo (Billy) Ford. This violence was recorded by media cameras and was soon aired on TV networks all over the United States.[37]

Throughout the crisis the White House consulted closely with congressional leaders of both parties, who indicated their firm support of the U.S. position as the situation rapidly escalated. Fearing for the safety of U.S. forces, their families, and other Americans in the area, the president directed that additional army and marine units, totaling about 2,000 in strength, be sent to reinforce the U.S. command in Panama and that service families and U.S. government employees living on the economy be move to protected American bases. Concurrently, the U.S. ambassador was recalled, leaving only essential personnel in the U.S. embassy. By 12 May the first contingents of army and marine reinforcements had arrived by air at Howard Air Force Base in the canal area, while endangered families and other Americans began moving onto U.S. military bases or returning to the United States. These moves were generally supported by U.S. officials, both civilian and military.[38]

Earlier the president had called on Latin American governments to join in condemning the elections and the violence, and by 12 May most had done so, while also warning the United States against military intervention. Meanwhile, other Western nations announced their firm support of the U.S. actions. On Sunday, 14 May, a statement by Panama's Roman Catholic bishops denouncing the fraud and violence connected with the elections was read at church services throughout the nation. The people welcomed it with enthusiastic approval before dispersing peacefully.[39] This action by the church may prove to have been of enormous consequence in resolving the situation peacefully.

President Bush also supported initiatives coming from Western Hemisphere governments to address the crisis through regional diplomacy. In order to clarify American intentions, he stated unequivocally that the United States would continue to abide by the Panama Canal Treaty.[40] As a result of an urgent appeal from Venezuelan President Carlos Andres Perez, the OAS foreign ministers met in Washington on 17 May and adopted a resolution condemning Noriega for electoral fraud. The OAS also sent to Panama the foreign ministers of Ecuador, Guatemala, and Trinidad, assisted by OAS Secretary General Joao Baena Soares of Brazil, to persuade Noriega to surrender power to civilian rule on 1 September 1989. Rebuffed by Noriega, the ministers reported back to the OAS on 6 July, and their mission was extended to 19 July. As of this writing, the chances for success appear to be slim. Nevertheless, the OAS efforts increase the political, moral, and psychological pressures on Gen. Noriega and further isolate him from Western democracies. In addition, such hemispheric efforts to defend beleaguered democracies in the region will help restore the sagging prestige of the OAS not only in the eyes of Latin America but also throughout the Free World.[41]

At this juncture, however, the OAS finds itself at its lowest ebb in its forty-one-year history, its financial situation so precarious that even after further personnel cuts early in 1989, it lacks sufficient funds to meet its reduced payroll this summer. This stems from frustrations with the OAS that have caused the United States, which has been paying for two-thirds of the OAS budget, to withold most of its dues, its arrears now amounting to over $50 million. U.S. dissatisfaction has been caused primarily by OAS insistence that a policy of nonintervention be the cornerstone of its actions affecting member states. Thus the OAS is extremely reluctant to support U.S.

proposals to take action against one of its members, as for example, Nicaragua. In any event, the Panamanian problem may not be solved at the OAS, although it is encouraging to note that Mexico, strongly on the side of nonintervention, has publicly blasted Noriega, thus denying him one of his few remaining sources of diplomatic support in Latin America.[42]

In my opinion, the president, in responding to the crisis in a measured, firm way after broad consultations, keeping the American people and other nations informed, is on the right track. Moreover, he has demonstrated that he understands the relationship between diplomacy and force and has skilfully orchestrated U.S. actions designed to bring about the desired end as peacefully as possible. For the moment, the prospects seem fair that the current impasse can be resolved without resort to military force. An early resolution, however, is highly desirable. Although control of the canal is supposed to pass to Panama at noon on 31 December 1999, the United States does not have the luxury of a decade to resolve the Noriega problem. At the beginning of 1990 the United States administrator of the canal is due to be replaced by a Panamanian, who must be approved by the U.S. Senate, which might reject any candidate nominated by a Noriega-controlled government unless the United States finds a way to finesse the situation.[43] Thus the United States still has a rocky road ahead, and before it is all over, stronger military moves, which will surely strain U.S.–Latin American relations, may become necessary.

Over the longer term, the problem of the final U.S. withdrawal from Panama at the end of the century is even more serious for the United States than the present contretemps. In my opinion, the political and psychological effect of such a total U.S. departure, after almost a century of continuous and substantial presence, will adversely affect the prestige and stature of the United States worldwide. Specifically, the lack of base rights in the area beginning in the year 2000, only a little over ten years away, will make it virtually impossible for the United States to keep the canal continuously operational after that date. Moreover, the absence of such base rights in the canal area will limit the ability of the United States to protect its interests in the larger Caribbean Basin. Once the Noriega problem is settled, the United States must sooner or later broach the subject with the Panamanian government and propose an amendment to the treaty that would allow minimal base rights and a small U.S. presence in the canal area. As a quid pro quo, the United States should offer to finance needed improvements of the canal that Panama cannot at present afford, or to reimburse Panama with an annual fee for the exercise of these base rights.

In this connection, it is interesting to note that the initial problem faced by the United States in the Dominican Republic in 1965, Grenada in 1983, and Panama in 1989 was the protection of U.S. citizens who were endangered. The protection of a state's own nationals in a foreign land has long been recognized as a legitimate, humanitarian act under international law. Since the taking of American hostages in Iran in 1979, an event that contributed significantly to President Carter's defeat in the 1980 U.S. elections, American presidents have become acutely aware of the political pitfalls connected with hostage taking. Reagan was well aware of this possibility in Grenada, and Bush likewise was undoubtedly influenced by this factor. In this age of international terrorism, the hostage nightmare will no doubt figure prominently in future presidential decisions with respect to international crises.

In the meantime, the United States must take steps to refurbish its historic special relationship with Latin America, especially the Caribbean region, and to revitalize the OAS, another urgent project to address being the Haitian problem. Any fresh approach on the part of the United States should be founded on a better and more sympathetic understanding of Latin American traditions and customs, as well as a sincere desire to develop mutual understanding and respect. Latin American instincts as to what is acceptable, what will work, and what will not in a Latin American environment are a good deal better than American judgments. On the economic side, trade rather than aid should be stressed, along with American initiatives to increase nontraditional exports from Caribbean region countries.[44] On the societal and cultural side, the United

States needs to expand its cultural exchange, language, and area studies programs. Non-Hispanic Americans need to know more about Latin America. There is no better way to accomplish this than by learning to speak and read Spanish.

Most thinking Americans have come to realize what a dangerous world we live in—a world haunted by the specter of nuclear war and unstoppable environmental pollution, a world held hostage by terrorists. How to survive in such a world and yet retain the traditions of a free people who respect law and human rights—this is the key question. In my view, all the more reason to provide for a more secure American homeland through the concept of an extended family of nations in the hemisphere, a region that encompasses Canada, the United States, Mexico, Central America, and the rest of the Caribbean Basin, and a region that is united by many ties of history as well as by common bonds of heritage.

This is not a "Fortress America" mentality nor an isolationist point of view. Such concepts are a thing of the past. The world is far too interdependent and the multinational aspects of today's financial, business, and industrial communities are too well developed to allow such a retreat. Nevertheless, forging stronger and more enduring links among the nations of this North American–Caribbean region can result in a stronger extended homeland for the peoples concerned, based on a mutually beneficial community of interests.

Glossary of Acronyms

AID	See USAID
ASA	Army Security Agency
AUSA	Association of the U.S. Army
C-1	assistant chief of staff, personnel, HQ, IAPF
C-2	assistant chief of staff, intelligence, HQ, IAPF
C-3	assistant chief of staff, operations, HQ, IAPF
C-4	assistant chief of staff, logistics, HQ, IAPF
C-5	assistant chief of staff, civil affairs, HQ, IAPF
C-6	assistant chief of staff, communications, HQ, IAPF
CBS	Columbia Broadcasting System
CEFA	Armed Forces Training Center
CIA	Central Intelligence Agency
CINCLANT	Commander in Chief, Atlantic Command
CINCSOUTH	Commander in Chief, U.S. Southern Command
CINCSTRIKE	Commander in Chief, U.S. Strike Command
CNO	Chief of Naval Operations
CP	command post
DCSOPS	deputy chief of staff for operations
DOD	Department of Defense
DZ	drop zone
FBI	Federal Bureau of Investigations
FIP	Fuerza Inter-Americana de Paz [IAPF]
GNR	Government of National Reconstruction
HQ	headquarters
IAF	Inter-American Force [renamed IAPF]
IAPF	Inter-American Peace Force [See also FIP]
IG	inspector general
IMF	International Monetary Fund
ISZ	International Security Zone
JCS	Joint Chiefs of Staff [U.S.]
JIB	Joint Information Bureau
LA	Latin America

LANTCOM	Atlantic Command [U.S.]
LAW	light antitank weapon
MAAG	Military Assistance and Advisory Group
MEB	Marine expeditionary brigade
MP	military police
MPD	Dominican Popular Movement [Maoist in outlook]
NSA	National Security Agency
NSC	National Security Council
OAS	Organization of American States
OCES	Organization of Eastern Caribbean States
OEA	Organizacion de Estados Americanos [OAS]
1J4	14th of June party [Castroite—named after an aborted Cuban invasion of the Dominican Republic on 14 June 1959; also known as the APCJ]
OPCON	operational control
OPLAN	operations plan
OPSDEPS	Operations Deputies [the group of five 3-star officers, consisting of the Director of the Joint Staff and the DCSOPS of the services, that meet regularly to handle matters of lesser importance for the JCS]
PCD	Partido Communista Dominicano [Communist party]
PIO	public information officer
PR	Partido Reformista [Reform party]
PRD	Partido Revolucionario Dominicano [Revolutionary party]
PSYOPS	psychological operations
PSYWAR	psychological warfare
R&R	rest and recreation
SAC	Strategic Air Command
SEALS	special operations forces [U.S. Navy]
SIM	Dominican Secret Police [during Trujillo era]
SOUTHCOM	U.S. Southern Command
SSO	Special Security Office [special communications elements used on a high-level personal basis for sensitive messages, often called "back channel" messages]
STRICOM	U.S. Strike Command
TAC	Tactical Air Command
UN	United Nations
USAF	United States Air Force
USAID	U.S. Agency for International Development
USIS	United States Information Service
USMC	United States Marine Corps

Notes

Prologue

1. Greenberg, *U.S. Army Unilateral and Coalition Operations*, p. 22.

2. Other civilian secretaries of uncommon ability and dedication with whom I have had the privilege to serve include Vivian Greene, Office of the Vice Chief of Staff, U.S. Army (Mrs. Greene served with distinction for over twenty-five years, providing continuity between the tours of fourteen successive vice chiefs); Margaret Norris, Office of the Deputy Chief of Staff for Operations and then Office of the Chief of Staff, U.S. Army; Aubrey Newman and Peggy Bisek, Office of the Secretary of the General Staff; Jean Harris, Office of the Deputy Commandant, U.S. Army War College, Carlisle Barracks, Pennsylvania; Ruby Campen, Office of the Commanding General, XVIII Airborne Corps, Fort Bragg; Eunice Perry, HQ U.S. 8th Army in Korea; and Betty Dinova, Office of the Commander-in-Chief, U.S. Readiness Command, MacDill Air Force Base, Florida.

3. Johnson, *Vantage Point*, pp. 199-201; Poole, "Dominican Intervention."

4. Later, I learned that General Wheeler wanted to promote Maj. Gen. Vernon P. ("Phil") Mock to three stars and make him the army's DCSOPS, the job I was holding at the time. This information confirmed my original suspicions that I was selected for the Dominican mission because I was "available" and my selection immediately created a choice spot for Wheeler's protégé. In retrospect, it was a good decision because Mock was an outstanding staff officer.

5. In the early 1970s Hardin was my deputy commander at HQ U.S. Readiness Command, a joint unified command at MacDill Air Force Base that succeeded the U.S. Strike Command in 1973 and had operational command of all army combat forces and air force tactical

units in the continental United States. With his command and staff experience, Hardin was admired in both army and air force.

1. Origins of the Revolution

1. Logan, *Haiti and the Dominican Republic,* pp. 14-17.

2. Langley, *Banana Wars,* pp. 149-54; Stephen M. Fuller and Graham A. Cosmas, "Marines in the Dominican Republic," pp. 49-51.

3. Fagg, *Cuba, Haiti, and the Dominican Republic,* pp. 157-65.

4. Greenberg, *U.S. Army Unilateral and Coalition Operations,* p. 24.

5. Beaulac et al., *Dominican Action—1965,* p. 4.

6. Johnson, *Vantage Point,* p. 187.

7. Beaulac et al., *Dominican Action—1965,* p. 8.

8. Greenberg, *U.S. Army Unilateral and Coalition Operations,* pp. 13-15.

9. Beaulac et al., "Dominican Action—1965," p. 17.

10. Today, however, unified command in the Caribbean is no longer divided, CINCLANT having been assigned complete responsibility for the region.

11. Greenberg, *U.S. Army Unilateral and Coalition Operations,* pp. 15-16.

12. Ibid., p. 17.

13. Ibid., pp. 17-18.

14. Walter Poole, *Dominican Intervention;* Yates, *Power Pack,* pp. 35-37.

15. Greenberg, *U.S. Army Unilateral and Coalition Operations,* pp. 18-20.

16. Bracey, *Resolution of the Dominican Crisis,* p. xv; Yates, *Power Pack,* pp. 44-45.

17. Greenberg, *U.S. Army Unilateral and Coalition Operations,* pp. 19-21.

18. In April 1966 Ambassador Bennett departed the Dominican Republic, having been replaced by John H. Crimmons. Bennett was then posted to the Air University at Maxwell Air Force Base, Alabama, as the university's political adviser, a sinecure after what he had been through in Santo Domingo. The assignment by no means indicated that he had been banished by State, but it was politically expedient because it did get Bennett at least temporarily out of the diplomatic mainstream until the Dominican affair cooled off. He returned to Washington with flying colors, serving with distinction for long periods in such positions as deputy to the U.S. representative to the

United Nations, U.S. ambassador to NATO, and the State Department's chief of legislative affairs.
19. Greenberg, *U.S. Army Unilateral and Coalition Operations,* pp. 32-35.
20. Ibid., pp. 33-34.
21. Ibid., pp. 34, 20-21.
22. Bracey, *Resolution of the Dominican Crisis,* p. xvi. Martin's efforts in the Dominican Republic are chronicled in his book *Overtaken By Events.*
23. Greenberg, *U.S. Army Unilateral and Coalition Operations,* pp. 62-64.
24. Ibid., pp. 21-23.

2. Initial U.S. Operations

1. Greenberg, *U.S. Army Unilateral and Coalition Operations,* pp. 23-24.
2. Ibid., pp. 35-36. To enhance the ability to conduct joint operations of the naval, marine, army, and air force elements earmarked for contingencies in the Caribbean, CINCLANT in 1964 began annual joint training and mobility exercises at sites in the southeastern United States and Puerto Rico. Similar exercises continue to the present time, normally involving naval forces from the Norfolk, Virginia, area, battalion-sized units from the 82d Airborne Division at Fort Bragg, and elements of the 3d Marine Division/Air Wing in the Camp LeJeune–Cherry Point area of North Carolina.
3. Ibid., pp. 36-39.
4. In August 1968, as vice chief of staff, U.S. Army, I selected Forrester (then a colonel) as my executive officer. Full of energy, smart, and aggressive, Forrester twice served in Vietnam with distinction, first as a brigade commander and then as an assistant division commander (a brigadier general slot). His later commands included the army's Recruiting Command during the transition period between the draft and the all-volunteer force, the 6th Army at the Presidio of San Francisco, the combined U.S.–Republic of Korea Field Army on the DMZ in Korea, and the Western Command in Hawaii. He retired in 1983.
5. Discussion with Lt. Col. Eldredge R. ("Rick") Long, 4 November 1986, at the National Defense University, Fort McNair, Washington, D.C. Long, commanding the 1st Battalion, 508th Airborne Infantry, had broken a leg in a parachute jump not long before the intervention

and was unable to join his battalion in the Dominican Republic until about midday, 30 April 1965, while it was establishing the Duarte bridgehead. He said that the Dominican commander of CEFA troops at the site had his men periodically fire at random into Santo Domingo, apparently just to stir things up. It was evident to Long that the Dominican soldiers were afraid of the rebels and had no intention of advancing into the city.

6. Greenberg, *U.S. Army Unilateral and Coalition Operations*, pp. 40-44.

7. Ibid., p. 65.

3. Stabilizing the Situation

1. Greenberg, *U.S. Army Unilateral and Coalition Operations*, pp. 49-50.

2. Ibid., pp. 50-51.

3. *Special Forces Operations Debrief*, pp. D2-D5. This paper is a good account of the special problems encountered in carrying out sensitive and clandestine missions during the Dominican crisis.

4. Bracey, *Resolution of the Dominican Crisis*, p. xvii.

5. Ibid., pp. xvii-xviii

6. Ibid., p. 1.

7. Alabaster, "The United States Commitment," dated July 1965, an unpublished case study of the U.S. military public information experience in Santo Domingo in the early days of the intervention (author's files), pp. 1-4.

8. Szulc, *Dominican Diary*.

9. Both Bennett and I testified during the hearings held in Washington in May 1971. Also testifying was the U.S. marine noncommissioned officer Corp. Gandia-Graulau, who had been in charge of the checkpoint where the shooting incident occurred. Afterward, he was approached outside the courtroom by Burt, who reportedly said in a friendly manner that he hoped any further meeting of the two would be under more pleasant circumstances. Gandia-Graulau responded, in effect, that if he met Burt under such circumstances again, he would make sure there were no survivors. Several spectators heard the exchange, including Burt's counsel, who recalled Burt to the stand and asked him about it; the testimony was allowed as relevant to the issue of whether the marines involved were "ill-disciplined, untrained, or immature." Besides confirming the old adage about getting your witnesses away from the courthouse as soon as possible, the incident

indicated the bitter animosity toward the press held by some marines. Needless to say, it did not help the government's case.

10. When I was invited to speak about the Dominican crisis at the meeting of the Association, U.S. Army (AUSA), in October 1965, General Wheeler sent me a back-channel message disapproving any such talk and telling me not even to come near Washington; the press, he implied, was in a foul mood about the Dominican affair. For the record, I eventually did speak on the subject at the 1966 AUSA meeting.

4. Creating the Inter-American Peace Force

1. "Dominican Crisis"; Greenberg, *U.S. Army Unilateral and Coalition Operations*, pp. 65-67.

2. Greenberg, *U.S. Army Unilateral and Coalition Operations*, pp. 67-68.

3. Ibid., p. 69.

4. Ibid., pp. 69-70.

5. Admiral McCain later commanded the U.S. Pacific Command with distinction. His son, a naval aviator, was shot down and captured in North Vietnam. After years as a POW in Hanoi, the younger McCain was elected as a Republican congressman from Arizona and is now serving as a U.S. Senator from that state.

6. According to Gen. Robert W. Porter, Jr., CINCSOUTH at the time, President Castello Branco of Brazil wanted Colonel Vernon A. ("Dick") Walters, U.S. Army, military attaché in Rio de Janeiro, to accompany General Alvim to the Dominican Republic. Branco was afraid that Alvim, an ardent rightist, would do something rash and felt that Walter's presence might be helpful. Alvim had served during World War II with the Brazilian Expeditionary Force that had fought in Italy; Walters was much admired by the Brazilians for his service as the liaison officer between the Brazilian forces and the allied command in the Mediterranean. Walters was an accomplished linguist but also outspoken in his anti-Communist and anti-Soviet views. State was concerned about his close connections with the Brazilian military, who where familiar with and accustomed to Brazilian-style military coups, and accordingly queried Bunker and Bennett, who asked for my reactions. Although I knew and admired Walters, I said I would prefer to get acquainted with Alvim on a one-on-one basis; inserting Walters, a man with an overpowering personality and strong personal views, into the picture would likely complicate my job. I pointed out, too, that assigning a senior American aide could give the impression

that Alvim was a U.S. puppet and add further fuel to the anti-U.S. propaganda campaign in Santo Domingo. Bunker and Bennett agreed, and Walters did not visit the Dominican Republic until well after Alvim had arrived. Walters never quite forgave us, but subsequent events demonstrated that we were right. With Walter's support, Alvim could have given us an even harder time on the occasions when he opposed actions proposed by the OAS and supported by the United States. (Walters later served with distinction as the U.S. ambassador to the United Nations during the Reagan administration.)

7. Gutierrez was later promoted to major general and for many years served as the Nicaraguan military attaché in Washington, where we renewed our Dominican association and became good friends. When the Sandinista revolutionaries began their final attack to overthrow the Somoza dictatorship, Gutierrez was Nicaragua's military attaché to Japan. During the belated efforts to find an acceptable *presidente* as an alternative to Somoza and to effect a peaceful transfer of power, Gutierrez's name was prominently mentioned because he was associated with the Sacassa family, powerful supporters of the Liberal party rather than the Conservative party represented by the Somoza family. In July 1979, when the Sandinistas took over in Managua, what little property Gutierrez owned in Nicaragua was confiscated, and he was not allowed to return to his country. With the help of the Japanese government he came to the United States in 1980 but moved to Europe not long thereafter.

8. The Paraguayan troop commander, whose name I will not mention in order to protect him and his family, returned to Paraguay in 1966, where he was greeted at the Ascuncion airport by a crowd of about 25,000 people. President Alfredo Stroessner, an army general, was displeased by the returning hero's popularity, and thereafter the colonel and his family were harassed, threatened, and intimidated by Stroessner's men until they gave up and moved to the United States. I helped the colonel's wife obtain a job with the World Bank but was unsuccessful in finding a suitable position for him.

9. The School of the Americas was a casualty of the U.S.-Panama treaty negotiations. Because some U.S. and Latin American officials had previously objected to the School of the Americas on the grounds that it allegedly helped train and motivate Latin American students— generally junior officers and noncommissioned officers—to revolt against their own governments, the United States agreed to discontinue the school in the Canal Zone; in 1984 it was reestablished at Fort Benning, Georgia. Curiously, however, the United States continues to operate an Inter-American Air Force Academy and a U.S. Navy

Small Craft Instruction and Technical Training School, both in the Canal Area. Part of the rationale for these latter schools is that their benefits go well beyond the military because the students will return to their homelands with both a better understanding of Americans and a better capacity to contribute to the growth of a middle class and to nation building—which was one of the basic objectives of the original School of the Americas.

10. Mottos later was promoted to major general in the Brazilian Army and during the 1970s was under consideration as a possible future president of Brazil. He apparently fell into political disfavor, for reasons unknown to me, and retired to become a private citizen. For several years he and his wife visited the United States annually, where my wife and I got to know them well.

11. York was transferred to Fort Benning in the summer of 1965 and took command of the Infantry Center and School, major elements in the army's training establishment; in 1967 he was promoted to three stars, returning to Fort Bragg to command the XVIII Airborne Corps and the post. Meanwhile, Maj. Gen. Joe Lawrie replaced York as the 82d Airborne Division commander but did not go to the Dominican Republic; an assistant division commander, Brig. Gen. Ed Smith, took command of the 82d elements there, and a forward echelon of division headquarters remained at San Isidro. In the fall of 1965, Brig. Gen. John R. Deane, Jr., replaced Smith in the Dominican Republic.

12. Bracey, *Resolution of the Dominican Crisis*, pp. 1-2.

5. Establishing a Provisional Government

1. Bracey, *Resolution of the Dominican Crisis*, pp. 1-2.

2. Ibid., p. 2; and Herz, *Conclusions*, p. 45. Herz, director of studies at the Institute for the Study of Diplomacy, School of Foreign Service, Georgetown University, Washington, D.C., produced a thoughtful analysis of Bunker's negotiating techniques and style, as well as an unforgettable tribute to Bunker the man; this essay about diplomacy and Bunker's masterful tour de force in the Dominican Republic is well worth careful study.

3. Bracey, *Resolution of the Dominican Crisis*, pp. 2-6.

4. Ibid., pp. 7-9.

5. Ibid., pp. 11-17.

6. Ibid., pp. 17-19.

7. *Stability Operations*, pt. 2 (covering 31 May to 25 October 1965, dated 16 January 1966), p. 7.

8. Ibid., pp. 8-9.

9. Ibid., pp. 6-7.

10. Bracey, *Resolution of the Dominican Crisis*, pp. 23-24.

11. Ibid., pp. 25-27.

6. Return to Normalcy

1. Bracey, *Resolution of the Dominican Crisis*, p. 31.

2. *Stability Operations*, pt. 2, pp. 13-14.

3. Bracey, *Resolution of the Dominican Crisis*, pp. 32-33.

4. *Stability Operations*, pt. 2, pp. 14-16.

5. *Stability Operations*, pt. 2, pp. 10-11.

6. Ibid., pp. 5, 11-12, 17.

7. Ibid., pp. 12, 17.

8. Bracey, *Resolution of the Dominican Crisis*, p. 34.

9. Ibid., pp. 34-35; *Stability Operations*, pt. 2, pp. 17-18.

10. *Stability Operations*, pt. 2, p. 17.

11. Ibid., pp. 19-20.

12. Ibid., p. 20.

13. Ibid., pp. 20-21.

14. Ibid., pp. 21-22.

15. Francisco Caamano's father was Fausto Caamano, who graduated from the Dominican Military Academy and rose to general officer rank during the infamous reign of Trujillo. Fausto Caamano served in the Dominican Secret Police (SIM), which Trujillo had created not long after he became chief of the national police in 1927 and used to keep himself in power during and after World War II. Reportedly, the older Caamano participated in the murder of thousands of Dominicans and Haitians during Trujillo's regime. His son Francisco had apparently attended but did not graduate from the Dominican Military Academy yet was commissioned in the Dominican Army while Trujillo was still in power. As a boy, Francisco was thought to be unstable and was nicknamed *El Loco*, "the crazy one."

16. *Stability Operations*, pt. 2, pp. 22-23.

17. Ibid., p. 24.

18. Ibid., p. 25.

19. Ibid., pp. 25-26.

20. Ibid., pp. 26-27.

21. Ibid., pp. 27-28.

22. Ibid., pp. 28-30.
23. Ibid., pp. 30-31.

7. The IAPF Completes Its Mission

1. Ford, "Dominican Republic Crisis." This informal memorandum, dated 17 October 1986, is based on extensive research of files made available to Ford by the U.S. Department of State and the OAS.

2. *Stability Operations,* pt. 2, pp. 31-32.

3. Ibid., pp. 33-34.

4. Klein went on to become a major general; he commanded an infantry battalion in combat in Vietnam (where he was wounded in action and won numerous decorations for valor) and served in a variety of other command and staff positions in the army, as well as on the joint staff of a unified command. In the summer of 1965 I acquired a junior aide, 2d Lt. Thomas H. Brett, a fine youngster from the Citadel. He too distinguished himself in Vietnam, commanding a rifle company in combat. Brett is now a colonel.

5. Abraham was a well-known figure in the ranks of the "old airborne troopers" of the U.S. Army. He had served in the mid-1950s in Vietnam as senior U.S. adviser to the South Vietnamese Airborne Brigade commanded by Col. Do Cao Tri (who, as a lieutenant general, was killed in 1970 during the allied incursion into Cambodia). Abraham played a key role in 1956 when the Vietnamese airborne brigade carried out numerous successful operations against various dissident groups challenging Premier Diem's efforts to consolidate his government's position. Abraham left his mark on the Vietnamese Airborne Brigade, later expanded to a division, which became the finest body of fighting men in the South Vietnamese Army.

6. In the summer of 1966, while I was commanding the XVIII Airborne Corps at Fort Bragg, I was invited to visit Brazil with General Bob Porter, CINCSOUTH, as guests of the Brazilian government. We met the top commanders of the Brazilian armed forces in Rio de Janeiro; called on President Branco in Brasilia, and visited several military bases and army units, including the Brazilian Airborne Center. We also addressed the Brazilian National War College, which is unique in that one-third of the students are civilians—industrialists, academics, clergy, businessmen, and various professionals; the result is that Brazil has a sophisticated and cosmopolitan approach to national security affairs. I was deeply impressed by the seriousness of our hosts'

views of Brazil's role as a major player not only in South America but also on the world scene. Despite its subsequent economic and political ups and downs, I believe that the country has the talent, the people, and the natural resources to take its place sooner or later as a major power in the world.

7. *Stability Operations*, pt. 2, pp. 36-38.

8. Ibid., pp. 38-39.

9. *Stability Operations*, pt. 3 (covering 26 October 1965–17 January 1966, dated 1 October 1966), pp. I-2, I-3; discussion with Colonel John Costa, June 1975, at Fort McPherson, Georgia; and Bracey, *Resolution of the Dominican Crisis*, pp. 36-37.

10. *Stability Operations*, pt. 3, pp. I-3, I-4.

11. *Stability Operations*, pt. 4 (covering 17 January–26 September 1966, dated 1 October 1966), p. I-1. For the record, not long after Balaguer became president on 1 July 1966, Caamano reportedly moved from London to Havana, where he apparently made plans to return to the Dominican Republic and foment resistance against the elected government. In the summer of 1973 he did return in secret, arriving by small craft on the northern coast, where he got into a gun battle with local security authorities and was killed.

12. Ibid., p. I-2; Bracey, *Resolution of the Dominican Crisis*, pp. 39-40.

13. *Stability Operations*, pt. 4, p. I-3.

14. Ibid.; Bracey, *Resolution of the Dominican Crisis*, p. 41.

15. Bracey, *Resolution of the Dominican Crisis*, p. 41.

16. Ibid.; *Stability Operations*, pt. 4, p. I-4.

17. *Stability Operations*, pt. 4, pp. I-4, I-5.

18. Herz, *Conclusions*, p. 49.

19. *Stability Operations*, pt. 4, p. I-5.

20. These casualty figures are derived from two sources: HQ XVIII Airborne Corps intelligence and operational estimates, plus personnel reports made at the time in the Dominican Republic; and "Commanders' Weekly Summary," dated late September 1966, published by the Office of the Chief of Staff, U.S. Army.

8. An Assessment

1. Fulbright, *The Arrogance of Power*, p. 84.

2. Ibid., pp. 93-95.

3. Ibid., pp. 85-86.

4. Ibid., pp. 87-88.

5. Gil, *Latin American–United States Relations*, pp. 255-56.
6. Ford, "Dominican Republic Crisis."
7. Krieg, *Peaceful Settlement*, pp. 78-82.
8. Fulbright, *The Arrogance of Power*, pp. 90-92.
9. Greenberg, *U.S. Army Unilateral and Coalition Operations*, pp. 25-26.
10. Ibid., pp. 14-15.
11. Quello and Conde, "Revolutionary Struggle," pt. 1, pp. 71-81; pt. 2, pp. 33-36.
12. Krieg, *Peaceful Settlement*, pp. 79-81.
13. Philips, *The Nightwatch*, pp. 162-63.
14. Barton Connett, wife of William Connett, the deputy chief of the U.S. mission in Santo Domingo, had courageously refused to be evacuated, despite personal threats on her life. It was she who appealed to the U.S. forces for help and assisted in organizing the effort to save the creatures in the Santo Domingo Zoo.
15. These principles, among others, are now taught at the UN-sponsored International Peace Academy in New York, which conducts international seminars on peacekeeping operations with participants from more than a hundred different countries. Established in 1970, the academy has conducted seminars in Mexico and Peru as well as several in Washington for the Inter-American Defense Board. The latter, in addition to studying UN peacekeeping experiences in such areas as Cyprus and the Congo, have included a case study of the IAPF experience in the Dominican Republic.

9. Caribbean Realities for the United States Today

1. LaFeber, *Inevitable Revolutions*, pp. 226-37; Ford, "Dominican Republic Crisis." After the fall of Somoza in 1979, the situation in El Salvador grew worse, reaching a critical point in the summer of 1983. This prompted Ellsworth Bunker to propose that the OAS negotiate a political settlement of the civil strife there, as it had done successfully in the Dominican Republic. A major missing element, however, was a completed "third force" such as the OAS Ad Hoc Committee backed up by the IAPF that was able to form a neutral interim Dominican government and keep the peace during negotiations; thus the proposal went nowhere.
2. Brands, "American Armed Intervention." pp. 612-15. According to Brands's account, the Department of State carefully drafted for

the OCES, presumably with its concurrence, the formal request for U.S. assistance.

3. White Paper, *Lessons of Grenada* (Washington: Department of State, February 1986).

4. Brands, "American Armed Intervention," pp. 618-19.

5. Ibid., pp. 617, 619.

6. Judgments on the performance of U.S. forces in Grenada are based in part on letter and videotape dated 10 June 1988 from Brig. Gen. Stephen Silvasy, Jr., Deputy Commandant, U.S. Army War College, Carlisle Barracks, Pennsylvania, who as a colonel commanded the leading brigade of the 82d Airborne Division that landed in Grenada on 25 October 1983; foreword to Assessment of Operation URGENT FURY (Grenada), dated 16 May 1985, Washington, D.C., signed by General John A. Wickham, Chief of Staff, U.S. Army; and *Army Times* (Washington, D.C.), 5 November and 17 December 1984.

7. White Paper, *Grenada, October 25 to November 2, 1983* (Washington: Department of Defense, 1983).

8. "Soviets in Caribbean Threaten Security of U.S. and the Americas," White House Briefing for Joint Congressional Iran-Contra Committee, 14 July 1987; Giovanni and Harvey, *Crisis in Central America*, pp. 25-26, 28-29.

9. Wiarda, *In Search of Policy*, p. 130.

10. Parker, "The Panama Canal"; Ryan, *Panama Canal*, pp. 88-93.

11. Parker, "The Panama Canal," pp. 58-60. HQ U.S. Southern Command is located at Quarry Heights on the southern side of the canal and the Pacific side of the isthmus, right next to Panama City, with a population of over 400,000 people; Quarry Heights has been on the front line during numerous riots and demonstrations against the U.S. presence and is vulnerable to such outside interference. Moreover, the command's mission concerns all of Latin America and is far broader than just the security of the canal; thus Panama does have a legitimate basis for wanting the headquarters to be moved.

12. Nuechterlein, *America Overcommitted*, is an outstanding exposition of U.S. goals, the ability of the nation to accomplish them, and the necessity of setting priorities for its efforts abroad.

13. "Five Key Issues for the Atlantic Community," address at George C. Marshall Public Service Leadership Conference, 21-22 October 1988, Lexington, Virginia.

14. "Report of the Dean 1988," excerpts printed under "For the Record" column, editorial page, *Washington Post*, 1 April 1989.

15. "Revolutionary Epoch Ending in Russia, Kennan Declares," *Washington Post*, 5 April 1989.

16. "US Urged to Cut Force by One-half in Europe," *Washington Post*, 15 April 1989. The plan is set forth in a study prepared for and published by the Atlantic Council of the United States, a NATO support group located in Washington. Goodpaster chaired the study group. Goodpaster has exceptional credentials when it comes to NATO. He helped Gen. Dwight D. Eisenhower, the first supreme allied commander of NATO forces, to organize NATO's military element in the early 1950s. In 1954-1961, he served in the Eisenhower White House in the key post of staff secretary, and in 1969 was appointed the supreme NATO commander by President Richard M. Nixon, holding the post for five years.

17. Shortly after he retired to his farm in Gettysburg, Pennsylvania, President Eisenhower visited the nearby U.S. Army War College at Carlisle Barracks, Pennsylvania, several times. In the spring of 1961, in an address to the War College, where I was deputy commandant at the time, he stated that U.S. force levels in Europe should be reduced to corps size, or about one-half the current force. He felt that sooner or later the United States would wear out its welcome and should take steps now to reduce its presence and pass more responsibility to Western Europe for its own defense. That was twenty-eight years ago.

18. "NATO Arms Cut Proposal Faulted as Too Cautious; White House Fears Position Could Be Undermined before Serious Negotiations Begin," *Washington Post*, 17 April 1989. Eventually bringing home a large number of U.S. forces from Europe will result in substantial reductions in U.S. defense expenditures only if those forces are inactivated, or converted to a reserve status, because personnel costs absorb a large percentage, about half in some instances, of total active force costs. On the other hand, if returning forces are retained in the active force structure, overall U.S. defense costs will rise because of the cost of building or reactivating the bases at home required to accommodate them and the fact that our NATO allies pay for much of the current support costs of U.S. forces in Europe.

19. Stephen S. Rosenfeld, "Is Bush Being Too Careful?" editorial page, *Washington Post*, 14 April 1989; Charles Krauthammer, "Kennan: Cold Realist," editorial page, *Washington Post*, 14 April 1989; "Bush Proposal to Cut Forces [in Europe]," *Washington Post*, 11 June 1989; "Soviet Leader Welcomes Bush Troop Plan in Bonn," *Washington Post*, 13 June 1989.

20. This listing is not intended to be all-inclusive. For example, Canada and Australia are not shown, but this does not mean that they are unimportant to the United States. For obvious reasons, the Soviet

Union, China, Eastern Europe, and other areas under Communist/Marxist control have not been listed.

21. Recent good news about dealing with the crushing foreign debts owed by Latin American nations to Western banks should make it less difficult to find the financial support needed for the Caribbean Basin. Western banks, the World Bank, and the International Monetary Fund are adopting a new debt strategy which emphasizes debt and debt-service reduction. "Mexico, Venezuela Debt Focus of Treasury Talks," *Washington Post*, 29 March 1989; "IMF and World Bank Pledge Fast Debt Plan Implementation," *Washington Post*, 5 April 1989.

22. Wiarda, *In Search of Policy*, pp. 77-84, 131-33; Lowenthal, "Changing Patterns in Inter-American Relations," *Washington Quarterly*, Autumn 1980, pp. 168-70.

23. Wiarda, *In Search of Policy*, pp. 80-81, 132-33.

24. Canada has made known its interest in joining the OAS but so far has not opted for full membership.

25. Wiarda, *In Search of Policy*, pp. 58-59, 83-85, 92-94.

26. Laurence Jolidon, "Refugees Flee Central America for Hope in USA," *USA Today*, 5 November 1987.

27. Larry Rohter, "Immigration Portends Uncertainty for Mex-America," *New York Times*, 7 June 1987; Leon F. Bouvier, "Immigration beyond Romantic Illusions," *Washington Post*, 25 October 1987.

28. David B. Ottoway, "Diplomatic Confrontation Looms on Regional Issues," *Washington Post*, 16 April 1989; Julia Preston, "Havana Summit: Forum for Gorbachev and Castro to Air Differences," *Washington Post*, 6 April 1989.

29. Ibid.; "Gorbachev Attacks U.S. Regional Role," *Washington Post*, 5 April 1989.

30. Ibid.; "Soviets in Cuba Criticize Export of Revolution," *Washington Post*, 4 April 1989.

31. Ibid.; "Gorbachev Attacks U.S. Regional Role," *Washington Post*, 5 April 1989.

32. John Goshko, "Bush Urges Gorbachev to Aid Peace Effort," *Washington Post*, 31 March 1989; "Arias Praises Bush's Approach," *Washington Post*, 5 April 1989.

33. Anne Devroy, "U.S. Rebukes Gorbachev on Nicaragua," *Washington Post*, 6 April 1989.

34. Tom Donnelly, "Terror in Panama; Violence against Americans on Rise; U.S. Response Hit," *Army Times*, 20 March 1989; Margaret Roth, "Caught in the Cross Fire," *Army Times*, 27 March 1989;

"In Panama: Bribes, Violence, Zonies, and U.S. Policy," *Army Times*, 24 April 1989.

35. Noriega is the de facto president. The former president, Eric Arturo Delvalle, was forced out by Noriega in March 1988 and is now in hiding under U.S. protection. The United States continues to recognize him as the legitimate president of Panama even though Noriega replaced him with his handpicked man, Manuel Solis Palma; "Opponents of Noriega Warn of Electoral Fraud; OAS Rights Unit Notes Voter List Complaints," *Washington Post*, 21 April 1989; "Panama Visa Curb Tied to Voter Fraud Scheme," *Washington Post*, 21 April 1989; "Lugar Urges Crackdown on Noriega; Strongman Seeks to Rig Panama's 7 May Election," *Washington Post*, 22 April 1989.

36. "Bush Urges Noriega to Quit, citing 'Irregularities' "; Panama Offers First Vote Result, Giving Lead to Noriega's Candidate"; "As Observer, Carter Proves Acute; Ex-President Puts Onus of Irregularities on Gen. Noriega," all three articles in *Washington Post*, 10 May 1989. In another article in the same issue of the *Post*, John Goshko reports that many members of Congress, including some who witnessed apparent election rigging on 7 May, are calling for tough measures, such as abrogating the Panama Canal treaties that took effect in 1979. But other U.S. leaders warn that such measures could have consequences much more damaging than Noriega's reprehensible acts.

37. "Panama Invalidates Election; Bush May Move to Strengthen U.S."; "Opposition Leaders Attacked; Bodyguard Killed; U.S. Dependents to Shift to Bases," all three articles in *Washington Post*, 11 May 1989.

38. "Bush Orders More Troops to Panama; Efforts to Isolate Noriega with Diplomacy Continue"; "The Crisis in Panama: Bush Says Democratic Nations Bear 'Enormous Responsibility' for Outcome," both in *Washington Post*, 12 May 1989. "First U.S. Reinforcements Arrive in Panama," *Washington Post*, 13 May 1989. According to George C. Wilson, reporting in an article, "Bush Turns to Gunboat Diplomacy in Move to Protect U.S. Lives," *Washington Post*, 12 May 1989, U.S. military leaders, including JCS Chairman Adm. William J. Crowe, Jr., advised against any direct military action to achieve U.S. political objectives in Panama.

39. "Latin Nations Denounce Noriega's Move on Vote; U.S. Warned Not to Intervene Militarily," *Washington Post*, 12 May 1989; "Bishops in Panama Denounce Vote Fraud; Letter Read in Churches Brings Applause," *Washington Post*, 15 May 1989.

40. "Venezuelan Leader to Press OAS to Denounce Noriega; Perez

Offers to Grant Panamanian Exile in Caracas," *Washington Post*, 13 May 1989.

41. Robert Pastor, "A Born Again Strategy for Panama," *Washington Post*, Sunday Outlook Section, 14 May 1989; William F. Buckley, Jr., "Noriega the Treaty Violator," *Washington Post*, 18 May 1989; "OAS to Ask Noriega to Step Aside," *Washington Post*, 18 May 1989; "OAS Extends Effort to Displace Noriega," *Washington Post*, 7 June 1989.

42. "OAS: A Troubled Forum on Panama," *Washington Post*, 16 May 1989.

43. "Bush Confronts Dilemma over Panama; President Must Choose between Actions Likely to Fail or to Endanger U.S. Interests," *Washington Post*, 10 May 1989.

44. In this connection, Richard T. McCormack, who was the U.S. Permanent Representative to the OAS during the Reagan years, deserves high marks. He was the first American to chair its Economic Council.

Selected Bibliography

This list includes only major sources and material that I found particularly useful or perceptive. Additional sources include personal notes and papers gathered from my service in the U.S. Army (1936-74) and with the CIA (1978-82) as a member of the Senior Review Panel, part of the agency's national intelligence analysis wing. I have also benefited from numerous discussions with governmental officials who have had to deal with the immensely complex and endemic problems found in the Caribbean Basin.

Alabaster, Harold L. "The United States Commitment in the Dominican Republic, 1965." Unpublished case study, 1965.

Barnet, Richard J. *Intervention and Revolution.* New York: World, 1968.

Beaulac, William L., et al. *Dominican Action—1965: Intervention or Cooperation?* Washington, D.C.: Center for Strategic Studies, Georgetown University, 1966.

Blasier, Cole. *The Hovering Giant: U.S. Responses to Revolutionary Changes in Latin America.* Pittsburgh, Pa.: Univ. of Pittsburgh Press, 1976.

Bosch, Juan. *The Unfinished Experiment.* New York: Praeger, 1965.

Bracey, Audrey. *Resolution of the Dominican Crisis, 1965: A Study in Mediation.* Washington, D.C.: Institute for the Study of Diplomacy, Edmund A. Walsh School of Foreign Service, Georgetown Univ., 1980.

Brands, H.W., Jr. "Decisions on American Armed Intervention: Lebanon, Dominican Republic, and Grenada." *Political Science Quarterly* 102, no. 4 (1987-88): 612-15.

Chomsky, Noam. *Turning the Tide: U.S. Intervention in Central America and the Struggle for Peace.* Boston, Mass.: South End Press, 1985.

Costa, John J. *The Dominican Republic: Intervention in Perspective.* Carlisle Barracks, Pa.: U.S. Army War College, 1968.

The Dominican Crisis: The Hemisphere Acts. Washington, D.C.: Department of State, 1965.

Dominican Republic—Case Study 4-01. Carlisle Barracks, Pa.: U.S. Army War College, 1971.

Dubois, Jules. *Operacion America.* Santo Domingo: Editora del Caribe, C. por A., 1964.

Fagg, John Edwin. *Cuba, Haiti, and the Dominican Republic.* Englewood Cliffs, N.J.: Prentice-Hall, 1965.

Ford, John W. "Dominican Republic Crisis of 1965." Unpublished memorandum, 1986.

Fulbright, J. William. *The Arrogance of Power.* New York: Random House, 1966.

Fuller, Stephen M., and Graham A. Cosmas. *Marines in the Dominican Republic, 1916-1924.* Washington, D.C.: USMC History Division, 1974.

Gil, Frederico G. *Latin American—United States Relations.* New York: Harcourt Brace Jovanovich, 1971.

Giovanni, Cleto di, Jr., and Mose L. Harvey. *Crisis in Central America.* Miami, Fla.: Advance International Studies Institute and Univ. of Miami, 1982.

Gleijeses, Piero. *The Dominican Crisis: The 1965 Constitutionalist Revolt and American Intervention.* Baltimore, Md.: Johns Hopkins Univ. Press, 1978.

Greenberg, Lawrence M. *U.S. Army Unilateral and Coalition Operations in the 1965 Dominican Republic Intervention.* Historical Analysis Series. Washington, D.C.: U.S. Army Center for Military History, 1987.

Herz, Martin F. *Conclusions.* Addendum to Bracey, *Resolution of the Dominican Crisis.*

The Inter-American Peace Force (IAPF). Santo Domingo, Dominican Republic: Public Affairs Office, HQ IAPF, 1966.

Johnson, Lyndon B. *The Vantage Point.* New York: Holt, Rinehart, & Winston, 1971.

Krieg, W.L. *Peaceful Settlement of Disputes through the Organization of the American States.* Washington, D.C.: Department of State, 1973.

Kurzman, Dan. *The Revolt of the Damned.* New York: Putnam, 1965.

LaFeber, Walter. *Inevitable Revolutions: The United States in Central America.* New York: Norton, 1984.

Langley, Lester D. *The Banana Wars: An Inner History of American Empire, 1900-1934.* Lexington: Univ. Press of Kentucky, 1983.

Larson, Eric M. "National Population Censuses, Dominican Republic, 1920-1981." Austin: Univ. of Texas, 1987.

———. "Immigration Research: The Case of the Missing Dominicans." Austin: Univ. of Texas, 1987.

Logan, Rayford W. *Haiti and the Dominican Republic.* New York: Oxford Univ. Press, 1968.

Long, Eldredge R. *The Dominican Crisis, 1965: An Experiment in International Peacekeeping.* Newport, R.I.: U.S. Naval War College, 1967.

Lowenthal, Abraham F. *The Dominican Republic: The Politics of Chaos.* Washington, D.C.: Brookings Institution, 1969.

———. "Changing Patterns in Inter-American Relations." *Washington Quarterly,* Autumn 1980.

Mallin, Jay. *Caribbean Crisis: Subversion Fails in the Dominican Republic.* New York: Doubleday, 1965.

Mann, Thomas C. *The Dominican Crisis: Correcting Some Misconceptions.* Washington, D.C.: Department of State, 1965.

Martin, John Bartlow. *Overtaken by Events.* New York: Doubleday, 1966.

Millett, Richard. *Guardians of the Dynasty: A History of the U.S.-Created Guardia Nacional de Nicaragua and the Somoza Family.* Maryknoll, N.Y.: Orbis, 1977.

Mottos, Carlos de Meira. *A Experienca do FAIBRAS na Republica Dominicana* (The experience of the Brazilian contingent of the Inter-American Peace Force in the Dominican Republic). Rio de Janeiro: Escola Superior de Guerra, 1967.

Nuechterlein, Donald. *America Overcommitted: United States National Interests in a Changing World.* Lexington: Univ. Press of Kentucky, 1985.

Parker, David S. "The Panama Canal and U.S. Security." *Armed Forces Journal,* Dec. 1987.

Philips, David A. *The Nightwatch.* New York: Atheneum, 1977.

Poole, Walter. *Dominican Intervention of 1965-1966.* Washington, D.C.: Historical Division, Office of the JCS, 1984.

Quello, J.I., and N. Isa Conde. "Revolutionary Struggle in the Dominican Republic and Its Lessons." 2 parts. *World Marxist Review* (Prague, Eng. edition), Dec. 1965, pp. 71-81; Jan. 1966, pp. 33-36.

Rodman, Selden. *Quisqueya: A History of the Dominican Republic.* Seattle: Univ. of Washington Press, 1964.

Rostow, Walt. *The Diffusion of Power.* New York: Macmillan, 1972.

Ryan, Paul B. *The Panama Canal: U.S. Diplomacy and Defense Interests.* Stanford, Calif.: Hoover Institution Press, 1977.

Sierra, Jimmy Guión, et al. *La Guerra de Abril.* Santo Domingo: Producciones La Causa, 1965.

Slater, Jerome. *Intervention and Negotiation.* New York: Harper & Row, 1970.

Special Forces Operations Debrief (Dominican Republic, 1965). Fort Belvoir, Va.: U.S. Army Combat Developments Command, 1966.

Stability Operations—Dominican Republic. 4 pts. Santo Domingo: HQ U.S. Forces Dominican Republic, 1965-66.

Szulc, Tad. *Dominican Diary.* New York: Delacorte Press, 1965.

Welles, Sumner. *Naboth's Vineyard: The Dominican Republic, 1844-1924.* 2 vols. New York: Payson & Clark, 1928.

Wiarda, Howard J. *In Search of Policy: The United States and Latin America.* Washington, D.C.: American Enterprise Institute for Public Policy Research, 1984.

Yates, Lawrence A. *Power Pack: U.S. Intervention in the Dominican Republic, 1965-1966.* Leavenworth Papers, No. 15. Fort Leavenworth, Kans.: U.S. Army Command and General Staff College, 1988.

Index